ON BECOMING AN EFFECTIVE TEACHER

On Becoming an Effective Teacher *describes exemplary practices like Teach For America, which highlight the power of person-centered teaching to bring about higher student achievement and emotional intelligence. Lyon situates the classic with the cutting-edge, integrating wisdom with research, anecdote with practical advice, to find truths that ward effective teaching.*
Jeffrey Cornelius-White, PsyD, LPC, Professor of Counseling, Missouri State University, USA, Author of *Learner Centered Instruction: Building Relationships for Student Success*

This fascinating book reveals through current research and contemporary applications that Carl Rogers' pioneering and radical approach to education is as relevant today as it was in the 1970s and 1980s.
Brian Thorne, University of East Anglia, UK
Carl Rogers is one of the most influential psychologists of the twentieth century. His influence is similarly outstanding in the fields of education, counseling, psychotherapy, conflict resolution, and peace.

On Becoming an Effective Teacher presents the final unpublished writings of Rogers, and as such has not only unique historical value, but also a vital message for today's educational crises, and can be read as a prescription against violence in our schools. It documents the research results of four highly relevant, related but independent studies which comprise the biggest collection of data ever accumulated to test a person-centered theory in the field of education. This body of comprehensive research on effective teaching was accomplished over a twenty-year period in forty-two US states and in six other countries – the UK,

Germany, Brazil, Canada, Israel, and Mexico – and is highly relevant to the concerns of teachers, psychologists, students, and parents.

The principal findings of the research in this book show that teachers and schools can significantly improve their effectiveness through programs focusing on facilitative interpersonal relationships. Teachers who either naturally have, or are trained to have, empathy, genuineness (congruence), and who prize their students (positive regard), create an important level of trust in the classroom and exert significant positive effects on student outcomes, including achievement scores, interpersonal functioning, self-concept, attendance, and violence.

The dialogues between Rogers and Lyon offer a unique and timeless perspective on teaching, counseling, and learning. The work of Reinhard Tausch on person-centered teaching for counselors, parents, athletics, and even textbook materials, and the empathic interactions of teachers and students, is among the most thorough and rigorous research ever accomplished on the significance and potential of a person-centered approach to teaching and learning.

This pioneering textbook is highly relevant to educational psychologists and researchers, as well as those in undergraduate and graduate university courses in education, teacher training, counseling, psychology, and educational psychology.

Harold C. Lyon, Jr. is a graduate of West Point, former US Director of Education for the Gifted, project officer for the development of Sesame Street, assistant to the president of Ohio University, has served on the faculties of Georgetown, Antioch, Dartmouth Medical School, Notre Dame College, Universities of Massachusetts, and Munich where he currently teaches physicians to be more effective teachers. He received the Gold Medal in the 32nd International Film & TV Festival of New York, a CINDY Award, and the Blue Ribbon in the American Film & Video Festival.

Reinhard Tausch is Professor Emeritus at the University of Hamburg and is the author of numerous popular books on psychology and teaching.

The Late Carl R. Rogers (1902–1987) has been called 'the most influential psychologist in American history'. His influence in the fields of education, counseling, psychotherapy, conflict resolution, and peace is similarly outstanding. The founder of humanistic psychology, he authored 16 books and more than 200 professional articles.

Advance Praise

'This book is a great bridge between person-centered psychology and learning. With a grand overview and infectious enthusiasm for teaching and learning, this book gives great insights in how person-centered psychology can advance your own teaching. And it contains the rare, lost dialogues between several of the founding fathers of person-centered psychology. If you care about education – read this book!'
Jan Kiesewetter, PhD, Clinical Psychologist, Member of the Munich Center of the Learning Sciences, Germany

'This unique book combines the largest body of convincing research ever assembled on the power of person-centered methods to bring about student achievement with practical ideas for parents, teachers, therapists, and managers to use with students in classrooms at every level. A "must have" book for every teacher and student of persons!'
George Rutherford , New York City inner–city high school teacher

'This book comprehensively presents us with contemporary and overwhelming evidence of the importance of person-centered methods. Tausch and Lyon share here for the first time, new research on empathy showing how lack of empathy on the part of teachers can lead to aggressiveness and violence, while empathic teachers result in peaceful classrooms and higher student performance and satisfaction.'
Master Teacher Gerhard Ekles, MA, EdD, San Francisco, California, USA

'This volume represents half a century worth of research and innovation in the human elements of teaching from three of the greatest of humanist educators. It's filled with intimate dialogues, speeches, research reviews, and practical tips. I'm sure you will profit from it and enjoy it as much as I!'
Jeffrey Cornelius-White, PsyD, LPC, Professor of Counseling, Missouri State University, USA, Author of Learner Centered Instruction: Building Relationships for Student Success

'This book is a model of the approach Carl Rogers used that inspired his students in the US and internationally. The empirical results in today's 21st century world more than demonstrate the power of permitting freedom to others and transforming a class of unruly students into a community of learners. I highly recommend this book to all educators, researchers, parents, and concerned community members.'
Barbara L. McCombs, PhD, University of Denver, USA

'This fascinating book reveals through current research and contemporary applications that Carl Rogers' pioneering and radical approach to education is as relevant today as it was in the 1970s and '80s.'
Brian Thorne, University of East Anglia, UK

ON BECOMING AN EFFECTIVE TEACHER

Person-centered teaching, psychology, philosophy, and dialogues with Carl R. Rogers and Harold Lyon

Carl R. Rogers, Harold C. Lyon, Jr and Reinhard Tausch

Routledge
Taylor & Francis Group

LONDON AND NEW YORK

First published 2014
by Routledge
2 Park Square, Milton Park, Abingdon, Oxon OX14 4RN

Simultaneously published in the USA and Canada
by Routledge
711 Third Avenue, New York, NY 10017

Routledge is an imprint of the Taylor & Francis Group, an informa business

British Library Cataloguing in Publication Data
A catalogue record for this book is available from the British Library

Library of Congress Cataloging in Publication Data
Rogers, Carl R. (Carl Ransom), 1902–1987.
On becoming an effective teacher : person-centred teaching, psychology, philosophy, and dialogues with Carl R. Rogers / Carl R Rogers, Harold C Lyon, Reinhard Tausch.
  pages cm
1. Teaching--Philosophy. 2. Effective teaching. 3. Student-centered learning. 4. Rogers, Carl R. (Carl Ransom), 1902-1987--Interviews. I. Lyon, Harold C. II. Tausch, Reinhard, 1921- III. Title.
LB1025.3.R635 2013
371.102--dc23

2013004279

ISBN: 978–0-415–81697-7 (hbk)
ISBN: 978–0-415–81698-4 (pbk)
ISBN: 978–0-203–72567-2 (ebk)

Typeset in Bembo
by Swales & Willis Ltd, Exeter, Devon, UK

DEDICATION

To my dear and loyal friends, the late David Aspy and Flora Roebuck, who took the original person-centered work of Carl Rogers and subjected it to the largest empirical field study ever done on effective teaching in forty-two US states and eight countries, including Germany, where Reinhard Tausch replicated it with what Rogers called 'Teutonic thoroughness'. To my dear friends Vince Giuliano and Tony Smith, who always support me and my writing as only true best friends can. To my wife, Karin, my love-for-life, person-centered partner. And to my children, Eric, Gregg, Kaela, and my wonderful grandchildren, whom I hope will have person-centered, empathic teachers.

A SELECTION OF BOOKS BY AND ABOUT THE AUTHORS

Carl R. Rogers

The Life and Works of Carl Rogers, a biography by Howard Kirschenbaum (PCCS Books) 2007.

Carl Rogers: The Quiet Revolutionary: An Oral History, Carl Rogers and David Russell (Penmarin Books) 2002.

A Way of Being (Houghton Mifflin) 1980, 1995.

Freedom to Learn, with H.J. Freiberg (Charles E. Merrill) 1994.

Carl Rogers Dialogues: Conversations with Martin Buber, Paul Tillich, B.F. Skinner, Gregory Bateson, Michael Polanyi, Rollo May, and Others, edited by Howard Kirschenbaum and Valerie Land Henderson (Houghton Mifflin) 1989

The Carl Rogers Reader, edited by Howard Kirschenbaum and Valerie Land Henderson (Houghton Mifflin) 1989

Freedom to Learn—A View of What Education Might Become (Charles Merrill) 1984.

Freedom to Learn for the 80's (Charles E. Merrill) 1983.

On Personal Power: Inner Strength and its Revolutionary Impact (Delacorte) 1977.

Becoming Partners: Marriage and its Alternatives (Delacorte) 1972.

On Encounter Groups (Harper and Row) 1970.

Man and the Science of Man (Charles E. Merrill) 1968.

Person to Person: The Problem of Being Human, with Barry Stevens (Real People Press) 1967.

On Becoming a Person: A Therapist's View of Psychotherapy (Houghton Mifflin) 1961, 1965.

Client-Centered Therapy: Its Current Practice, Implications, and Theory (Houghton Mifflin) 1951.

Harold. C. Lyon, Jr.

Angling in the Smile of the Great Spirit (Deep Waters Press) 2004, 2009, 2012

A Love Affair with Angling (Deep Waters Press) 2006.

Tenderness is Strength (Harper Row) 1978.

It's Me and I'm Here! (Delacorte) 1976.

Learning to Feel—Feeling to Learn (Charles E. Merrill) 1974.

Reinhard Tausch

Hilfen bei Stress and Belastung (Rowohlt) 2010.

Sanftes Sterben (Rowohlt) 2000.

Wege zu Uns und Andren (Rowohlt) 1999.

Erziehungs-Psychologie (Hogrefe) 1998.

Gesprächs-Psychologie (Hogrefe) 1990.

CONTENTS

ACKNOWLEDGEMENTS

Thanks to Natalie Rogers, Carl's daughter, for her support and permission to use her father's name, writing, and for her comprehensive bibliography; the late Dave Aspy and Flora Roebuck and Cheryl Aspy, for their loyal support and updated research chapter; Reinhard Tausch and Renate Hüls for their research—especially their recent research chapter on empathy; Jef Cornelius-White, Adam Harbaugh, and SAGE Publications for their comprehensive meta-analysis of person-centered teaching, *Learner Centered Instruction: Building Relationships for Student Success*, and especially to Jef for his foreword and gracious critique of this manuscript. To Florian Eitel for his Introduction, sincere interest in this book, and eagerness to drive me to Stuttgart for inspiring meetings with Reinhard Tausch over the past years. To Martin Fischer for his personal and professional support; Thomas Brendel for his translation of Chapter 14 of this book, and other support; Howard Kirschenbaum and Peter Sanders at PCCS books for their thorough biography, *The Life and Works of Carl Rogers*; Wendy Kopp and Steven Farr, for their Teach For America program; Jossey-Bass for Steven Farr's *Teaching as Leadership: the Highly Effective Teacher's Guide to Closing the Achievement Gap*; PublicAffairs Books for Wendy Kopp's *One Day, All Children … The Unlikely Triumph of Teach For America and What I Learned Along the Way* and *A Chance to Make History: What Works and What Doesn't in Providing an Excellent Education for All*; and Carl Rogers' granddaughter, Frances Fuchs, for photos of Carl. Special thanks to Bruce Roberts, Publisher and Hamish Baxter, Senior Editorial Assistant at Routledge for their patience with me. And thanks to Nikky Twyman for her thorough copy editing and Kristin Susser for excellent proof editing.

Special thanks to my wife, Karin, who has not only translated much of the German content of this book, but who has also been a loving wife and midwife in helping me through the final gestation years and birth of this long-coming book.

FOREWORD

Hal Lyon has assembled an impressive body of work with his mentor, the late Carl R. Rogers, father of person-centered philosophy, and Reinhard Tausch, Germany's renowned humanistic education researcher. *On Becoming an Effective Teacher* offers teachers, counselors, administrators, professors, and parents a rare combination of historically interesting material – revealing timeless, venerable dialogues and speeches – and fresh ideas that bring light to enduring challenges in teaching and learning, psychology, and parenting. The book links little-known, but well-conducted and replicated, older studies with contemporary meta-analyses showing that person-centered practices result in student achievement and many other positive outcomes. It describes exemplary practices like Teach For America, which highlight the power of person-centered teaching to bring about higher student achievement and emotional intelligence. Lyon situates the classic with the cutting edge, integrating wisdom with research, anecdote with practical advice, to find truths that reveal paths toward effective teaching.

On Becoming an Effective Teacher is about the human dimensions of teaching – how to be, what to do, and especially how to relate. The original stories, never-before-published vulnerable dialogues, research, and practical advice are bolstered by an enormous, indisputable body of evidence in person-centered and constructivist education on teacher–student relationships. My own meta-analysis (e.g. see descriptions from 2007 and 2010) has shown that teacher–student relationships characterized by empathy, warmth, congruence, and trust are strong predictors of student success. Student success in twenty-first-century outcomes like social skills, self-initiative, participation, critical thinking, and self-esteem are particularly helped by strong person-centered student–teacher relationships. But vital traditional concerns like student achievement and attendance are also helped. These relational factors appear universal and relevant regardless of the race, gender, and geographic location of the teachers or students. This book also contains unique insight into special needs children, including gifted and talented students, from Lyon's decade of national leadership in this field.

In these pages, I know you will enjoy the inspirational tone, the originality of material, and the solid, accessible research base this book offers as much as I did. I especially appreciated how the vulnerable dialogues between the famous Rogers and his colleague, Lyon, reveal rare insights into this empathic man, Carl Rogers, who is widely acknowledged as the most influential psychotherapist in American history. Hal Lyon's view of teaching as the combination of 'grit', compassion, and empirically validated factors such as empathy will help any teacher, psychologist, physician, administrator, or parent create the person-centered context and practices to help students and patients excel.

Jeffrey H. D. Cornelius-White, Psy.D., LPC
Missouri State University

INTRODUCTION

Prof Dr Med Florian Eitel

Harold Lyon and I met for the first time in 1989, Hal as an educator and I as a medical teacher, united by our combined efforts to help our colleagues improve their teaching skills. When he told me about the manuscript for this book, it immediately aroused my curiosity in that it would highlight effective teaching and psychology, comprising the remaining unpublished work of Carl Rogers, the 'Father of Person-Centered Therapy'. Hal knew Rogers personally as a mentor. In the late 1970s, they made the decision to write this book together. Hal assembled much of it before Rogers died. The manuscript went into a file cabinet in Hal's attic as Hal mourned the loss of his mentor and one of psychology's greats. But thankfully it came out of the attic and, after revision and updating, it now presents what Rogers and person-centered methods and philosophy can offer contemporary teachers, students, and parents for becoming effective teachers.

I had studied Rogers' work as a freshman at the University of Cologne in the early 1960s. However, Rogers was far back in the recesses of my mind when I began working on the opportunity to help reform undergraduate medical education at the University of Munich in 1985. But I immediately understood the importance of Hal's project, giving visibility to the value of Rogers' person-centered work for educating today's teachers, psychologists, and medical students. Hal shared that he had met a German professor who, according to Rogers, had replicated his earlier research on effective teaching in Germany with 'Teutonic thoroughness'. To my great surprise, he was Reinhard Tausch.

There it was. A seeming crossing of life's trajectories: Rogers', Tausch's, Hal's, and mine. I vividly recalled a huge lecture hall at the University of Cologne, crowded with hundreds of students, with a tall, slim professor up front lecturing in an undertone and a clear voice on empathy, congruence and

positive regard. It was Professor Reinhard Tausch who conveyed by his lecturing style the clear impression that he lives what he talks. This deeply impressed
me and I recalled wishing I had Tausch as my mentor but was too shy to ask
him, as after his lectures crowds of students always surrounded him. He soon
left Cologne for the University of Hamburg, where he chaired the Institute of
Psychology until his retirement, while I went on to other challenges.

Hal told me that Reinhard Tausch, now Emeritus Professor at Hamburg,
was living nearby in Stuttgart and that he was updating the contribution he had
made years earlier to the Rogers–Lyon book. Hal invited me to go with him to
visit and speak personally with Tausch, as one of my admired role models. We
drove to Stuttgart together in 2010 and had a wonderful day with Reinhard,
who graciously hosted us in a lovable way. We had the opportunity to be in
the presence of a man of profound intellect and charm. When driving back to
Munich, I felt our lives had become richer.

Among the tidings of this story are the power of person-centered attitudes and
relationships among colleagues in the process of human learning and teaching.
That's just one of this book's messages. The book contains many other unique
contributions, including never-before-published writings of Rogers and a unique
historical dialogue bridging the eclectic chapters of the book with the mentor
(Rogers) and his pupil (Lyon) discussing informally issues of person-centered psychology and education, taped and transcribed back before Rogers' death but as
relevant to teaching as if spoken today. These rare dialogues reflect experiences of
the past and render them understandable for the future.

Good teaching creates a longing for learning, fosters motivation to experience new knowledge, wisdom, and performance. Without this human longing,
it is unlikely that our trajectories of life will merge to build bonds of positive
regard, empathy, and congruence. Understanding this longing for learning elu-
cidates the basics of mentorship: a mentor's humanity helps his students grow.

What does this book offer to you, the reader? Lyon and Tausch reopened
my mind to understanding person-centered teaching and learning. I am
convinced this will happen to you, too, whether you are psychologist,
doctor, teacher, parent, or student. Through its unique real-life conversations between the great Rogers and his student, the large field studies of
Aspy and Tausch linking person-centered teaching to student achievement, or the powerfully disturbing voices of students who, in Tausch and
Hüls' recent research, cry out desperately for more empathic teachers in
Chapter 14, this book will lead you to an understanding of the value of
person-centeredness as a context of personality and a means of teaching,
learning, and being. Beyond pedagogy, this understanding will enable you
to use person-centeredness as a means for tying ideas, feelings, and lifelines
to your own web of human trajectories that will help you grow in a humane
learning environment. The great advantage of this book is that the experiences of Rogers, Aspy, and Tausch in the past are now validated by the

largest meta-analyses ever done on effective teaching and achievement by Hattie[1] and Cornelius-White.[2]

In addition, this outstanding book provides insights into the last of the unpublished work of Carl Rogers, who has been called 'the most influential psychologist in American History', supporting a deeper understanding of his contributions to person-centeredness. Rogers', Aspy's, Tausch's, and Lyon's timeless insights make this book a 'must-have' for all teachers, psychologists, and students of persons.

The authors, along with the contributions of Drs Aspy and Roebuck, who conducted the most ambitious field study of effective teaching ever done (presented in Chapter 12), provide scientific evidence for the effectiveness of one of the most important conditions for teaching and learning: person-centeredness. Let me amplify this with some brief findings from educational research in my field of medical education.

Person-centeredness

Physicians' attitudes toward medical students and patients, even more so than their professional capabilities, make the crucial difference between effective and ineffective doctors and teachers.[3] Their empathy, unconditional positive regard, congruence, and their facilitative behaviors are associated with positive outcomes.[4] Medical students with higher empathy scores obtain higher ratings of competence in core clinical clerkships.[5] Empirical findings show a strong positive correlation between teachers' facilitative behavior and students' perception of the learning value of educational measures. The recent randomized research study of Lyon and his colleagues at two medical schools presented in Chapter 17 shows that medical teachers can be efficiently and effectively trained using person-centered interventions.[6]

Intrinsic learning motivation

The experience of self-efficacy and control over one's life is a necessary, though not sufficient, prerequisite for learning.[7] The experience of being competent is correlated with a feeling of autonomy that is an intrinsic motivation for learning.[8] This is a rationale for person-centered learning environments that allow students to experience feelings of competence during the course of their learning. Intrinsic learning motivation is necessary for sustained, lifelong learning so needed in rapidly changing modern times. Adaptation to change does not happen without intrinsic motivation to learn.

Feedback

An important determinant for feeling competent is positive feedback, informing students about their successful goal attainment, supporting them to seek actively for successes in their performances on tasks. The strongest determinant for achievement is feedback: 'Achievement is enhanced as a function of feedback';[9] 'Feedback does have a positive effect on physicians' clinical performance.'[10]

Mentoring and evidence-based learning

There are good reasons for enhancing traditional teaching by person-centered methods, including mentoring and evidence-based learning.[11] Evidence-based learning is a synthesis of problem-based, case-based, outcome-based mastery learning with quality assurance measures in teaching and tutoring, respectively. Evidence-based learning can be transferred to other domains like 'quality circle work' or quality management in education. Lyon presents the essentials for effective mentoring in Chapter 16.

Best Evidence Medical Education

Best Evidence Medical Education (BEME) consists in the application of research findings, educational experience, and student-centeredness. The literature clearly shows a need for formalization in medical curricula on the basis of empirical findings, i.e. evidence.[12] Educational research advantageously drives curricular management. Best evidence medical education is an example of introducing more effectiveness in teaching and students' achievement.

This book underpins these research points from the field of medical education. *On Becoming an Effective Teacher* is a highly enjoyable book to read. The authors have congruently combined scientific evidence from the past and present with empathetic storytelling. It is impressive and convincing when such empirical work is presented in a humane way. It's an eclectic and entertaining book, quite apart from its important empirical value. It ranges from Rogers speaking to thousands of people on the 'Man of Tomorrow' who Lyon suggests is 'the effective teacher of today', to Rogers' revealing dialogues with Lyon, on a wide range of educational and psychological issues. It gives long-overdue visibility to perhaps the most important large field study ever done on teaching by Aspy and Roebuck, which found that the most successful teachers are also the most person-centered. And one important outcome of their students is higher student achievement. And Tausch's replication, broadening, and deepening of the research in Germany, including startling new research on empathy presenting students' voices clamoring for more empathic teachers, adds corroboration to Rogers', Aspy's, and Roebuck's research, while Lyon's specific example of teaching a university psychology class using person-centered methods provides a useful model for the newly aspiring person-centered teacher. Finally, the recent huge meta-analyses of teaching, correlated with achievement by Hattie and Cornelius-White, bridge the past with the present. Reading this book is a fun, stimulating, and aesthetic learning experience. It will become classic reading for teachers, researchers, psychologists, students, and parents. We can all learn from it.

Florian Eitel, MD

Reinhard Tausch (foreground) and Florian Eitel, July 2010 (photo by H. Lyon)

Notes

1   Hattie, John (2009) *Visible Learning – A Synthesis of Over 800 Meta-Analyses Relating to Achievement*. London/New York: Routledge.
2   Cornelius-White, Jeffrey F. D., and Adam P. Harbaugh (2010) *Learner-Centered Instruction: Building Relationships for Student Success*. Thousand Oaks, CA/London/New Delhi/Singapore: Sage Publications.
3   Tang, F. I. , S. M. Chou, and H. H. Chiang (2005) 'Students' Perceptions of Effective and Ineffective Clinical Instructors'. *Journal of Nursing Education* 44, no. 4 (April): 187–92.
4   Kendrick, S. B., J. M. Simmons, B. F. Richards, and L. P. Roberge (1993) 'Residents' Perceptions of Their Teachers: Facilitative Behavior and the Learning Value of Rotations'. *Medical Education* 27, no. 1 (January): 55–61.
5   Hojat, M., J. S. Gonella, S. Mangione, T. J. Nasca, J. J. Veloski, J. B. Erdmann, C. A. Callahan, and M. Magee (2002) 'Empathy in Medical Students as Related to Academic Performance, Clinical Competence and Gender'. *Medical Education* 36, no. 6 (June): 552–57.
6   Lyon, H. C., M. Reincke, T. Brendel, A. Hesse, J. Ring, M. Holzer, and M. Fischer (2009) *Improvement of Faculty Lecturing by a Modified Flanders Interaction Analysis*. Published Proceedings of the International Association of Medical Science Education (IAMSE) Annual Meeting, University of Leiden, Netherlands, 29 June.

7   Prenzel M., F. Eitel, R. Holzbach, R. J. Schoenheinz, and L. Schweiberer (1993) 'Learning Motivation and Teaching Surgery'. *Journal of Education Psychology* 7, no. 2/3: 125–37.

8   Csikszentmihalyi, M. (1985) 'Reflections on Enjoyment'. *Perspectives in Biology and Medicine* 28, no. 4: 469–97.

9   Hattie (2009), *Visible Learning*.

10 Veloski, J, J. R. Boex, M. J. Grasberger, A. Evans, and D. B. Wolfson (2006) 'Systematic Review of the Literature on Assessment, Feedback and Physicians' Clinical Performance. BEME Guide 7'. *Medical Teacher* 28, no. 2: 117–28.

11 Eitel, F., and S. Steiner (1999) 'Evidence-Based-Learning'. *Medical Teacher* 21, no. 5: 506–12.

12 Eitel, F., K. G. Kanz, E. Hortig, and A. Tesche (2000) 'Do We Face a Fourth Paradigm Shift in Medicine – Algorithms in Education?' *Journal of Evaluation in Clinical Practice* 6, no. 3: 321–33.

INTRODUCTION TO THE AUTHORS

Carl Rogers

by Natalie Rogers

Carl Rogers (1902–1987) has been called 'the most influential psychologist in American history'. His influence in the fields of education, counseling, psycho-therapy, conflict resolution, and peace is similarly outstanding. The founder of humanistic psychology, he has impacted the world through his empathic presence, rigorous research, and his authorship of sixteen books and more than 200 pro-fessional articles. Among his best-known books are: *On Becoming a Person, Client Centered Therapy, Freedom to Learn, A Way of Being, Carl Rogers on Personal Power, Carl Rogers on Encounter Groups,* and *Becoming Partners: Marriage and Its Alternatives.*

His lifetime of research and experiential work focused on demonstrating the psychological conditions for allowing open communication and empow-ering individuals to achieve their full potential. He pioneered the move away from traditional psychoanalysis, and developed client-centered psychotherapy, which recognizes that 'each client has within him or herself vast resources for self-understanding', for altering his or her self-concept, attitudes, and self-directed behavior. Carl believed, and acted on the belief, that the client has the most important answers to his or her own personal issues within him- or herself, and the job of the therapist or teacher is to create a supportive environment in which the client can discover those answers.

Carl's last decade was devoted to applying his theories in areas of social conflict among nations. He traveled worldwide to accomplish this. In Belfast, Ireland, Rogers brought together influential Protestants and Catholics; in South Africa, blacks and whites; in the United States, con-sumers and providers in the health field. In November of 1985, Carl Rogers and his colleagues implemented their Peace Project – a conference in Rust,

Austria, bringing together high-ranking diplomats from seventeen Central and South American countries to discuss 'the Central American Challenge'. Carl said of this experience, 'This was a new experience for diplomats. It's a fluid process, but it worked. We wanted a gathering where influential international figures could meet "off the record" and talk, argue, shout and embrace in a situation where the staff makes it safe to do so, until they come to know each other deeply, to trust one another more fully and work together for peaceful solutions.' One of his last trips, at age 85, was to the Soviet Union, where he lectured and facilitated intensive experiential workshops fostering communication and creativity. He was astonished at the number of Soviets who knew of his work, since none of it had been published in Russian. His presence opened the field of Russian psychology to humanistic practices and values.

Recognition of his work has come through many honorary awards and degrees bestowed on him from throughout the world, among them the American Psychological Association's Distinguished Scientific Contribution Award, the first year it was given. A few years later he also received its Distinguished Professional Contribution Award. The day he died, February 4, 1987, also happened to be the day that he was nominated for the Nobel Peace Prize. The nomination states: 'your work in Central America, South Africa, and Northern Ireland is truly deserving of consideration for the Nobel Peace Prize'.

Five of his books have been published posthumously: *The Carl Rogers Reader*, a collection of his most influential writings, and *Carl Rogers: Dialogues* (both by Howard Kirschenbaum and Valerie Henderson), which features his interchanges with such other giants in the field as Paul Tillich, B.F. Skinner, Gregory Bateson, and Rollo May; *The Life and Works of Carl Rogers,* the impressive biography by Kirschenbaum; and *Carl Rogers: The China Diary*, edited by Jef Cornelius-White. Most importantly, Carl Rogers modeled the compassion and democratic ideals that he voiced. Jerry Freiberg has loyally updated Carl's excellent book *Freedom to Learn* to the eighth edition after Carl's death.

by Harold Lyon

I first read Carl Rogers' writings in 1964 in graduate school. My first personal contact with Carl came about in 1968, while I was serving in a political appointment in the Johnson Administration in the US Office of Education with responsibilities for improving the management of that Federal agency. This contact was a phone meeting between us discussing the possibilities of his working with us to improve communications among top managers. He was quite pessimistic about chances for achieving any breakthrough working in a large government bureaucracy using his small group techniques, unless all echelons, from the top to the bottom, were included. And he begged off of taking on such a commitment while recommending to me Chris Argyris, who had considerable experience working in large organizations and who later worked with us in our sometimes futile attempts to make the bureaucracy a more humane place to work.

My next contact with Carl came about just after the student rebellion crisis at Columbia University, when I was invited with a group of outsiders to attend a conference called 'Columbia – After the Crisis'. This was a unique attempt, in the wake of the riots at Columbia, to bring together the students, faculty, administration, and trustees with a group of outsiders who it was hoped would provide some objectivity to the meetings. I was honored to be among these outsiders along with Erik Erikson, John D. Rockefeller III, and Carl Rogers, who was asked to organize the meeting into small encounter groups, each containing a diverse mix of people to attempt to foster a climate of vulnerable honesty. By chance I ended up in the group Carl led, which was a fascinating experience.

Carl later invited me to contribute a book, *Learning to Feel – Feeling to Learn*, as part of his 'Studies of the Person' series of educational texts. He honored me by writing the foreword to that book, as he did with a subsequent book, *It's Me and I'm Here!*[1] Carl wrote of how strange it was that he and I were drawn together philosophically, given my vastly different background as a West Point graduate and former Ranger paratrooper military officer and his largely pacifist orientation. After we became friends, I invited him to my home in Washington, DC when I hosted him while he gave a series of workshops for Congressional staff leaders in the federal government and a large address to the nation's Capitol community. This inspirational address appears in this book as Chapter 3, 'The Man of Tomorrow'.

Just before Carl's visit to my home, I had a strange dream that I later shared with him. In the dream I had two guests at my home, General Maxwell Taylor, one of my military heroes, and Carl Rogers. In my dream I was rushing home on the eve of the arrival of my two distinguished guests, fearful that two such opposites might get there before I arrived and have nothing to say to each other. I was late and, when I arrived, I found the two making themselves at home in my garden, sitting on a bench together in animated conversation. When I shared the dream with Carl, he said that he was not at all surprised by the dream. That these two visitors in my dream clearly symbolized who I am – a seemingly paradoxical mix of the military combined with the person-centered therapist and educator. But he added that it was a bit arrogant of me in the dream to worry, as they both clearly had the skills to get along well. I enjoyed getting to know this quiet, humble, yet very strong man as a mentor, therapist, and friend during vulnerable visits with him and his wife, Helen, at their hillside home in La Jolla, California and at other meetings.

In the 1970s I visited Carl in La Jolla at the Center for Studies of the Person. My flight arrived late and, when I finally got to Carl's office, I was led by a graduate student into an ongoing encounter group being led by Carl, mostly of staff, graduate students, and interns dealing with internal issues. What happened was a bit disconcerting for me. After introducing me to the group and continuing the encountering for thirty minutes or so, Carl got up and, much to my surprise, said, 'I have a meeting. Please continue. Hal will take over leadership.' Carl left and did not return for over an hour until we broke later for lunch! Actually, in spite of Carl's ill-placed confidence in me, it went well, riding on the waves of here-and-now honesty, as we were, as we dealt openly with personal and professional issues and conflicts. Fortunately, I had led encounter groups at Esalen Institute and other growth centers and had also experienced my first encounter group with Carl as leader for the first time at Columbia University at their post-riot conference.

Though I feel Carl and I had a refreshingly open relationship with each other, I was recently surprised to learn that Carl was brought up in a fervent Christian home with daily prayer and Bible readings. I learned this from the excellent book edited by Jeffrey Cornelius-White, *Carl Rogers – The China Diary*,[2] a fascinating daily journal the young 20-year-old Carl kept during his six-month 1922 YMCA-sponsored trip to the Orient. On several occasions I shared my own faith with Carl and inquired about his, but in spite of his usual openness I had the feeling that this was a subject he preferred to keep to himself.

In the late 1970s, Carl and I agreed to put together a book for teachers which would bring together his various writings on education with some of the material from my book *Learning to Feel – Feeling to Learn*, plus new material from Carl, David Aspy, Reinhard Tausch, and others, along with some of my experiences in the field of education for the gifted and talented. That proposed book, to be called *On Becoming a Teacher*, was to highlight the excellent research on person-centered teaching done by my close friends David and Cheryl Aspy, Flora Roebuck, and corroborated by Reinhard Tausch in Germany, whose collective work, Carl and I both believed, had not had the wide exposure it deserved.

He cautioned me that he had not had any successful experience collaborating on a book together with anyone before and, in fact, had aborted one other failed attempt at doing so – a surprising admission from my mentor, who was a world-renowned expert in bringing adversaries together! He said he would agree to this only if I took full charge of it, integrated the writings he furnished, and if it generated no more work for him other than a final reading. I was optimistic and naive enough to think that this was possible. It was not. I was living on the edge then and my life imploded that year, after which Carl and I met privately at his home, and I sadly withdrew my name from the project.

For a time I regarded not completing that book successfully as one of my biggest failures … that is, until I made much more colossal ones! Some of the material we gathered for that book was later published in *Freedom to Learn for the*

80s, which has been well updated to many editions by Jerry Freiberg. Twenty years later, I was rummaging in my attic and found there the mouse-nibbled transcript of the dialogue which Carl and I had recorded, freely discussing an agreed-upon list of questions about education, along with the tape I had made of several of Carl's presentations. This dialogue had been sent to Carl after we recorded it, and he made some edits in it and sent it back to me. And then it disappeared with the original aborted manuscript, only to be resurrected by my visit to the attic. As I read this unpublished dialogue between us, I found it to be humbling as well as somewhat timeless – especially Carl's writings – and it appears here in this book for the first time, as Carl and I created it over three decades ago. It's a historical and vulnerable glimpse into the fine mind of my distinguished friend.

I have been blessed to have had Carl as one of my mentors and it is an honor to share these contributions of Carl's posthumously (with the permission of his daughter, Natalie), which corroborate the vital findings of his life's work: that learning facilitators, as he liked to call us – teachers, counselors, therapists, and parents – who use person-centered methods and who have the traits of empathy, genuineness, and unconditional positive regard for others, are the most effective teachers, therapists, managers, and parents.

I've had the opportunity personally to corroborate these person-centered principles in my own life in several diverse professions, from person-centered leadership of a combat-ready rifle company in the 101st Airborne Division, to management in many levels in government, including being part of the integration of both the universities of Mississippi and Alabama, early contributions to *Sesame Street*, the academic world, and in my current work teaching physicians to be more effective teachers, presented in Chapter 17 of this book. In 2009, John Hattie published the largest study of effective teaching ever done since the research studies presented in this book by Aspy, Roebuck and Tausch. Hattie synthesized over 800 meta-analyses of more than 200,000 studies, distilling it all into 'effect sizes' showing the power various educational innovations have to bring about student achievement.[3] Hattie's colossal work validates the research and person-centered philosophy presented in this book, showing that the teachers who care about their students, who empathize and plan with them, and give frequent supportive feedback, have powerful effects on their achievement. Jeffrey Cornelius-White has done a recent meta-analysis of the research since 1948 focusing on person-centered interventions that provides specific evidence that Learner Centered Instruction leads to positive student outcomes and achievement.[4]

Finally, an apt description of how Carl worked with others comes from Hermann Hesse's classic book *The Glass Bead Game*, written not about Carl, but accurately reflecting his mode of being with his patients, students, and friends:

Harold Lyon and Carl Rogers at Rogers' home, La Jolla 1978 (Photo by Helen Rogers)

All the complaints, confessions, charges, and qualms of conscience that were brought to him seemed to pass into his ears like water into the desert sands. He seemed to pass no judgment upon them and to feel neither pity nor contempt for the person confessing. Nevertheless, or perhaps for that very reason, whatever was confessed to him seemed not to be spoken into the void, but to be transformed, alleviated, and redeemed in the telling and being heard … Rarely did he give advice, let alone any order. Such did not seem to be his function, and his callers apparently sensed that it was not. His function was to arouse confidence and to be receptive, to listen patiently and lovingly, helping the imperfectly formed confession to take shape, inviting all that was dammed up or encrusted within each soul to flow and pour out. When it did, he received it and wrapped it in silence.[5]

Harold Lyon
by Carl R. Rogers, February 1980

I have known and grown to admire and respect Hal Lyon, as one of the more courageous and dedicated professionals I have encountered over the years. We first became acquainted in January 1969, while he was serving as Assistant Deputy US Commissioner of Education in the federal government – a position of considerable responsibility for a young man in his mid-thirties. During our first personal meeting he was a member of a small group I facilitated composed of faculty members, administrators, students, leaders, and other educators attempting to sort out the aftermath of the riots and crises that had occurred at Columbia

University the year before. From that time on our paths frequently crisscrossed in the worlds of psychology, education, and government.

Over the past, in my opinion, he made a most unique contribution toward bringing a more humanistic viewpoint toward education within the federal government. In what was sometimes an underground battle and other times a head-on attack, he consistently fought to give legitimacy within the federal establishment to those innovative programs that stand for a more humanistic approach toward education. For example, he chaired the federal Task Force that enabled North Dakota to install the statewide humanistic education programs that Charles Silberman acclaimed in his book *Crisis in the Classroom.*[6]

He successfully worked to insure that students, the real consumers of education, have a voice in the development of federal programs and priorities. His efforts helped establish a precedent for federal support of person-centered education.

His textbook on humanistic education, widely used on campuses around the country, *Learning to Feel – Feeling to Learn*, is a most comprehensive general overview of the person-centered education movement. Perhaps an excerpt from the foreword I wrote for this book will explain some of my feelings toward Hal and his professional work:

> This is a vital book for those responsible for classroom learning at every level. It is a book one cannot help but use, tempting everyone to try out some of the practical ways described for humanizing learning. It will stimulate innovation in all but the most torpid. Hal Lyon is a sensitive person who has learned deeply from his experiences in the military, in teaching and educational administration, in personal living and personal crises, and these lessons have come together in a deeply felt series of beliefs about the human being which shines through every page. It will make every reader a student of persons.

As a result of Hal's eight years of leadership as Federal Director of Education for the Gifted and Talented, a growing concern for gifted and talented youth emerged. Teams of leaders were trained from virtually every state, private foundation support was stimulated, and national mentor programs were developed. Through Hal Lyon's leadership a humanistic thread of concern for the whole person, affective as well as intellectual, has been woven throughout this national effort for bright and creative youth. Hal was also one of a small group of creative educators who helped launch the successful children's television program *Sesame Street*.

Hal has been a uniquely non-bureaucratic leader within the bureaucracy. His was an uphill battle, surviving public criticism, including Congressional inquiries stimulated by the John Birch Society over his sometimes unpopular humanistic beliefs and private lifestyle.

I also wrote the foreword for another book of Hal's, *It's Me And I'm Here!* which is a psychological account of his own pain, growth, and work as a

David Aspy, Carl Rogers, and Harold Lyon at the American Psychological Association Annual Meeting in Washington, DC, 1976

therapist and educator. It was in the reading of this highly personal manuscript that I realized the extent to which my writings and thinking have influenced his life. I find that his philosophical and personal outlook is very congenial to my own. From my foreword to that book:

> All in all I found this book a rich and poignant account of painful, exciting, enriching strides toward a growing and a becoming. It is written for persons: men, women, young people; partners and parents – I have difficulty in thinking of any who would not find it a compelling personal document. It stands as a sort of challenge to each one of us in his own private world. Here is a person who has risked, changed, grown. Do we possess equal courage?

The richness of his experiences, coupled with his warm and human presence toward students and associates, cause me to feel highly confident that whatever individuals or organizations are fortunate enough to gain his association and hear his thoughts will benefit and grow through his contributions.

Reinhard Tausch

by Harold Lyon and Inghard Langer

Reinhard Tausch (1921–) is known as the champion in the German-speaking world of person-centered psychotherapy and teaching, following in the footsteps of Carl R. Rogers. Together with his wife Anne-Marie Tausch (1925–1983), he has been Germany's leader in research on person-centered education and psychology.

As a young boy, Reinhard hated the inhumanities he experienced in the schools under the National Socialist regime and resisted joining the Hitler

Youth. He experienced in his schooling a painful lack of person-centered teaching and behavior on the part of his own teachers. After high school, he was forced to join the military in 1939. Six years later, in this painful period of his life, he sustained a serious wartime injury followed by a year's recuperation in a military hospital. These horrific World War II experiences had a powerful effect on his determination to devote the rest of his life toward contributing to Germany a more humanistic approach toward people and students, especially on the part of teachers and psychotherapists.

In 1947, he passed the examination as an elementary teacher. He studied Psychology at the University of Goettingen, earning his Ph.D. in 1951. From 1952 to 1954 he was an assistant professor at the University of Marburg, where he learned rigorous scientific research skills. In 1954, he married Anne-Marie, his partner for life. They worked closely together on cutting-edge person-centered research projects until her passing in 1983. Together, they performed the most thorough and important research ever done in Europe on person-centered teaching and psychology, following in the footsteps of the famous American father of client-centered therapy, Carl Rogers, with whom Tausch frequently corresponded and befriended.

From 1954 to 1960, Reinhard Tausch taught psychology at the Institute of Pedagogy in Weilburg/Hessen. In 1961, he completed his dissertation at the University of Marburg, followed by a professorship in psychology at the Paedagogische Hochschule Kettwig-Duisburg, where he headed a psychology research institute until 1964. This was followed by distinguished teaching and counseling at the University of Cologne. In their early years, Reinhard and Anne-Marie's studies showed how ineffective teaching usually was at schools, with persistent lecturing by teachers and often disrespectful treatment of students, and autocratic punitive behavior, beginning as early as kindergarten and progressing all the way through graduate school. Their studies caused an uproar in the press when, supported by their sound research, they encouraged teachers to radically change their behavior toward more person-centered methods. They were often under attack by school officials and sometimes their own conservative academic colleagues. In repeated empirical studies, the Tausches courageously showed that teachers who showed considerably respect or caring toward students, and were empathic and genuine, produced pupils who were motivated to study better and achieve more. Their evidence, captured on tape, was irrefutable. This led to many publications espousing the advantages of person-centered teaching in small groups as compared to the classic lecture format so prevalent in Germany. Their research showed that even athletics, school and scientific textbooks, and parenting could be much more effective if coming from a person-centered context.

After receiving his diploma, a book by Carl Rogers fell into the hands of Reinhard Tausch. He was fascinated, and soon, by himself, he started person-centered interviews with test persons who had asked for his help in using his 'perception experiment'. One year later, when he was working as an assistant in Marburg, he began to do therapy with patients who were emotionally disturbed. The therapy interviews were recorded with a *Drahtspulengeraet*, a primitive, early version of the tape recorder, while students observed these live therapy sessions through a one-way mirror. Shortly after, he introduced his first research results during a large psychology congress and his colleagues were much impressed by his results. But it wasn't until he became a professor in Hamburg in 1965 that he could perform larger scientific studies about the effectiveness of client-centered therapy. One of these studies that showed impressive and significant results in favor of client-centered therapy involved over 400 patients in person-centered group psychotherapy, compared to 500 in conventional individual therapy. Over 150 diploma theses and 25 doctoral dissertations resulted from this research work.

Some members of the faculty at that time objected to Reinhard Tausch's establishing a psychotherapeutic counseling center apart from the medical curriculum and were not pleased with the increase in graduate students in clinical psychology who were becoming advocates of client-centered therapy. Psychotherapy was seen at that time as exclusively part of the medical curriculum and profession. But finally the president of the university created three separate institutes for psychology. The institute III was reserved for Tausch's impressive clinical psychology.

Research in 'dialogue psychotherapy' included persons with clinically recognized disorders, to the dismay of the medical doctors, who saw 'the clinical' as their sole domain. Anne-Marie Tausch also pioneered controlled research studies and group client-centered psychotherapy treatment sessions with diverse groups including prisoners, elderly people over 70 years of age, the poor and hungry, cancer patients, and with schoolchildren.

Beginning in 1974, Reinhard and Anne-Marie participated as members and leaders in small-group discussions led by Carl Rogers in La Jolla, California, which began their personal friendship with Carl Rogers.

The psychotherapy philosophy of Carl Rogers, which was originally not translated into the German language, convinced the Tausches to publish their own research studies in the book *Gespraechspsychotherapie*. This title was chosen by Anne-Marie and Reinhard to underscore that in Germany, psychotherapy was done by *talking* with the patient, which then was all that was allowed by a person who was not a physician. Characteristic of this popular psychology book is clear and understandable language, statements on the basis of scientific results, and extensive personal experiences of single and group psychotherapy results the two achieved. They made their work transparent for thousands of others in a series of twelve German television programs about successful person-centered group therapy for psychologically disturbed people.

Rather than challenging the psychotherapy philosophy of Carl Rogers, Tausch is convinced that Rogers' person-centered methods are the optimal approach.

But he emphasizes that 'dialogue psychotherapy' can be improved by the person-centered approaches, better language, and methods of relaxation. In the book *Gespraechspsychotherapie*, he advocates dialogue therapy for serious chronic conditions and behavior therapy in the treatment of behavior disorders.

For fifteen years, Reinhard Tausch worked intensively in this research area. He believes that people can help themselves when they are emotionally distressed, along with the help of professionals. In that sense Tausch mirrors the view of Rogers that all patients have within themselves the answers to the questions which trouble them. And the work of the therapist is to create the facilitative environment in which the patient can discover those answers. In the last couple of decades, Tausch has performed more than twenty-five empirical studies, with the goal of finding out what people find helpful when they were distressed, and empathy was one of those important findings. Out of this work came the popular book *Hilfen bei Stress und Belastung*.

Reinhard Tausch, together with Anne-Marie, performed significant scientific research in three different but connected areas, passing on their wisdom in educational psychology and 'dialogue therapy' as well as greatly influencing the field of self-help therapy. In addition to his popular books, including his *Erziehungs-Psychologie*, which has sold over 160,000 copies, the backbone of his contribution, irrespective of his books, is his solid empirical research. Reinhard Tausch's empirical methods led to useful results in meaningful areas of life that are useful for human beings.

From 1965 to 1987, Tausch taught psychology as a tenured professor at the University of Hamburg, where he is still Professor Emeritus. In 1991, he was honored with the Hugo-Muensterberg-Medal of the Association of Professionals of German Psychology for his outstanding achievements in the field of applied psychology. In 2002, he was honored by the German government when they presented him with their most distinguished honor, the Order of Merit, Highest Category.

Rogers was to describe Anne-Marie and Reinhard Tausch's research with children in schools, teachers, parents, and even the effects of person-centered books for children, as having been done with 'Teutonic thoroughness'. When Rogers and I first planned this book, we both agreed that the most important research to include was the person-centered large field studies done by my close friends David and Cheryl Aspy and Flora Roebuck, which had not received the visibility it deserved. Rogers told me that this work had been replicated and expanded in Germany by his friend Reinhard Tausch, whose work was essential to be featured in this book. Shortly thereafter, Reinhard sent us the story of his person-centered research, which was edited by Flora Roebuck from its rough translation into what appears here as Chapter 14.

In 2000, I first traveled to Stuttgart to meet this sparkling-eyed, brilliant man personally for the first time. He was still playing tennis four or five times per week

Reinhard Tausch and Harold Lyon, 2010 (Photo by Florian Eitel)

at age 80. We agreed to seek the right publisher for this rare book and I began to organize it for us. I visited him again in 2010 with my surgeon–educator friend and former student of Reinhard's, Florian Eitel, to discuss his contribution to the book and shared a lunch and gracious visit with this distinguished man. Just before the manuscript for this book was due to the publisher, Reinhard appropriately insisted that it should include his most recent research with Renate Hüls on empathy to insure that the loud and desperate voices of students crying out for more empathic teachers was presented in this book. I'm honored to appear as coauthor with Reinhard Tausch and Carl Rogers.

Notes

1   Lyon, H. C. (1974) *It's Me and I'm Here!* New York: Delacorte.
2   Cornelius-White, J. H. D. (ed.) (2012) *Carl Rogers – The China Diary.* Ross-on-Wye: PCCS Books.
3   Hatttie, John (2009) *Visible Learning: A Synthesis of Over 800 Meta-Analyses Relating to Achievement.* London/New York: Routledge.
4   Cornelius-White, J. D. H., and A. P. Harbaugh (2010) *Learner-Centered Instruction.* Thousand Oaks, CA: Sage.
5   Hesse, Hermann (1943) *The Glass Bead Game.* London: Random House/ Vintage, pp. 466–67.
6   Silberman, Charles E. (1979) *Crisis in the Classroom – The Remaking of American Education.* New York: Random House.

PART I
Person-centered freedom

1

A DIALOGUE BETWEEN CARL ROGERS AND HAROLD LYON

CARL: Schools can, if they wish, deal with students in ways that stimulate and facilitate significant and self-reliant learning. This approach is based on person-centered freedom – to learn and to live. It eliminates every one of the elements of conventional education. It does not rely on a carefully prescribed curriculum, but rather on one that is largely self-chosen; instead of standard assignments for all, each student sets his own assignment; lectures constitute the most infrequent mode of instruction; standardized tests lose their sanctified place; grades are either self-determined or become a relatively unimportant index of learning.

HAL: Your statement supports what we found about maximizing the potential of exceptional children – those with special needs as well as the gifted and talented child. We found that the classroom, which is geared to the average child, is not suitable for many children. Both gifted children, who wish to go faster or learn in depth, and special needs children who should approach learning in a unique way, need education tailored to the individual person. Federal legislation prescribed that these needs point schools toward mainstreaming children: providing special needs or gifted children special programs with special services, but placing the child, for at least part of each day, in a classroom that has diverse children. There are some concerns about this. Studies show gifted children tend to drop out of school, as they are often bored and not challenged, and they will sometime rebel from the educational system which moves at the pace of the average child, or even slower. In a national study, over 30% of dropouts were found to be gifted and talented children, turned off and bored by the traditional lock-step classroom.[1] Special needs children also have some problems when you mainstream them. They tend to have better peer associations and friendships when they're in small groups for at least a few hours a day with their own peers. They tend not to make friendships as well in the normal classroom and need time with their own peers and then they often blossom. But they also have much to gain from their average classmates and vice versa. I am not in favor of segregating the gifted in special private or public schools, separate from other youngsters. They also need to have a few hours a day with other gifted children to go deeply in a richer curriculum, to have more creative opportunities, to have more independent study, to be free to learn and grow at their own pace and in their own direction.

CARL: Well, this is not a field of expertise for me. My one comment is of a general nature: I do see one positive opportunity in bringing together all these different kinds of children. I think they do need to be in the kinds of small groups that you mentioned, but I also see another opportunity. If teachers and parents of these special needs children and normally functioning children could meet in small groups with a competent facilitator, important changes would follow. We know that from our experience. There could be open expression of the feelings of each group – an open facing of the fear or prejudice most of us feel in dealing with the disabled, and the jealousy that many people feel in dealing with the gifted or unusually talented child. And so, facing of those prejudices and fears would mean growth for all concerned. I know from my experience in workshops for handicapped persons that they hold the possibility of the handicapped individual being treated as a person; not always supported; not always treated gingerly; but sometimes being confronted honestly, instead of with deference. I've seen individuals confronted – people in wheelchairs – who were told that they're taking up too much time, or 'You're using your handicap as a lever to manipulate us.' And that honesty has been a very constructive experience for those people. They need that kind of solid confrontation as well as the more usual sympathy and understanding of their condition. This has been a lesson personally for me because I've had this same discomfort of dealing with a handicapped individual as just a person, but one can overcome that. When I've been able personally to overcome that, it's a freeing thing to all concerned. So the mixing of different kinds of children in the same classroom does have an opportunity for growth if we can take the initiative and have the imagination and the skill to use that opportunity.

HAL: I'm reminded of a friend who is blind and who shared with me about going to a program with you at La Jolla many years ago. After he emerged from this program, he said that for the first time in his life he had received honest feedback from sighted people about himself. He had always been treated with deference because he was blind. It was the first time he had any sense of his own being as a solid person because he knew what he was getting in the way of feedback was honest, even though it wasn't always complimentary. It was the first time that he really emerged with a sense of who he was as a person. Before he went to the program, he was having a lot of difficulties, had taken drugs, and was very depressed. Since then, he has completed his Ph.D. and now he is leading a national program of cross-country skiing for blind people, including an international competition for cross-country skiing on established trails. It's interesting how that one intense experience was pivotal in his life: being integrated with sighted people and having that workshop experience without being treated as a special disabled individual but, instead, being treated as a person.

CARL: That's a beautiful illustration and it's the kind of thing I would hope might occur in the schools. Education that centers on the individual as a person can have a really freeing impact. I believe that any factor that helps the young, growing child to realize that learning is important is bound to have a lasting effect on his or her life. I'm really not surprised at the findings of an organization called the Consortium for Longitudinal Studies which indicated that the positive effects on children of early intervention projects, such as *Sesame Street,* a program I know you helped in its early stages, are showing up later as greater social and intellectual maturity as those students reach adolescence. The fact that the original effects of these interventions seemed to have been washed out by third grade may have been because the impact was something that goes deeper than the qualities which are tapped by third grade achievement tests. I think, for many children, it's a significant experience to receive special attention at an early age. It helps to build self-esteem and self-esteem makes for greater maturity in the child. I am excited and pleased to know that the kind of attention they receive, this kind of building of their self-confidence, does show up in later years, even if it doesn't show up in the very early years of school. I might add that even elderly people show very positive changes from an hour or two a week in which they are the focus of caring and attention. This statement is based on a thorough research study made by Reinhard and Anne-Marie Tausch in Germany. They demonstrated that, at any age, when special attention is given to a group of people, positive and constructive effects result. I think whether the early learning programs are ideal from the point of view of instruction or not, the basic element of attention and of making the child feel important, helping the child feel confident – those elements are bound to last.

HAL: As we do more research, I think we'll find even more significant results accruing from the earliest interventions. And I'm not just talking about the first couple years at school. I'm talking about from conception on. Even the first nine months in utero, the nutrition of the mother and her personal experiences make a difference: whether she smokes or not; whatever she takes into her body – all this has an effect on that child's early development. And the birth process itself makes a difference. I was intrigued by the follow-up research done by the French Association for Psychology on the Leboyer children who are now much older. The initial sample of 126 of these children were birthed in a tender candlelit environment without an anesthetic – being handed to the mother, in a natural way, caressed and massaged immediately after birth; the umbilical was kept intact for ten minutes or so as a supplementary oxygen source, and then the children were immersed in warm water to simulate being in utero. This is in contrast to the traumatic experiences of our modern technological birth process, where the mother often gets a saddle block anesthetic, which goes straight to the child's lungs when it needs to breathe for that first moment, where the child gets a sudden spank on the rear end and then placed in a crib to bond with a plastic bottle. These Leboyer children were largely free of most of the early childhood diseases and problems. They're very happy. They held up their heads and smiled significantly sooner than children whose mothers had an anesthetic and they are exceptionally bright. Out of 126 of them, 100 seemed to be ambidextrous, which says something about the damage that we may be doing to one-half of the brain in our modern, technological birth process.

Some years ago Burton White at Harvard showed that, between 8 and 22 months, a child is literally consumed by curiosity. This is a vital period when creativity is formulated. Yet, it's the same period when the child is reaching for every breakable object in the household, and mother is saying, 'No, no, no, no!' punctuated by a slap on the hand, which tends to stifle that creative development at this important formative time. Burton White showed that you can train mothers to set up stimulating 'childproof' environments during that crucial period. So, before the child ever gets to school, parents have a special opportunity to nourish creativity.

I think parents are the most important teachers and, for this reason, this book is written for parents as well as classroom teachers. Parents are the most important influence during the years where much of growth, learning, attitudes and directionality are established for later growth and development in school.

And let me say something about *Sesame Street,* for which I take no credit. I was fortunate to be there with a great man, Harold Howe II, then the US Commissioner of Education, and a small group of other very creative divergent thinkers when we brainstormed how we might create one program which would survive, reach young inner-city children and build long-term success. The TV antennas on each roof seemed the best route to get into inner-city homes and we had to reach them before school began. But how to start one major initiative that would survive the current administration and continue beyond that, was the real challenge. Howe and Lloyd Morrisett, his friend from the Carnegie Foundation, who got the idea for a TV show for teaching children by watching his own children remembering TV ads, went out to foundations and told of their vision of something unique which would survive beyond the Johnson Administration and keep being well funded. We needed long-term private, as well as short-term federal, money to insure its success. The foundations responded.

We were also lucky to find the most creative and motivated people in Joan Ganz Cooney and her Children's Television Workshop (CTW). As the federal project officer for these efforts, I was honored to sit with the CTW Research Advisory Board and was a witness to one of the most amazing and successful examples of 'person-centered' education ever created. Every show involved constructive 'arm wrestling' between the technical video people and the educators. We had cognitive objectives for each show (e.g. learn the numbers 1 and 2), plus affective objectives (e.g. honesty, caring about others, respecting the elderly, 'the Golden Rule', etc.). Before a show was aired, CTW tested the tapes with children in day-care centers along with very interesting toys and the show had to hold the attention of the children, in spite of the competing toys, while, at the same time, achieving the educational objectives. I loved it that every show had affective as well as cognitive objectives, which was the theme of a book of mine.[2]

My favorite has always been the show where the little boy has lost his mother, whom he describes as 'the most beautiful woman in the whole world'. The villagers and the chief do a big search and no one can find her. After a day of searching, an ugly-appearing old hag comes limping down the street. The little boy runs up shouting, 'Mother!' They embrace and the village chief scratches his head and mumbles, 'Beauty *is* in the eye of the beholder.'

CARL: I would like to add my hearty endorsement to what you said. I've been fascinated, also, by the Leboyer birth process. One of my colleagues has said, 'That makes the birth process a really person–centered thing,' and I believe that's true. It treats the newborn infant with the real respect which is his due and it does make a tremendous difference in their development, their early start on becoming fully functioning persons. And *Sesame Street* is truly one of the most indelible examples of 'person–centered' teaching that has caught on internationally. Children all over the world benefit from it and you were, indeed, fortunate to have been a part of its beginning.

HAL: I was interested in what you said about positive changes for elderly people resulting from focused, caring attention for an hour or two a week. That seems important to me – the idea that we are never too old to benefit from person-centered interaction. We are an aging population, while the proportion of young people in the population is getting smaller. We older people are finding that we can do things that we didn't expect to do later in life, and continuing education about what it means to be old is of growing importance. Our expectations about what it means to be old are being knocked down. For example, sexuality for older people is something that is quite common up through the eighties and later, but young people don't realize or appreciate that. Often in nursing homes older people are treated like children and they are deprived of their privacy and opportunities to experience their sexuality – to keep growing. I was delighted to learn in a visit to a retirement village that the older people are speaking out about their right to have their own sexuality. Ongoing educational opportunities for the elderly are essential. We need to have teachers who are responsive and sensitive to the needs of the elderly, who still have an incredible amount to contribute from their experience.

The elderly also make excellent teachers at times. We've lost so much of our family continuity, such as grandparents teaching grandchildren traditions. We can reinstitute it by mentor-type programs where retired older people can work with younger people, which can be a growth experience for both ages.

Older people tend to be 'out of touch', literally and figuratively. They are not touched very much. A program of massage therapy was introduced in a community's nursing homes in California and the results were astounding. Seniors involved in the massage program who had not been able to get out of bed for several years began walking, and morbidity and mortality among those being touched dropped significantly. The power of such a natural and normal person-centered act such as touching is amazing.

CARL: I would concur with what you said about sexuality among older people and also their ability as teachers. I would add one other general thought: as our population becomes older, it would be a horrible thing if they simply settled into rigid, traditional attitudes. It's very important that the elderly be a growing learning group in our country. Otherwise, they may find themselves frozen in a most unfortunate psychological rigidity. Person-centered freedom can happen in any age group and any setting; we don't have to be bound by patterns of the past. It is in the hope of letting teachers know that it is not necessary to follow the conventional pattern that this book presents the conceptual material and examples of person-centered ways in which people may learn. It seems important to show that such significant, self-initiated, experiential learning is possible in sharply different kinds of educational situations, including senior homes, and that it produces self-reliant learners, capable of fully functioning in all aspects of life.

Notes

1   Marland, S. P., Jr (1972) *Education of the Gifted and Talented,* Vol. 1, *Report to the Congress of the United States by the US Commissioner of Education.* Washington, DC: US Government Printing Office.
2   Lyon, H. C. (1974) *Learning to Feel – Feeling to Learn.* Columbus, OH: Charles Merrill.

2

WHO WANTS A PERFECT TEACHER?

Harold Lyon

Another learning I would like to mention briefly is one of which I am not proud but which seems to be a fact. When I am not prized and appreciated, I not only feel very much diminished, but my behavior is actually affected by my feelings. When I am prized, I blossom and expand, I am an interesting individual. In a hostile or unappreciated group, I am just not much of anything. People wonder, with very good reason, how did he ever get a reputation? I wish I had the strength to be more similar in both kinds of groups, but actually the person I am in a warm and interested group is different from the person I am in a hostile group. Thus, prizing or loving and being prized or loved is experienced as very growth enhancing, A person who is loved appreciatively, not possessively, blooms and develops his own unique self. The person who loves non-possessively is himself enriched. This, at least, has been my experience.[1]

Carl R. Rogers

In contrast to the violence in our classrooms we read about so often today, my educational dream of the future is that we as teachers could take off our roles and masks and be individual human beings relating with other human beings instead of playing the teacher role – then we'd have the warmth and motivation in the classroom that we lack.

I'm not advocating that we become amateur therapists in the classroom or elsewhere – teachers are not legally or professionally qualified to do that – but I am saying that we can be authentic or genuine in the classroom. When this happens, we begin to allow people to be.

It's not easy to take such risks. But to stand up in front of a classroom as a genuine person can be a freeing experience. This is the difference between what I call 'status' and 'natural authority'. Status authority comes from hiding behind a podium, a degree, or a title, lecturing down to an 'inferior' group of students, waiting to be filled with your superior knowledge. Natural authority is earned from sharing in a learning experience with a group of colleagues by bringing together all your resources, books, experiences, friends, feelings – and the students in the classroom, who are the most important resource of all.

How many teachers think of bringing a friend, who may be visiting, into the classroom to share with the students? Friends are so rare. As I get older, I begin to realize that if I have two or three on whom I can really count, I am indeed blessed. To bring a friend into your classroom to share with your students can be a peak experience for you and your friend, as well as for the students. Friends are one resource that you have. And the students in the classroom are the most important resource of all. They learn more from one another than they do from the teacher. The teacher who is most effective is a good catalyst, a facilitator who can implement that kind of discovery. This is a teacher who doesn't have all the answers. You never will, so why pretend?

The thing that is beautiful about us is not our perfection but rather our imperfection. This is what makes us human. A human being is not perfect. The hothouse fruits of life, grown in the 'perfect' protective environment of the greenhouse, don't have nearly the flavor of those that are exposed to the wind and the rain and the elements. The same thing is true of people. Those people who are overly protected – who look perfect – don't have the flavor of those who are more natural. What's beautiful is our humanity, which may be imperfect but real.

Who wants a perfect teacher? A perfect teacher is phony. Who wants a perfect wife, a perfect husband, a perfect boss? Those people are not genuine. You lift a tremendous burden off your shoulders when you shed your need to be perfect – to look as though you have all the answers. And this, for me, is a vital discovery!

My over-achieving image of perfection began when I was five years old and my father left for World War II. As he left, he said: 'Now, you be good; you're going to be the man of the house. You take care of your mom. You be good and I'll hurry home!' That stuck in my mind through childhood and adolescence. I had tried so hard to be good, and he hadn't come home for three and a half years, and I had kept trying, thinking I just wasn't 'good' enough.

In wanting so badly to take care of my mother, I instantly 'grew up', skipping over the tender times of childhood. That's when I first became an over-achiever, trying to gain all those accomplishments in order to let them speak for me. But what I really wanted was for my father to come home. I wanted to be held and loved to make up for what I didn't have enough of as a baby – few of us do. I suspect that's how many of us become over-achievers. If we're fairly bright or fairly talented, we climb all the ladders to get the rewards held up by society rather than seeking for the rewards from within.

But when we finally discover we can get important rewards from within, this discovery frees us in a new way. It's a freeing from being dependent on everyone else. It's growing from environment support to self-support. This is what maturity is about – leaving the support of the environment and being able to get most of our approval from within ourselves.

Alfred North Whitehead once said: 'After you understand all about the sun and the stars and the rotation of the Earth, you may still miss the radiance of the sunset.'

During a crisis in my life − a 'peak experience' of intense loneliness − I found I could no longer evade the pain of my own loneliness. In the past I had gathered friends around me or had gotten busy accomplishing things to evade my loneliness but this was a time when I didn't quite outrun it; it caught up with me. So I spent time crying for the first time in my life and deeply admitting to myself that I was very lonely. Beneath my tough veneer, in my loneliness, I found new strength; I found tenderness (which my alma mater, West Point, didn't exactly nourish) − a new creativity: an undiscovered part of the essence of me. I even found a rather likable little-boy part of me that 'growing up fast' had almost completely bypassed, and it's now a favorite part of me.

This was a kind of 'Men's Liberation' for me − a freeing from the 'macho' toughness I had thought was my strength, and an allowing of the tenderness that I had thought to be my weakness when it was really my strength.

Society teaches us in many ways, and so do schools and parents, to have a fixed set of responses to things. Certainly West Point conditioned a fixed set of responses in me to many things. Society encourages this and calls it 'character'. And that means that we have a small, narrow, ego boundary in which we're secure and which generates a fixed predictable set of responses. To the extent that we're stuck that way, we realize a fraction of our potential and numb a tremendous amount of our essence and vitality.

I'm convinced that if we can deal with the whole person with feelings and intellect in the classroom, if teachers can begin to deal with children as feeling human beings instead of just intellects to be developed, then there's hope for education in this country. We have many one-dimensional half-men teaching all around the country, often brilliantly developed intellectually but stunted emotionally. Many of these people are afraid to deal with their feelings − the affective side of man. And I believe acknowledging the affective reduces violence and has many other benefits, as the research of Tausch, the Aspys, and Roebuck will show in this book.

You can integrate the cognitive with the affective within the classroom. For example, if you are an English teacher teaching *The Red Badge of Courage* or *Lord of the Flies*, break the class down into five-person groups; have each group get rid of a member. And those who were rejected could perhaps form their own groups and talk to the rest of the class about how it feels to be rejected, comparing that with how Piggy felt in *Lord of the Flies* or how the hero felt in *The Red Badge of Courage* when not accepted by one regiment or another.

While I worked briefly with the White House Task Force on the Gifted in 1968, we interviewed some of this country's most successful citizens. We asked them to identify what helped them most in realizing their potential. Most had the same answer to that question. Some person − a teacher, a coach, a respected adult − had stepped out of his or her role and rank, taken off his or her mask and status, and built an intimate one-to-one human relationship with these individuals

– encouraging them to believe in themselves, to take risks and try things they wouldn't have tried without such encouragement.

How we can build such mentor relationships with students was a concern in our efforts for gifted and talented students some years ago, and it continues in not enough schools today. What traits does such a mentor or teacher have? I think they are the same traits which Carl Rogers' research found to be significant in therapists and Tausch, the Aspys, and Roebuck have found in their extensive studies: *realness*, genuineness, or congruence in the teacher; *prizing* or high regard toward others; and *empathy* out of which grows trust between teacher and learner.

But these are traits very few schools or teacher training institutions are fostering. Is it difficult to teach these traits? The Aspys and Roebuck show us that this is not nearly as difficult as one might think. We also recently found that we could teach medical teachers in these person-centered traits in a cost-effective process which I present in Chapter 17.

You have to let people discover these traits in an environment in which such discoveries can take place. This is the kind of environment where we tend to be human beings instead of superior cognitive intellectuals lecturing at students.

When you reach that independent place of self-support, you are so free that another strange thing happens for which I have no explanation. You become 'a mirror'. When other persons look in your eyes, they can feel their own beauty in your reflection. It is as though you mirror their beauty and they feel good about themselves. Now, I have no cognitive explanation for that. It's just something that happens. My hope is that teachers or facilitators can free themselves enough to become mirrors for their students in which the students can see the beauty of themselves as real human beings, or that managers can be that way with their employees.

When that happens, we begin treating people the way we treat sunsets. Carl Rogers once said that, when we look at a sunset, no one says, 'It needs a little more orange in the cloud cover, a little more pink on the right hand side.' You allow it to be. That's one of the joys of sunsets – they're all unique. You allow them to be just what they are. This is what this book is about ... and we present the research to support this person-centered viewpoint.

Note

1   Rogers, C. R. (1988) *A Way of Being*. Boston: Houghton Mifflin, p. 23.

3

THE MAN OF TOMORROW

A speech given to the Washington, DC
community on February 22, 1978

Carl Rogers

This unpublished address of Rogers speaks of the person Rogers saw emerging in the late 1970s – the generation we now know as the 'Baby Boomers' now in their fifties and sixties and at the peak of influence in their lives and careers. What has happened now at the turn of the century to this minority and their individualistic courage that Rogers speaks about? Have they become the leaders of their generation, or have the more conservative of them emerged at the helm? Do these people Rogers described more than thirty years ago still survive as part of the fabric of modern society? Do we still value their traits today? How has this Man of Tomorrow (now our man of today) been shaped or diluted by our schools and our society? Have we killed off Rogers' Man of Tomorrow? Are such persons able to survive in today's schools, businesses, and society? Is there hope that he and his values have been woven into the fabric of our society and represent hidden strengths in our academic institutions, schools, businesses, and governments? These are but a few questions stimulated by Rogers' historical and provocative prophecy about the Man of Tomorrow spoken many years ago. The violent terrorists of today certainly do not have the positive values of Rogers' Man of Tomorrow, but do a few irresponsible people of today forebode a new violent man of the coming decades and, if so, what can we do as teachers to prevent that? Chapter 4 suggests that Rogers' Man of Tomorrow is today's most effective teacher. This speech was taped in Washington, DC and was part of a series of addresses and seminars Rogers gave to influential government officials, elected representatives, and profession-als at the invitation of Hal Lyon in 1978 when he served as Director of Education for the Gifted and Talented in the US Department of Education.

Introduction of Carl Rogers by Harold Lyon

It's a special privilege for me to have the honor of introducing our distinguished speaker, as he has inspired me in both my professional and person life. I could spend twenty minutes listing his impressive achievements in the fields of psychology, education, research, or even horticulture (he's quite a gardener). Or I could talk about his books, several of which have been bestsellers and many of which you've read. Or I could speak of his courageous pioneering over the past half-century, which has resulted in the most significant contribution toward making psychotherapy and education a humanistic growing process of becoming a person with major emphasis – his emphasis – on the precious uniqueness of the person. However, he has been publicly recognized throughout his impressive career by many organizations, such as the American Psychological Association which singled him out as the only American psychologist ever to be awarded both of its major awards, the Award for Scientific Contribution and the Award for Professional Achievement.

Over the past few decades, the 'Rogerian' or 'Client-Centered' approach has become a household word throughout the world of psychotherapy, where change occurs almost as slowly as it does in the world of education, and where until the emergence of our speaker, Freud and his therapist–centered approach has reigned rigidly for over a century. Carl has served as President of the American Psychological Association, American Academy of Psychotherapists, and serves presently as a member of the National Advisory Committee on the Gifted and Talented.

Rather than dote more on his accomplishments, I'd like to share with you a bit of what he has meant to me personally.

I first discovered Carl only five years ago, perhaps long after many of you had already read *On Becoming a Person*, which, incidentally, was named in a national survey of students as one of 'The Ten most Popular Textbooks in the US'. The book which really turned me on to him was his *Freedom to Learn*, a beautifully written book where I found strong reinforcement for my views that, not only can the student be trusted to pursue his own paths, but that when he encounters a teacher or learning facilitator, as Carl likes to call teachers, who is genuine or real, who prizes or cares about students, and who possesses empathic understanding, the student will often grow in ways far beyond expectations. These are the same traits that Carl's research has shown to be most effective in a therapist.

Carl has said that it is difficult to reach a person through a book. But he has reached me remarkably through his writings. It's as though many of the peak discoveries I have arrived at through crises and experiences in my life have been reinforced for me in his written views.

I share his view that one must experience 'here-and-now' discovery for significant learning to take place. More often than not, the usual sequence is for one to read or learn about the theory in books or in the classroom, and then, if the course was one of those rare relevant ones, perhaps the person later in his life's paths experiences something akin to the theory he learned in school. For me it seems to have been the reverse. Most of my early academic experience seems largely irrelevant in terms of what I now value in life. As I have lived my life, I've had many peak or crisis experiences with no earlier theoretical background as a reference. Carl's writings have provided a kind of reinforcing person theory of life for me after the experiences rather than before.

And after I read his book *Becoming Partners*, I realized that in that excellent book Carl's realness, his sense of prizing, and his empathic understanding shine through beautifully as he opens himself to the reader.

Through later personal meetings with Carl Rogers, I have grown to deeply admire and respect his humility and wisdom. Though I have never been in his classes or his patient, I feel I am his pupil and he has been my therapist and teacher. It's a pleasure to introduce to you tonight the man who has perhaps done more than any other toward making this world a viable place for the 'person of tomorrow', Dr Carl R. Rogers.

Carl speaking

Thank you Hal for that … I think I would call it a tribute. It always perplexes me when I hear – it always makes me feel very ambivalent – because you're saying a lot of very nice things that I know he means, and on the other hand it sounds almost uncomfortable; like an epitaph or something like that and I'll hope it isn't that, though I get closer to it all the time. It's been a long time since I've been to Washington; it's a pleasure to be here again. I'm also a little appalled by what I've heard that people have been left standing out in the cold as the auditorium is full, and some group came from West Virginia and cannot get in … and all kinds of things like that. I don't know what my fatal attraction is but it really sort of bowls me over each time when I run into something like this, especially when I doubted that I would begin to fill a theater holding several thousand people!

As I sat here looking over the audience, I was glad to see that from a quick inspection it looked to me as though there were a lot of young people here. I certainly want to talk to people of every age but it does please me that young people think I have something to say. I hope that you'll find that's true because tonight I want to talk about the person who's emerging for the future.

I'm fascinated these days by what I'm convinced is a very significant phenomenon. I'm seeing a new man emerging; and when I say man, I mean man and woman, it's one of the difficulties in our language that you can't say it all in one word. I believe that this new man is the person of tomorrow and I would like to talk to you about him. I've seen him emerging partially from encounter groups, sensitivity training, so-called 'T' groups.

I realize that for many years I saw facets of him emerging in the deep relationship that is psychotherapy. I see him showing his face in the rapidly growing trend toward a humanistic or human psychology. And though I'm not speaking about just one age group, I see him in the new type of student emerging in our colleges and in the persistent, even if less violent, campus unrest all over the world and in the impressive number of high-caliber dropouts from our educational institutions. To me, he's not all lovable; in fact, sometimes he's rather frightening, but he is emerging.

I see him in the surge toward individualism and self-respect in our black population, in and out of the ghettos, and in the racial unrest, which runs like a fever through all of our cities. I see elements of him in the philosophy of the hundreds of communes in this country and in the lifestyle of the groups of people called 'hippies'. I see him, strangely enough, in the younger members of industrial management today. I catch what to my older eyes is a confusing glimpse of him in the musicians, the poets, the writers, the composers of this generation. I'll just mention the Beatles and you can bring it up to date with many, many others.

I have a feeling that the mass media, especially television, have helped him to emerge, though on this I'm not very clear. But I've named, I think, some of the areas and trends, which perhaps have caused his emergence and certainly permit us to see the qualities of this new man. Though I am excited and full of anticipation about this person of tomorrow, there are aspects of the situation, which are very sobering.

I believe the new man has characteristics which run strongly counter to the orthodoxies and the dogmas and the forms of the major Western religions: Catholicism, Protestantism, Judaism. He doesn't fit at all in the traditional industrial management in organizations. He contradicts in his person almost every element of traditional schools, colleges, and universities. He certainly is not suited to become a part of bureaucratic government and he doesn't fit well into the military. Since our culture has developed all these orthodoxies and forms of present-day life, we have to ask ourselves seriously if this new man is simply a deviant misfit or whether he is something more hopeful?

There's another reason for thinking deeply and soberly about him. He's almost the antithesis of the puritan culture, with its strict beliefs and controls, which founded our country. He's very different from the person admired by the industrial revolution, with those persons' ambition and competitiveness and productivity. He's deeply opposite to the communist culture, with its controls on individual freedom of thought and behavior in the interest of the State. He in no way resembles the medieval man – a man of faith and force, of monasteries, and Crusades. I don't think he would be congenial with the man produced by the Roman Empire – the practical, disciplined man. He's also very alien to today's culture in the United States, with its emphasis on computerized technology and on the man in uniform: whether military, police, or government inspector.

If, then, he's new in so many ways, if he deviates so deeply from almost all of the gradually developed norms of the past and even the present, is he just a spot in the evolutionary line, soon to die out or be discarded? Personally, I don't believe so. I believe he's a viable creature. I have the conviction that he's the person of tomorrow and that perhaps he has a better chance of survival than we do. But I'll admit that's only my own opinion.

I've talked about him at some length but I have made no attempt to describe his attitudes, his characteristics, and his convictions. I'm going to try to do that very briefly. I would say that I don't know of any one individual to whom all of the following statements would apply. I'm also keenly aware that I'm describing a minority, probably a small minority, of our present-day population. But I'm convinced that it's a growing minority. What follows is a groping, uncertain characterization of what I see as the new man.

Some of his qualities are probably temporary ones as he struggles to break free from the cocoon of his culture. I'll try to indicate those. Some, I believe, represent the processed person that he's becoming. Here, then, are some of his characteristics as I see it. He has no use for sham, facade or pretense, whether in interpersonal relationships, in education, in business, in politics or in religion. He values authenticity. He will not put up with double-talk. He hates statements such as these: 'cigarette smoking is a romantic, exciting, pleasurable, satisfying thing' (and, of course, it kills a great many people through lung cancer). Or, 'we followed an honorable pathway in protecting South Vietnam from its enemies and living up to our commitments'. I guess you've guessed the second half: 'But in doing so it killed thousands upon thousands of men, women and children, many of them completely innocent, others whose only crime is that they have a goal for their country, which is different from ours.' But he hates that kind of thing with a passion.

He has seen Madison Avenue phoniness on TV. He has heard the double-talk of high government officials. He has seen our governments' strong stand for law and order and that same government sending out some of its trusted members, closest to the seat of power, to bug the offices of political opponents. He has heard our leaders talk of peace while pouring tons of bombs on defenseless villages of friend and foe alike. So he is not impressed by high-sounding words. He has seen our world as largely phony, a world of pretense, and he's not willing to believe what he is told. It's become almost a slogan to 'Tell it the way it is, baby.' He regards our current culture as almost completely hypocritical. I believe that this deep hatred for phoniness is perhaps the most significant mark of this new man.

He's opposed to all highly structured, inflexible institutions. He wants organizations to be fluid, changing, adaptive, and human. It will be clear from what follows how deep is his dislike for bureaucracy, rigidity, or form for form's sake. He simply will not buy these qualities. He finds educational institutions most irrelevant and futile so far as he's concerned. His unrest in college and high school arises out of a hundred specific issues, but none of these issues would be important if his school were truly meaningful for him. I think he sees traditional education as it is: the most rigid, outdated, incompetent institution in our culture.

I believe he would agree with me in the stance, which I have taken in my book *Freedom to Learn*, that teaching is a vastly overrated function and only the facilitation of learning is important. He doesn't particularly care to be instructed, but he's eager to learn if he's given a chance. He wants his learning to involve feelings, to involve the living of learnings, the application of relevant knowledge, a meaning in the here-and-now. Out of these elements, he sometimes likes to become involved in searching for new approximations to the truth, but the pursuit of knowledge purely for its own sake is not particularly characteristic.

Religious institutions are perceived as definitely irrelevant and frequently damaging to human progress. This attitude toward religious institutions doesn't mean at all that he has no concern for life's mysteries or for the search for ethical and moral values. This person of tomorrow has, in fact, revived interest in all the ancient searches for the heart of mystery: yoga and Zen, and the stuff of dreams, and the uniting of spirit and body, of Yang and Yin. He is deeply concerned with living in a moral and ethical way, but the morals are new and shifting, the ethics are relative to the situation, and the one thing that is not tolerated is a discrepancy between verbal standards and actual living values.

He's seeking new forms of community, of closeness, of intimacy, of shared purpose. He's seeking new forms of communication in such a community, verbal and nonverbal, feeling as well as intellectual. He recognizes that he will be living his transient life mostly in temporary relationships and that he must be able to establish closeness quickly. In his mobile world, he doesn't live long in one community. He's not surrounded by family and relatives. He's part of what Warren Bennis called the 'Temporary Society'. So he realizes that if he is to live in a human context he must be able to establish an intimate, communicative, personal bond with others in a very short space of time. Also he must be able to leave these close relationships behind without excessive conflict or mourning.

He has a distrust of marriage as an institution. A man/woman relationship has deep value for him only when it is a mutually enhancing, growing, flowing relationship. This attitude is certainly as true with a woman of tomorrow as it is with a man. Each has little regard of marriage as a ceremony or for vows of permanence, which prove to be highly impermanent. He's a searching person without any neat answers. The only thing he's certain of is that he is uncertain. And sometimes he feels a nostalgic sadness in his uncertain world. He's sharply aware of the fact that he's only a speck of life on a small blue and white planet in an enormous universe. Is there a purpose in this universe, or only the purpose he creates? He doesn't know the answer but he's willing to live with this anxious uncertainty.

There's a rhythm in his life between flow and stability, between changingness and structure, between anxiety and temporary security. Stability is only a brief period for the consolidation of learnings before moving on to more change. He always exists in this rhythm of process.

He's an open person, open to himself, close to his own feelings. He's also open to and sensitive to the thoughts and feelings of others and to the objective realities of his world. It is certainly true that he is a highly aware person. He's able to communicate with himself more clearly than any previous man, I believe. The barriers of repression, which shut off so much of man from himself, are definitely lower than in preceding generations. Not only is he able to communicate with himself; he's also often able to express his feelings and thoughts to others, whether they are negative and confronting in nature or positive and loving. His likes and his dislikes, his joys and his sorrows, are passionate and are passionately expressed. He is a vitally alive person. He's a creative person and turns his energies to new styles in art, craftwork, music, clothing, food, and to new materials and forms in furniture and building. He's a spontaneous person willing to risk newness, often willing to risk saying or doing the wild and the very far-out thing. His adventuresomeness has an almost Elizabethan quality: everything is possible – anything can be tried.

Currently he often likes to be turned on by many kinds of experiences or by drugs. This dependence on drugs for a consciousness-expanding experience is, I believe, gradually being left behind as he discovers that he prefers to be turned on by deep and fresh and vital interpersonal experiences or by meditation. Currently he often decides to obey those laws, which he regards as just, and to disobey those, which he regards as unjust, taking the consequences of his actions. He refuses to be drafted when he regards a war as reprehensible. He gives out secret government documents when he believes the people should know what has been going on. This is a new phenomenon.

We've had a few Thoreaus, but we've never had hundreds of people, young and old alike, willing to obey some laws and disobey others on the basis of their own personal moral judgment. He's active, sometimes violently, intolerantly and self-righteously active in the causes in which he believes. Hence, he arouses the most extreme and repressive antipathies in those who are frightened by change. He can see no reason why educational organizations, urban areas, ghetto conditions, racial discrimination, unjust wars should be allowed to remain unchanged. He has a sustained idealism, which is linked to his activism.

He doesn't hope that these will be changed in fifty years; he intends to change them now. He has a trust in his own experience and a profound distrust of all external authority. Neither pope nor judge nor scholar can convince him of anything that is not borne out by his own experience. He has a belief in his own potential and in his own direction. This belief extends to his own dreams of the future and his intuitions of the present. He can cooperate with others with great effectiveness in the pursuit of a goal which he is convinced is valid and meaningful. He almost never cooperates simply to conform or just to be a good fellow.

Curiously enough, he has a disregard for material things and material rewards. He's been accustomed to living an affluent life and readily uses all kinds of material things, taking them for granted. But he's quite unwilling to accept material rewards or material things if they mean that he must compromise his integrity to do so.

He likes to be close to elemental nature, to the sea, the sun, the snow, flowers, animals and birds, to life and growth and death. He rides the waves on his surfboard. He sails the sea in a small craft. He lives closely with gorillas or lions. He soars down the mountain on his skis. Those are a few of the qualities that I see in this new man and the man who is emerging as the person of tomorrow. They make him a highly controversial person because he challenges so many of our values.

Now since I've talked of his qualities largely in the abstract, I'd like to give some specific examples to help you picture him more concretely. Take, for example, the commencement address given by Melvin Levine to the Harvard Law School, for he was a graduate student with degrees from three universities. Speaking to the students, their parents, and the faculty, but particularly addressing the older members of the audience, he says:

> You've told us repeatedly that trust and courage were standards to emulate. You've convinced us that equality and justice were inviolable concepts. You've taught us that authority should be guided by reason and tempered

by fairness. We have taken you seriously. We have accepted your principles and have tried to implement them. Students chose to work with poor people in Appalachia and the black people in Mississippi and in urban ghettos. They persevered in calling attention to the injustices in Vietnam despite accusations of disloyalty to their country. Now for attempting to achieve the values that you have taught us to cherish, your response has been astounding. It has escalated from the presence of police on the campuses to their use of clubs and tear gas. When this type of violent repression replaces the search for reasonable alternatives, Americans are allowing their most fundamental ideals to be compromised.

I think that, in his talk, we see something of a sustained idealism – the activism, the contempt for a two-faced culture, and the willingness to risk a direct and probably unpalatable communication of his own feelings. I believe that perhaps I can sharpen the outline of this new person by indicating the way in which he relates to organizations and institutions. I'll give several examples.

For the past five years I've had the privilege of being associated in various ways with priests, nuns, ministers, theological students, mostly men and women in their thirties and forties. It has been fascinating to see person after person among them slowly coming to trust himself rather than external authority. Coming to perceive the pretense in his own institutionalized religion, developing a growing willingness to risk himself in various ways and gradually separating himself from the ties of institutional religion. Sometimes the person has stayed within the framework of the church; sometimes he's left it.

In either case, it's clear that his experience constitutes the guideline for his living – not the dogma or authority of the religious institution. So, priests have married, nuns have left their orders, ministers have sought to promote significant experiences outside of the church. Let me give another example of persons who are living their values.

Though not highly publicized, there are many corporate executives who are dropping out of the gray-flannel rat race. A successful executive, an engineer, leaves his firm and becomes a raiser of chickens. A stockbroker drops out and becomes a ski instructor. A commercial airline pilot with thousands of flying hours just quits to live as he wants to. Another executive now works around boats in a small east coast marina, thoroughly enjoying his work. Others join communes with their wives and families. They are quietly saying 'no' to the high salaries, the stock option plans, and all the other inducements that corporate life can offer and choosing to live in ways that they can value. I think they constitute another facet of this new man.

Even on the assembly line, workers are refusing to be cogs in our great technological fields. Some refuse to come to work, hence the high rate of absenteeism. Some work carelessly, hence the dropping quality of our automobiles. And others, with or without formal approval, form teams in which they trade off jobs or handle two jobs at a time and in other ways pronounce by their actions that they are self-directing persons not automatons. They, too, exemplify this new man.

Another simple example of living one's values is provided by Catholic wives. Of those under the age of 30, over 75% are using birth control methods of which the Church disapproves. Over half the Catholic women of all ages that go to communion – in other words, the 'good Catholics' – follow the same course. I'm not aware of any demonstrations against the Pope's 1968 encyclical. As far as I know, there are a few vehement letters of protest. These women are simply living by their own personal judgment of what is right and sound and disregarding the authority of the institution to which they belong. They, too, are part of this new person.

I think we learn the same lesson wherever we turn. Some students and faculty in our colleges and universities are demanding that they be permitted to learn and to function in their own way. Failing to receive such permission, they drop out; and that applies to both the faculty as well as the students. Someone recently pointed out that we shouldn't refer to the students as dropouts, since many of them are among the most capable and creative persons within their respective schools. He suggests that they be called 'peak-outs'. They have gone straight through the ceiling of the conventional institution to live and learn in their own way. I know a college freshman dropout who is now heading up a small private school and, as you might expect, that school has a very flexible and open curriculum. Let me give you another example from a younger school level.

A sixth grade in a forward-looking school was holding its year-end ceremonies before moving on to junior high school. In the midst of this the teacher told the group, 'Some of you are not paying attention and yet this is your final culmination; it's your graduation', whereupon a sixth grader, whom I must admit had previously been a participant in an encounter group, rose to his feet and said, 'Why do you call it our commencement? You planned the ceremony, you selected the people who could speak, you chose the songs we would sing; it's your ceremony, not ours.' Here is the openness, the confidence in self, the willingness to communicate, and the spontaneity of which I've been speaking; and you might be interested to know that this year's ceremony will be planned by the students.

Even in the military we see signs of choosing to live by personal values. The B-52 pilot who resigned rather than continue senseless killing is not alone. The black sailors who held a sit-down strike on a large carrier accepted a terrible risk in acting upon their convictions. Even the beards and sideburns on sailors represent a small triumph of personal values over ancient rigidities.

In the institution of marriage, which is not an organization but certainly is a structure of social expectations, we find an equally remarkable emergence of the new. Varied options are now open. Thousands of couples are living together without marriage in partnerships of varying duration. There are thousands of communes with enormous diversity, from highly organized to stoutly anarchistic, from monogamous to sexually experimental. And within marriage itself there are openly discussed options. Shall the partners be free to engage in sexual relationships with persons outside the marriage; shall a couple become swingers; shall they try group marriage? Now a great many of these experiments, which are being tried, are failures, but it is clear that conforming to a set picture of social expectation, 'until death do us part', is no longer the only possibility. These persons of tomorrow are carving out their own way.

Most of the examples that I have given indicate that the new man and the new woman are simply not content to remain in the traditional institution or organization. What will take its place? I don't know, but we're going through a period of incredible experimentation. I've mentioned many of the alternatives to conventional marriage; so far as schools are concerned, the university without walls, is suggestive of the trends. When men leave corporations, they tend to engage in small personal enterprises. But the way in which this person of tomorrow will function in productive groups is still unclear.

It does come to mind – there's a possible illustration of a transitional trend – in the organization of which I am a part, the Center for Studies of the Person. Initially a number of our policies were adopted out of dire financial necessity as well as dislike for structured organizations. Gradually we've come to realize that we are perhaps building a non-organization in which the person of tomorrow could be quite happy. Let me try to describe very briefly a few of its unusual features.

If you should wish to join, you couldn't apply for a job, because there are no jobs in the ordinary sense. You'd have to find a way of getting involved in some of the activities that members of the Center are carrying on. If you became significantly involved over a considerable period of time and wished to join, then the group would vote on whether they wished to have you as a member. And the criterion for membership is: Are you really a member of my psychological community? If the majority of the group feel that way, then you'd be voted in.

If you were taken into membership, you would know that you must be responsible for finding your own support. This might be through getting a research grant or through carrying on educational or group projects, accepting a job as a teacher or counselor, writing and making your money from royalties, making films or any way that made sense to you. You would know that, if you lost your source of support, the group would be definitely concerned and would try to suggest any other means they possibly could. But the group would not guarantee your further income.

You would be almost completely on your own as to what you wished to do. Our director, quite correctly, calls himself the 'non-director', but he prizes the title because it enables him to speak for the Center to outsiders and to develop various opportunities for Center members. If you wish to start a new project it wouldn't be necessary to obtain the approval of the group unless there was a chance it would interfere with our non-profit status. Since all of these comments may seem somewhat strange, why is it that we have so many inquiries, so many visitors, and so many people who would like to join?

I think it's because the heart and essence of the Center for Studies of the Person is the spirit of community with which we are bound together. We don't, in any sense, have to be together. Consequently we can more freely share our hopes and frustrations, our feelings of interpersonal friction, our disappointments in the group as well as our pride in it. We can occasionally undertake some big venture, which includes the whole staff and gives us a great feeling of being together and being unified in some sort of work. We have an organization that is a psychological home which we all cherish but from which we go out to do a myriad of things of highly diverse sorts, in Rome, in Northern Ireland, in Kenya, in Nepal and all over the United States.

The only element, which perhaps ties our activities together, is that nearly all of the members have, as a part of their goal, the enrichment and improvement of life for persons and the gaining of further understanding as to what constitutes such enrichment and fulfillment. We're getting rather large now, with approximately forty members. If some of our group should wish to spin off into a new organization, they certainly would have the blessing of the staff in doing so. We also have no investment in the perpetuity of the Center. We have in fact discussed whether it might not be wise to put an end-point to it − to say, for example, at the end of ten years it must dissolve and be reorganized in some other form or forms. If it sounds as though the outfit is so loose and unstructured that it must necessarily fall apart, this is also the greatest source of its strength.

Our conflicts and differences can be open ones, but so also can our real love for each other. Each of us, I believe, feels a great deal of support in being himself. I think of one of our members, who is a department chairman of one of the colleges, and when he achieved that and tenure and all I asked him was, 'Why do you stay on as a member of the center?' He said, 'Because when things come across my desk and I know I'm supposed to handle them in a certain way, I keep thinking, "Yeah, but there's that gang back there who would say: 'Do what you feel is best, Tom.'"' So a lot of the stuff gets thrown in the wastebasket, a lot of it gets treated in most unorthodox fashion, but that's why I stay in the Center.'

I was attempting not long ago to tell a group of forward-looking corporation presidents something about my view of the person of tomorrow but also about this strange, unstructured group of which I am proud to be a part. I really was quite hesitant in telling them, because I didn't think they would understand the person of tomorrow and I thought that surely they wouldn't understand the incredible flexibility of our psychological ties at the Center. To my amazement they seemed fascinated by the whole story. They felt that this person of tomorrow is the very person they are finding it so puzzling to deal with in their own organizations and they felt there were many lessons they could learn from this non-organization that I was describing. So, incredible as it may seem, we may find ways of making organizations a place where free human beings can live.

Without giving examples of, and statements about, this new person who is emerging, and the sort of personal and institutional experimentation in which he's engaging, will our culture be able to accept him? Frankly, I don't know. There are many who are frightened by his actions, his lifestyle, and his freedom to try new modes of living. There are tremendous forces of reaction and fear − fear of the change in us that he represents. I think that in this period of reaction there are a great many who would like to suppress him.

He doesn't fit well into the world of the present and he'll have a rough time trying to live in his own way. Yet if he can retain the qualities that I have listed so briefly, if he can create a culture which would nourish and nurture those qualities, then it may be that he holds a great deal of promise for all of us and for our future. In a world marked by incredibly rapid technological change, we desperately need his ability to live as a fluid process. And in a world characterized by overwhelming psychological sham and pretense we certainly need his uncompromising integrity.

Perhaps some of you in this audience will have resonated to my description because you see in yourself some of these same qualities emerging in you. To the extent that you are becoming this person of tomorrow and endeavoring to sharpen and refine his qualities in a constructive fashion, I wish you well. May you find many enduring satisfactions as you struggle to bring him to being within yourself and in your relationships with others, the best of this new man. Thank you. [Sustained applause]

Hal Lyon moderating

The best part of an evening with Carl Rogers is the interaction. Carl has said that this is the part he enjoys most and he's consented to spend the next thirty minutes or so interacting with some spontaneity to whatever you may have in the way of questions or thoughts or comments. This is pretty tough in a large place this size with several thousand people, but let's give it a try. Carl, maybe you can recognize them and repeat the question so that everyone in here can hear it, as well as you – so stand up and sound out with any question that you may have. If that doesn't work, we'll try something with the microphone up here and you can come around. Let's give it a try right from the auditorium.

Carl speaking

If you're too far from the mike, I can perhaps catch your question and repeat it but if your close enough to the mike, I hope you'll come to it. I hope we'll turn up the house lights so that I can see you a little better. Anyone have a question or a comment that they'd like to raise?

Carl answering the first question

Yes. The question was wondering what my reaction is to biofeedback training, especially compared to the 'alpha greenline'? I'm certainly no expert in that field but I've been enormously impressed with what I've been reading recently about it. It's interesting in many, many ways to me because it indicates what a tremendous amount of control the individual has over his organism without really being aware of the control that he has. He can produce specific effects in himself; he can raise the temperature of his hand just by thinking about it. It seems some of that material seems absolutely fantastic and certainly helps to greatly modify this strictly machine picture of man as an organism.

Next question

The point made was that the new Man of Tomorrow sounds a lot like Daniel Boone. That could be because as a boy I was a great reader of frontier stories. I used to like them. But I would also point out that there are really many differences. I would say, in spirit, he is very much akin to Daniel Boone. In many of his characteristics he is, I think, quite different, and so there is both a kinship but also, to my mind, a very real difference.

Next question

The question is, 'Would it be accurate to say that there's a great deal of similarity between my approach and that of Lao Tse?' That opens up a kind of interesting area for me. When I was 20 years old, I went to China as part of a student delegation for the United States, took part in a conference there, traveled all around, both Japan and China.

It's a little embarrassing when people say, 'Have you ever been to China?', meaning, of course, 'Have I been there recently?' I haven't been there recently. I say, 'Yeah, 51 years ago I was there.' But I don't specifically remember. I know that I did quite a lot of reading in preparation for that trip. I don't specifically remember being greatly influenced by oriental philosophy.

So, it was a great surprise to me when, quite a number of years ago, Leona Patter, a psychologist in Oregon, wrote to me saying that she thought that my thinking was sort of a bridge between Eastern and Western thought. Since then, I've come to feel that could conceivably be true. And certainly in recent years I've become more and more interested in Lao Tse particularly. He may be the right person. I've recently been quoting him, but I'm afraid I can't quote him from memory. He gives a marvelous definition of a facilitator-leader which runs something like this … I'd hate to butcher him by not quoting him correctly, but, 'A leader is best when people hardly notice him', something like that. 'He is worst when people despise him', and then he goes on a bit but it ends with a notion: 'But about the good leader, when his work is all done and his mission accomplished, then the people will all say, 'We did this ourselves,' which to me is just great. I think that is a mark of real leadership. So I have become, yes, much influenced … no, that's probably not quite true, I've become much confirmed, by some of his reading that I've done recently in oriental philosophy.

Next question

All right. Let me see if I get the gist of your question. I've commented about people dropping out of the corporate rat race. Would I also comment on people who are now in, or who might drop out of the 'denim rat race' – the current faddish customs. Is that essentially your question? I see … that such hippiness may become as much a conformity as anything else we've had? Yeah, in the name of being different. I regard that kind of thing as always a possibility and a risk.

It is somewhat horrifying to look back and see the way in which good, new, original lifestyles, ideas and so on, quickly become institutionalized, organized, run by tradition. Well, the example that comes to mind is one of the most horrifying to me. In encounter groups, not infrequently these days, you run into people who tell the other members in the group, 'No, you can't talk like that because you're not speaking in the here-and-now! No, you can't do this because that's not a feeling.' In other words, the very opportunity which was expected to provide for spontaneous expression now comes to have its own rules and norms and you can do this and you can't do that, and so on. To me, that seems a sad but typical corruption of a new way of being. And I am sure that the same thing can happen – probably to a very considerable extent is happening – to what you call the 'denim rat race'.

It's a personal matter as well as an organizational matter. I've felt this so often myself in working with people, in therapy, or in working with groups. Suppose you do something quite spontaneously on one occasion, which just has a remarkable effect; it really moves things forward. You realize, 'I've been a real help by doing that.' What is the temptation? The great temptation is to think, 'Boy, now I'll do this the next time.' Only, the next time you try it, it doesn't have the same effect at all because it's not spontaneous. It's not really new at that moment; it simply doesn't work. So, I think this tendency to institutionalize, to repeat, to become repetitious, rather than really forging ahead, is a temptation to individuals as well as to organizations – as well as to trends and subcultures. I think it runs all the way through.

Next question (about Skinner)

Yes. I think I've heard of Skinner [*laughter*]. And he's a very nice person. I've held some very interesting debates with Skinner. Some are published and several others are unrecorded and unpublished [*laughter*]. I feel that the whole motive-operant conditioning, and work in the behavior modification field, has added a good deal to the technology with which we can deal with people. I think the point on which I disagree most deeply with Skinner is in the philosophy that he holds about human beings – even about himself.

I won't soon get over the shock that I had at one meeting when, after he'd finished expounding his ideas (this was a rather small group), I said, 'Well, if I understand you correctly, you didn't choose to come here for this debate and these sounds that you've emitted are simply ones for which you've been rewarded in the past by your environment' [*laughter*]. I spun it out pretty well. And he said, 'Well, essentially that's correct' [*laughter*]. Now, I guess my feeling is that conceivably he could be factually right, but you cannot live a life that way. You can't live a life feeling that what comes out of your mouth is simply something that you're conditioned to do by your environment. You can't live a life acting on the belief that everything you do is simply inevitable. It is rarely pointed out, but, having spent one year in seminary, I think it's worth finding out that there is a great relationship between the behaviorist philosophy and the Calvinist philosophy. Just as the Calvinist could show that logically there is every reason to believe that some infants are damned at birth, which seemed a little horrifying to the people in that day, so an extension of the behaviorist philosophy leads to the conclusion that the world must have been wound up at some point and from then on it has gone on its inevitable way with every conditioning cause leading to its behavioral effect, etc., etc. [*laughter*]. And that seems to me to be not a philosophy that I would choose to live by and I think there are an increasing number of people who would agree.

Another comment that might be made is that the behaviorist point of view, I think, appeals enormously to our culture because it gives a nice technology for dealing with people. You don't have to worry about them as persons. You can decide how their behavior is to be modified. You can set the environment that will modify it and you do get changes. And we're hooked on technology in every other aspect of our life, so why not in dealing with human beings, as well? And, as I say, in many ways it does offer a technical resource that I think shouldn't be overlooked. But in other areas of technology I believe we're beginning to raise all kinds of questions and I suspect that we will begin to raise a lot of questions about whether it is really the thing we wish to do, to deal with people with that philosophy. I certainly have no objection to the notion of using such operant conditioning for limited uses; it's very meaningful that way, I think.

One of the best uses I heard of was in Louisville, Kentucky, where they really have revolutionized the whole school system into a much more humanistic mode. They found that some of the children, coming from underprivileged homes into schools that had been just straight experiences of failure, simply didn't know how to act. You couldn't even get them to sit down; you couldn't get them to do anything. You couldn't reach them. So they used good operant conditioning procedures until they got them to the point where they could really respond to human beings as persons and then they became far more amenable to a person–centered learning environment. That's a good melding of the two points of view right there.

Next question

What do I think of bioenergetics as an encounter technique and as a therapy technique? I don't like to comment on other points of view, because I know that I don't understand them as well as I do my own, so my comments will be quite brief and general.

I think that in putting an emphasis upon bodily tensions and blocking or energy flow, and that kind of thing, bioenergetics may be doing a very useful thing and may lead to real significant changes. I also feel that we are going through a period of faddishness that I hope people don't take too seriously. I think of one chap I know. At first, one year of gestalt therapy was the answer. The next year it was bioenergetics; the next year it was primal screaming, and he's gone on from there. I think new points of view in therapy and in dealing with people are fruitful and eventually feed into the main stream of thinking. I do tend to be quite skeptical of thinking that each new thing that comes along is salvation. I'm not saying that you raised that question, but that's one comment that comes to my mind, because so many people do tend to feel that this new thing that comes along is *the* answer. I suspect nothing is so simple; I think that life is not so simple that anything is *the* answer.

Next question

The comment is that Tom Gordon has taken a number of ideas from 'client-centered' therapy and has made from them a – well, a course – a series of learnings, which parents can learn to deal with their children or which teachers can adopt in dealing with their students.

I know I have been really concerned with the somewhat mechanical way in which some of that has been done – as I've tried to follow it – as it has developed. I guess here's my honest opinion. I'm sorry Tom isn't here to probably disagree with me. I think that for people who are perhaps very rigid, who've never thought of understanding another person and so on, a sort of structured way of approaching the child or the student may be a useful first step. It seems to me that's the kind of thing that he's provided. As I've known people who have led the groups of parents and so on. The ones that I think have had the best results are those who use his rather structured approach as a takeoff point. From there on, it becomes much less structured and, in my mind, much more real – perhaps much more effective.

Next question

OK. You've practically taken the answer out of my mouth [*laughter*]. The comment is that she agrees with my notion of the emerging new man … and I thought this was the question, 'But how can he function effectively in groups?'

I think that if he rushes into organizing, he's falling into the same trap of our present society. That's part of our trouble. You can't have anything without immediately organizing it to produce something, if it's got to be task-oriented. And that's why I'm more impressed with people who are living their values either as individuals or in natural groups that have formed themselves. But not with a great stress on 'we're going to organize to conquer society' or something like that. I have a very strong feeling that change will come about more rapidly, even in this technological culture, with people living sets of values that are quite different from the ones that the culture tends to accept.

Next question

Mmm … hmm … The question is: 'Wouldn't this person of tomorrow be characterized also by loneliness, perhaps even by alienation – what would my comment be on that? How can those tendencies stop short of being suicidal despair?' Is that fairly close?

In my own mind I make some distinction between loneliness and aloneness (being alone). This person I've been talking about might be lonely or he might feel a very deep kinship with a few other people. And, after all, none of us need hundreds of people as a support group; we need a few. He will feel – he's almost certain to feel – alone, because he is tending to stand against his culture. I think that the thing that can keep that aloneness from becoming despairing is the linkage with a few other people who share the same values and who live those values. I can't think of anyone I know that I feel fits at all into this picture of the new man who really is so despairingly alone that suicide has been a particularly prominent thought. I may be too optimistic about that. I sometimes am.

Next question

The question is, 'Do I agree with Reich's 'Consciousness Three' person?' I think that what I've been talking about – especially in the last few minutes – about living one's values, and so on, is to my mind, quite similar to his 'Consciousness Three'. I feel that the individual who senses the newness in himself, endeavors to live that newness, judging his course by his own inner experience and not by the conventions of society, is the kind of person that will change society and is, I believe, not too far different from Reich's Consciousness Three.

I think you've been sitting a long time. You're a very appreciative audience. But I think probably we should call it quits. Thank you. [*Prolonged applause*]

4

ROGERS' MAN OF TOMORROW IS TODAY'S EFFECTIVE TEACHER

Harold Lyon

The portrait Carl paints of the Man of Tomorrow sounds very much like the effective teacher of today. Carl Rogers described the Man of Tomorrow as valuing genuineness, empathy, spontaneity, caring about others and being more process than content oriented:

> He values authenticity. He will not put up with double-talk ... He finds educational institutions most irrelevant and futile ... He sees traditional education as it is: the most rigid, outdated, incompetent institution in our culture .... He wants his learning to involve feelings, to involve the living of learnings, the application of relevant knowledge, a meaning in the here-and-now ... He's also open to and sensitive to the thoughts and feelings of others and to the objective realities of his world ... He's a vitally alive person. He's a creative person ... He can see no reason why educational organizations ... should be allowed to remain unchanged.

Aspy and Roebuck found in their large field studies, which we present in Chapter 12, that the most effective teachers had what Aspy called 'grit' and were able to inspire their students to higher achievement and more creativity. These teachers, too, sound like Rogers' Man of Tomorrow.

When one observes or reads about the Teach For America teachers who are able to raise students' grade levels two to three levels in a year, they sound like Rogers' Man of Tomorrow.

When one looks at what teacher traits help students achieve and the powerful effect sizes John Hattie has found for them in his analyses of the meta-analyses, they sound like Rogers' Man of Tomorrow. And when one reads Jeffery Cornelius-White's meta-analysis of Learner Centered Instruction and sees what teacher behaviors in the classroom lead to higher cognitive and affective performance, these effective teachers of today sound even more like Rogers' Man of Tomorrow.

The effective teacher is a person who cares enough about students and is committed to them to work tirelessly to help them reach lofty goals and raise their achievement, which addresses the achievement gap that exists today between students of ineffective and effective teachers.

International student rankings

Arguably the UK, Germany, and US have the best higher education in the world, with students coming to our universities from all over. But our elementary and secondary students perform poorly when compared to students globally. Many other countries, including China, South Korea, Finland, Japan, Canada, New Zealand, Australia, Netherlands, Belgium, and Norway have surpassed the US (ranked 14th in reading, 21st in science, and 30th in math), the UK (ranked 19th in reading, 14th in science, and 27th in math), and Germany (ranked 16th in reading, 12th in science, and 16th in math).[1]

You hear the excuse that America, as the former 'melting pot' of so many other cultures, no longer does the melting it historically did. Has America lost its 'exceptionalism'? This is a complex question we are facing for the first time since the Sputnik era.

The international tests from the Program for International Student Assessment (PISA), which ranks nations, are given in native English in America and the UK and native German in Germany when rapidly growing segments of our populations taking the tests are no longer native speakers, hence pulling down the test scores. But, whether or not we like the test results, the current diverse culture is our America, UK, and Germany. Sheldon Kopp once said, 'It is very important to run out of scapegoats.' We need to find out why our students – all of them – are not doing better and work to close the achievement gap which exists between the less advantaged students and those with advantages and between our schools and those in other countries rather than making excuses about our low rankings.

PISA has also found that more teaching is not necessarily better. Students from Finland and South Korea, where teachers teach an average of only 600 hours per year, perform much better than students in the US, where teachers average 1,100 hours per year. We also pay our teachers considerably less then the better-ranked countries and apparently do not value the teaching profession as much as other countries do. Only 1% of American fourth and twelfth graders scored at the Advanced Level on national science exams in 2009, and only 4% of American degrees were awarded in engineering in 2008 compared to 31% in China.[2]

These are among the challenging education problems we face today. And the solutions are not clear ones, given the numerous complexities and confounds in such issues. First we must more clearly define the problem, as it is easy to get lost in the research on these issues. But a research vehicle called meta-analysis can help us see more clearly.

Meta-analysis – a research method to see the forest from the trees

'A meta-analysis is a synthesis of thousands of studies in a particular field. Meta-analyses have also themselves been combined, creating syntheses of syntheses, which allow one to get an entire snapshot of a field, not just a particular area. Syntheses of syntheses allow one to compare the results of a particular body of research (e.g. learner-centered relationships) against the entire field (e.g. education) to assess the significance of a finding.'[3]

Thanks to meta-analyses of thousands of quality studies and very large field studies, we begin to arrive at some data in which there are answers – answers as to what leads to better achievement as well as other important outcomes.

But how can we tell what is really worth our while in pursuing and investing our educational dollars? We need a benchmark for viewing the research on what works in classroom teaching. Seminal syntheses of meta-analyses were first done in 1987 synthesizing 134 meta-analyses from 7,827 studies with over 5 million participants, which showed that all educational interventions from classroom size to instructional methods result in an overall average improvement.[4] So most interventions make a difference, but how much of a difference do we need to make the intervention worthwhile?

The Hattie and Cornelius-White studies

Two new contemporary studies of what teaching practices lead to student achievement are now available to us for the first time and they both corroborate the earlier research of Rogers and the large field studies of Aspy, Roebuck, and Tausch, presented in later chapters. And they go a giant step farther today in showing just how powerful person-centered teaching is in improving student achievement. Both of these studies are unique meta-analyses. The larger the numbers of quality studies analyzed in a meta-analysis, the better the likelihood of finding good answers to the research questions. John Hattie[5] and Jeffrey Cornelius-White[6] and their colleagues have done two impressive studies. Hattie has carried out syntheses of meta-analyses of most of the research studies done in the past half-century to determine what actually leads to student achievement at all levels of education.

Taking a broad view, Hattie synthesized over 800 meta-analyses to determine what teacher behavior leads to achievement. The busy teacher or layperson is often frustrated with the task of interpreting statistics. Knowing this, Hattie presents his results in easy-to-compare 'effect sizes', which show the power of an intervention to bring about change. Effect size can be shown as d or r, which can be changed back and forth, depending upon the design of the original study. Hattie, in his huge analysis of the meta-analyses, publishes his very useful list of the effect sizes, showing the power of hundreds of interventions leading to student achievement using the effect size of r as the measure. An effect size of 0 means that there is no change resulting from the intervention. An effect size of 1.0 is equivalent to one full Standard Deviation of change, which is huge, amounting to two to three grade levels of improvement in student performance. Hattie, after studying millions of interventions intended to bring about change in student performance, realized that most any intervention will bring about some change, but many of these interventions are costly and create insignificant change. Hattie asked: What is the threshold point of effect size that makes an intervention worthwhile?

In earlier work, Fraser and Hattie both concluded that an effect size of $r = 0.20$ is 'well worth pursuing' and any correlation greater than $r = 0.30$ 'should be of much interest' in pursuing. Any effect size larger than this is perhaps worthwhile investing in, while those below $r = 0.20$ are hardly worth our time, though in the past we have invested millions of dollars in some of these less-than-effective interventions. But we just did not know what makes a difference. Now, thanks to these meta-analyses of Hattie, Cornelius-White, and their colleagues, we are beginning to learn what behaviors make a teacher an effective teacher. In his classic analyses of the meta-analyses, to make sure we invest in interventions which will truly result in significant results, Hattie sets this useful higher 'pivot point' for effect sizes of 0.40 as being those interventions definitely worth our investment to bring about higher achievement. Certainly effect sizes of interventions near $r = 0.50$ or higher have enormous power to bring about change.

Focusing more narrowly on our topic of person-centered learning, Cornelius-White and Harbaugh have done the largest meta-analysis of Learner Centered Instruction ever done. Their huge meta-analysis includes the large field studies of Aspy and Roebuck (including forty-two US states and eight countries), presented in Chapter 12, and the research of Tausch, presented in Chapter 13. And it also corroborates their findings.

> Overall, learner-centered teacher variables have above-average associations with positive student outcomes. Positive relationships, nondirectivity, empathy, warmth, and encouraging thinking and learning are the specific teacher variables that are above average compared with other educational innovations. Correlations for participation, critical thinking, satisfaction, math achievement, drop-out prevention, self-esteem, verbal achievement, positive motivation, social connection, IQ, grades, reduction in disruptive behavior, attendance, and perceived achievement are all above average and are presented in decreasing order. Researchers, policy makers, teachers, administrators, students, parents, and others involved in schooling can advocate for increasing the awareness and practice of positive learner-centered relationships.[7]

So, whether you call it Learner Centered Instruction or person-centered, we are talking about the same thing—person-centered teaching, learning, relationships and principles. Thorough research over the years shows that person-centered teaching results in positive student achievement and other positive outcomes.

Since 1990 there is a much wider, larger body of research and professional acceptance of Learner-Centered Instruction, especially since the American Psychological Association (APA), under the leadership and writings of Barbara

McCombs, has endorsed a new APA education paradigm, 'Learner Centered Psychological Principles'.[8]

In Cornelius-White's meta-analysis, he focused on person-centered interventions, which he calls Learner Centered Instruction (LCI). He defines LCI as 'an approach to teaching and learning that provides facilitative relationships, the uniqueness of every learner, and the best evidence on learning processes to promote comprehensive student success through engaged achievement.'[9] This definition is very close to what we call person-centered teaching throughout this book.

The Cornelius-White study of all the highest-quality studies conducted 'between 1948 and 2004, involved over 350,000 students, nearly 15,000 teachers, and 1,450 separate findings from preschool to graduate school'. This meta-analysis found that Learner Centered Instruction (LCI), which includes empathy, warmth, and non-directive teaching, leads to both higher cognitive and affective performance outcomes of students.

These studies have great relevance to the theme of this book and to all who are concerned with effective teaching. They build upon and include the earlier work of Rogers, Aspy, and Tausch, corroborating these earlier findings as relevant for today and presenting them in their meta-analyses as evidence of the power that person-centered instruction methods have to bring about student achievement.

Student outcomes from the Aspy-Roebuck person-centered teachers[10]

The student achievement outcomes which correlated with person-centered teacher behaviors from the large Aspy and Roebuck field studies included the following:

- increased standard achievement scores
- less absenteeism
- fewer discipline problems and less violence
- increased IQ scores (if the students were young children)
- increased self-concept scores
- improved attitudes toward learning
- increased levels of cognitive functioning (more thinking)
- increased creative responses
- increases in teacher energy and satisfaction levels.

Though Aspy and Roebuck did the largest field study ever done back in the 1970s and 1980s and their results are solid, every research study needs corroboration and now Cornelius-White and Hattie recently have done just that in their huge meta-analyses.

Cornelius-White's LCI student achievement outcomes

Cornelius-White's meta-analysis also showed an impressive list of both cognitive and affective student achievement outcomes correlated with his Learner Centered Instruction (LCI) teacher variables, as follows.

Cognitive achievement outcomes correlated with LCI teaching (from highest to lowest) included the following:

- critical and divergent creative thinking
- math achievement
- verbal achievement
- IQ increases
- higher grades
- perceived achievement (teachers' evaluation of students' progress)
- scientific achievement
- achievement test batteries
- social science achievement.

Affective/behavioral achievements correlated with LCI teaching methods (in order from highest to lowest impact) included the following:

- participation
- student satisfaction
- dropout prevention
- self-efficacy/mental health
- positive motivation (such as curiosity or subject interest)
- social connection/skills
- reduction of disruptive behavior
- attendance
- reduction of negative motivation (such as work effort or work avoidance).

The cognitive results of LCI are above average in effect size, and affective and behavioral results are superior to nearly all other instructional variables investigated in the earlier classic synthesis of syntheses by Frazer et al. (1987).[11] And these outcomes are nearly identical with those in the large field studies by Aspy, Roebuck, and Reinhard and Anne-Marie Tausch, as you will see in later chapters.

Cornelius-White's meta-analysis effect sizes (power of these person-centered behaviors to bring about student achievement)[12]

- Empathy: $r = 0.32$
- Warmth: $r = 0.32$
- Composite (relationships of the above two as a whole rather than just empathy or warmth): $r = 0.36$
- Nondirective teaching: $r = 0.35$
- Encourage learning: $r = 0.23$
- Encourage thinking: $r = 0.29$
- Adept to differences: $r = 0.20$
- Learner-centered beliefs: $r = 0.05$.

(The low effect size of learner-centered beliefs $r = 0.05$, above, indicates that real actions, much more than mere beliefs, are needed to foster performance.)

To define the quality of a study for his meta-analyses, Cornelius-White used the Scientific Methods Score (SMS), which rates the quality of the findings based on the characteristics of the original studies, with 1 being the lowest quality and 5 being the highest quality. The findings presented here from Cornelius-White and Harbaugh were taken from only the highest-quality studies with a SMS of 5. That means that the researchers in these studies employed quality experimental or quasi-experimental designs, so he has captured the wheat and little of the chaff in his meta-analysis of the high-quality research studies.

Cornelius-White presents the interesting table below of opposites for discussion about the congruence of educational goals with methods, cautioning that this polarization might not show ways which learner-centered and traditional teaching methods might be similar or combined. He also cautions that 'learner-centered' does not mean a lack of structure by a teacher, such as the stereotype people often held about earlier 'humanistic education'.

Learner-centered facets contrasted with traditional facets[13]

Learner-Centered approaches	Traditional approaches
Person centered	Curriculum-centered
Self-directed	Teacher-directed
Democratic	Hierarchical
Child-centered	Teacher-centered
Process (how)	Content (what)
Constructing understanding	Covering subject matter
Inquiry-based	Knowledge-based
Thinking	Memorizing
Relationship	Instruction
Experiential methods	Lecture
Cooperation	Competition or individualism
Active	Passive
Learning	Teaching
Criterion referencing	Norm referencing
Showing	Telling
Facilitating	Professing
Liberatory pedagogy	Banking model

In summary, we now have very impressive research building on Rogers' classic person-centered philosophy from the past research of Aspy and Roebuck, and replicated by Tausch, showing that high student achievement results from person-centered teaching. And these older studies have been corroborated recently by Hattie and Cornelius-White in their important large syntheses of studies. In Chapter 17, I also present the results of a small but recent randomized controlled trial showing that we were able to significantly change medical teachers toward seven person-centered criteria – many of the same criteria shown to be effective in the earlier and current studies – in a cost-efficient, empathic training program using as a vehicle a modified Flanders Interaction Analysis, which Aspy and Roebuck used back in their large field studies to diagnose the interpersonal skills of hundreds of thousands of teachers.

Let's look at how one might practically apply the results of this research to actually pick and train teachers facing today's classroom challenges.

The Teach For America innovation

Rogers' Man of Tomorrow also sounds like one of the over 37,000 teachers who have served during the past two decades through Teach For America, a non-profit organization that has been carefully selecting, training, and sending highly motivated teachers into high-needs urban and rural classrooms. What is unique about many of these teachers? The most effective seem to have combinations of skills that help enable some to raise student achievement two to three years in one year. External evaluations about the impact of different teacher-preparation programs suggest that Teach For America is among the most effective sources of new teachers in low-income communities. Statewide studies, conducted between 2009 and 2012, found that corps members often help their students achieve academic gains at rates equal to or larger than those for students of more veteran teachers.

When teacher effectiveness results in high student performance, Wendy Kopp and Steven Farr, originators of Teach For America, call this, 'Transformational Teaching'. It is 'transformational' in that it is much more powerful than mere 'change'. Two to three grade levels is an enormous improvement akin to effect sizes of $r = 1.0$. Behind the scenes, Teach For America has been doing careful research, studying what unique behaviors these effective transformational teachers possess that others do not.

I need to back up a bit to tell a story. When I first entered the U.S. Office of Education back in 1966 in a political appointment, everyone was excited by the landmark Coleman Report. This large study suggested that the poor achievement low income children were experiencing was not the fault of their teachers or schools, but was ninety percent due to the students' socioeconomic issues – their neighborhoods, families, and school facilities. For many decades this viewpoint let the schools and teachers off the hook. It has taken us nearly fifty years to learn that school performance is mostly dependent upon one thing: effective teaching. I recall many accomplishments of the Johnson Administration's Great Society programs including breaking the back of segregation, special education of special-needs students, starting programs like *Sesame Street* and *The Electric Company,* programs for the gifted and talented, and providing equal opportunity to education for millions of children.

But, I also recall many costly programs the Coleman Report's message spawned that pumped hundreds of millions of dollars into updating old school buildings and huge block grants into lower income school districts, hoping throwing money at the problem would somehow result in higher achievement and help close the achievement gap. Hattie's meta-analyses show that many of these interventions we thought would increase learning, in fact, have little or no effect on student performance. In fact many interventions we thought would enhance achievement, such as the physical attributes of the class including class size, use of television, retention (keeping students back a grade), team teaching, more money, audio-visual aids, ability grouping, and programmed instruction all have such small effect sizes ($r = 0.18$ and lower), that they hardly make any difference in student performance. But effective interactive relationships between person-centered teachers and their students do.

Teach For America is a unique organization as one of the contemporary successes in addressing teacher selection, placement, and the issues of what works in the classroom to raise student performance. Teach For America has provided teacher training and support to over 37,000 college graduates and professionals in the two decades since its beginning in 1990 who are recruited mainly from universities, but also from careers, intensively trained, and placed for two years in high-need urban and rural schools where the achievement gap is most pronounced.

'These dedicated teachers have worked with over 4 million low-income children and have made an enormous contribution toward closing the achievement gap.'[14]

The founder of Teach For America, Wendy Kopp, was a young Princeton student back in 1990. Her senior thesis at Princeton addressed ideas to help eliminate educational inequality in the US. In the next twenty years she worked to design and then implement this unique program and wrote about her efforts in an interesting book.[15] Ten years later, Kopp, with Steven Farr, now the chief teacher-trainer-researcher at Teach For America, wrote another book documenting the methods, research findings, and success of Teach For America.[16]

What makes Teach For America effective

What makes this teacher training program so different from so many we have spent millions of dollars on in the past? First of all, this program studies and compares the specific behaviors of teachers who seem to have 'mystical' skills to make big improvements in student performance with other teachers whose students do not make large achievement gains. What they have found is that these behaviors and skills are not mystical at all and that teachers can be trained to behave with these skills. Aspy and Roebuck found many years ago that they could train teachers to have high empathy, caring, and congruence (genuineness) in several weeks. My colleagues and I found that we could train medical teachers to be more effective in seven person-centered behaviors in a very short time, as presented in Chapter 17.

Teach For America is finding they can select and train effective teachers in in-service training better than most pre-service training. They make comparisons between seemingly similar teachers in inner-city schools, analyzing why and how one teacher is able to achieve great student gains while a competent-seeming teacher down the hall is unable to do so. These effective teachers' behaviors are analyzed and, from year to year, the next year's recruitment is based upon selecting teachers who appear to have these persistently effective teacher behaviors. It is clear that the effective teachers care so much about their students that they do not give up – they have grit, helping them reach the high achievement goals that they work with individual students to set and achieve. The importance of person-centered behaviors is apparent in observing these successful teachers in their classrooms.

The new person-centered movement to reward teachers who facilitate student achievement

Teachers – especially those in low-income schools – are the ones on the firing line, facing classrooms with too many students, many of whom do not want to be there. Often their students are aggressive, sometimes violent, and lack positive motivation. Teachers in the trenches rightfully feel that they need a powerful advocate and influential spokespersons, and the teacher unions have filled that role for them over the years, fighting for better conditions, higher pay, better retirement, and benefits. Though teacher unions in the past have done great service – especially in raising the low salaries of teachers – unfortunately this has been based mostly upon their seniority rather than the achievement of their students. The unions have traditionally identified with more liberal or Democratic causes in America.

A new paradigm – rewarding teachers based on their students' achievements

But now there is an important new bipartisan movement to promote and reward teachers based upon their students' performance rather than seniority and, as might be expected, the unions have become the scapegoats even after all their positive work for teachers. Teach For America and many of its alumni, along with other new organizations representing both the left and right, are now fomenting this vital transformation throughout America to reward teachers based upon their students' performance.

Michelle Rhee, a former Teach For America alumna and controversial former Chancellor of the Washington, DC School System from 2007 to 2010, fought valiantly to transform the District of Columbia's failing school system, challenging teacher unions to implement a program to pay teachers according to their ability to raise student grade levels. In addition to being the founder and the CEO of the New Teacher Project, Rhee is now heading up Students First, another non-profit advocacy organization for more effective teaching. She is fighting head-on, and has always been, in her attempts to remove teacher tenure as the criterion for teacher performance, and instead to promote teachers based upon the achievements of their students. Armed with her experience as a school reformer, Rhee is a controversial figure in education today, as are most who make a difference in this world.

In its first year, 1990, Teach For America trained and placed 500 young teachers, focusing on low-income schools. This program is extraordinarily popular with recent university graduates who have little or no experience teaching. These new inexperienced teachers are recruited based upon having the traits found among their most successful predecessors who have successfully raised student achievement. In some ways, it is a program emphasizing careful recruitment of the few right young teachers for these high-need urban and rural schools where the achievement gap is most pronounced. This is followed by intensive summer in-service training, when school is out for these teachers. Rather than traditional long pre-training of many teachers to become gradually better with experience and training, Teach For America bets on a few new teachers who have the right traits and/or can be quickly trained to have these person-centered traits. Such an approach, though apparently working well, understandably threatens some experienced teachers who see these inexperienced young teachers performing as well as, if not better than, they are able. And if teachers whose students are not achieving can be fired for this – the procedure Rhee used – the threat becomes very real. So this is one of the challenges such an out-of-the-envelope, but successful, program creates. But if students are achieving, one can hardly argue with that important measure of success.

In 2012, Teach For America received more than 48,000 applications from students at over 1,500 schools across the country, including 10% of the seniors at Morehouse College, 8% at Howard University, and 4% of California-Berkeley. At the Ivy League schools, one in seven African-American seniors and one in seven Latino seniors applied. And the Teach For America teachers and alumni are becoming activist catalysts throughout American education.

Many of these radical new organizations, both Democratic- and Republican-based, are challenging the power teacher unions have traditionally held over how teachers are promoted and are now lobbying for rewarding teachers based upon performance of their students. Over half of the Teach For America teachers continue to teach in their schools for a third year. Others go on to teach or become leaders at various charter schools or other schools founded by Teach For America alumni. This is becoming a growing and powerful pedagogical leadership group – a critical mass of over 28,000 young change agents or, I should say, 'transformation agents' – infecting American education all over the country. Two-thirds of its alumni remain in the field of education mostly as classroom teachers.

School administrators face the difficult challenge of also acknowledging other more experienced teachers, many of whom also are raising student achievement and who also have the person-centered behaviors their younger, less experienced Teach For America teachers also seem to possess. So in American education a promising new paradigm is evolving. The raising of student achievement becomes the criterion for effective teacher recruitment, training, and acknowledgment. And there is more impressive evidence we share later in this book that person-centered methods result in higher achievement. One might hope that the teacher unions will let go of seniority and join this new movement based upon student performance. There is evidence that some unions are.

What are the specific behaviors this highly person-centered program seeks when it selects and trains its corps of teachers? According to the 2005 National Teacher of the Year, Jason Kamras, a Teach For America alumnus, the answer is perseverant leadership:

> Teachers who are successful at closing the achievement gap do exactly what all great leaders do when they face seemingly insurmountable odds: they set big goals, invest in their organization (students) in working hard to achieve those goals, plan purposefully, execute effectively, continuously increase their effectiveness, and work relentlessly toward their objective of closing the achievement gap for their students.[17]

Within a context of person-centeredness, these specific skills which Teach For America seeks to identify in its selection process and train in its intensive summer training program are the same skills successful leaders in all walks of life possess.

Grit

One of my most significant learnings as a cadet at West Point was the discovery that to succeed as leaders we must possess something Teacher of the Year Jason Kamras feels is an essential for transformational teachers: 'grit'. Rogers suggested that his Man of Tomorrow is a person of grit. A West Pointer, Colonel John Roosma, father of two of my West Point classmates and one of collegiate basketball's greatest players, defined 'grit' to me when I was about to enter West Point as a young cadet: 'that determination which will not be denied, commonly known as guts'. West Point now also labels it 'grit' and has research showing that it is the most important trait to predict retention of cadets at the academy and a trait that officers must possess to achieve success as leaders. Teach For America calls it perseverance. It's the same strength I call grit.

In a carefully controlled prospective longitudinal study, Angela Duckworth, a psychologist at the University of Pennsylvania, and her colleagues researched grit, defined as 'perseverance and passion for long term goals'. Duckworth found that teachers with grit were 31% more likely then their less gritty peers to facilitate academic performance in their students.

Are these traits of perseverance and life satisfaction the same person-centered traits of Rogers' Man of Tomorrow? From my personal experience in the military, the academic world, and government, I would say yes. The revealing words of this first-year teacher with grit explain how:

> These young children needed help with reading and mathematics, but they also needed much more in their lives. They needed imagination and self-confidence. So we sang, happily and frequently. We recited, clapped, danced, and wiggled. We explored sounds and ideas. We discussed issues and concerns. We drew pictures and made up songs and stories, injecting into the grimness of many of their lives small pockets of joy. I could feel the love growing between us.[18]

This teacher showed an unwavering trust in students' ability to learn when given a flexible, caring, but firm environment. She did not turn away from their broad needs or believe they had too many problems, but instead engaged them head-on in a person-centered way that showed the same qualities of openness and commitment to persons and their goals that Rogers discussed as qualities of his Man of Tomorrow.

These qualities are among the same person-centered leadership skills Teach For America continues to find in its transformational teachers. Every year the researchers at Teach For America revise this list, based upon their ongoing research to learn what it is that certain teachers have which result in raising grade levels of students. The applicants with the traits below are the ones it currently seeks to identify in its selection process and promote in its training.

Student-driven selection criteria for Teach For America teachers[19]

- a deep belief in the potential of all kids and a commitment to do whatever it takes to expand opportunities for students
- demonstrated leadership ability and superior interpersonal skills to motivate others
- strong achievement in academic, professional, extracurricular, and/or volunteer settings
- perseverance in the face of challenges, ability to adapt to changing environments, and a strong desire to do whatever it takes to improve and develop, or grit!
- excellent critical thinking skills, including the ability to accurately link cause and effect and to generate relevant solutions to problems
- superior organizational ability, including planning well and managing responsibilities effectively
- respect for individuals' diverse experiences and the ability to work effectively with people from a variety of backgrounds.

Despite these admirable criteria qualities, as I observe and read accounts of these effective teachers firsthand, I see that they are not 'perfect teachers'. They are human, genuine persons building upon their unique strengths and weaknesses. They care for students deeply. They enhance and facilitate student motivation and empower students to reach their goals in their own personal ways. They are, in effect, real, congruent persons, who also happen to have honed person-centered leadership skills.

Robert Carkhuff, with whom David Aspy worked in his large field studies on effective teachers, analyzed thousands of data in Aspy's field studies and concluded that these effective, person-centered teachers were also very organized. From this he developed what he called the ROPES method[20] of organizing teaching (i.e Review, Overview, Present, Exercise, Summary = ROPES). These effective teachers organized their teaching in a way which:

1. Reviewed the content to access learner's abilities
2. Overviewed the content with the students, motivating them and showing why it will be important to them

3.   **P**resented the content in small simple steps, asking frequent questions while doing this
4.   **E**xercised the content to provide learners time to practice the skills
5.   **S**ummarized to obtain their own evaluation of their learning ('What have you learned this hour?').

Effective teachers often integrate these steps in three multi-sensory Tell–Show–Do steps, resulting in a ROPES fifteen-step matrix. The average teacher uses only two or three of these fifteen steps. More effective teachers tend to use seven or more steps.

Many of these steps are also apparent in the list of Teach For America's important skills. In our recent study to help medical teachers become more effective, this was one of the criteria we used: Did the teachers organize their person-centered teaching using the ROPES matrix? The most effective teachers from the Aspy-Roebuck studies used many of these steps without anyone having been taught to use them, as did our more effective medical teachers. We'll discuss this in later chapters in more detail.

An effective exercise of federal concern for reforming education

Our Constitution calls for federal concern, state responsibility, and local control of education in America. In this decade, one of those appropriate and unique 'federal concern' initiatives with high multiplier-effect was launched by Secretary of Education Arne Duncan, with the support of President Obama, called 'Race to the Top'. This is a one-time highly competitive stimulus program to be awarded to states who are able to demonstrate that they can change their policies and reward teachers with promotions and salaries who demonstrate skills to significantly raise student achievement.

Conservative groups who believe that government has no federal role to play in education are obviously among this program's enemies. This program invites states to compete for millions of federal education stimulus dollars by submitting proposals that include state reforms such as expanding charter schools and evaluating teachers on how well their students do on tests.

This program gives states huge financial incentives in several rounds of competitions to change their often-antiquated laws, many of which support teacher tenure based upon seniority and stifle transformation instead of rewarding teacher performance in raising student achievement. For example, to compete in the program, Massachusetts, and other states who wished to compete successfully, changed their laws to make it easier for children in low-performing schools to change to a charter school, often the only quality route to a higher education for some inner-city children. Race to the Top uses large grants to leverage change, which normally would never happen. Forty-eight states rushed to adopt common standards for all children in K through 12 so that they would be eligible to compete for the large funding from Race to the Top. Without this carrot, these states would not have changed.

Needless to say, this has incurred resistance from teacher unions, who have a history of fighting on behalf of teachers, but historically have pushed to pay teachers based upon seniority regardless of how well they teach. Strange that a Democratic Administration would initiate a program which appears to be anti-union, but this initiative and that of other bipartisan organizations are not anti-union, but pro-student achievement. It is beginning to transform the unions' policies even from within. It is not the unions being attacked but the antiquated policy of rewarding teachers based upon seniority and not performance.

Other encouraging initiatives on the part of non-profit activist organizations, including some below, offer new optimism for national educational reform in the US.

Non-profit organization activism for reforming education

Never before have I seen such encouraging bipartisan support for reforming the status quo. There is promising new evidence of conservative and liberal organizations working together to reward teachers for their ability to raise their students' performance, even if in the Congress they can't seem to compromise to reach agreement on most everything.

Stand For Children, founded by Jonah Edelman, son of the famed activist/leader Marian Wright Edelman, is a grassroots group lobbying states to reform teacher evaluations and more equitable school funding.

Students First, Michelle Rhee's new organization, is reaching out to millions of teachers, lobbying for student-performance-based promotions for teachers.

Educators 4 Excellence, founded by two Teach For America alumni, lobbies against union policies from New York and Los Angeles de-emphasizing teacher seniority.

Democrats For Educational Reform, a wealthy group of bankers and CEOs, is providing support for Democratic politicians who alienate the unions by pushing for educational reforms. What more strange bedfellows could one hope for than bankers and CEOs supporting Democratic lawmakers!

The New TLA, a progressive group of Los Angeles union teachers, is working to reform the 38,000-member LA union from within. So here are unions joining in the fight to overturn their practices of the past!

The Foundation For Excellence in Education, founded by former Florida Governor Jeb Bush, supports states expanding charter schools and efforts to link teacher pay to student performance.

The role of private foundations in educational transformation

Private foundations are also seeing the priority need to transform teaching. One significant initiative is that of the Bill and Melinda Gates Foundation, which has pledged a significant amount of its resources toward identifying what makes an effective teacher. I had the opportunity to meet Bill and Melinda Gates in 2006 when they were awarded the Fulbright Medal by the Fulbright Foundation. They have been investigating what makes an effective teacher and, not surprising to me, Melinda Gates told me that they are finding that it is a combination of the same person-centered qualities Aspy, Roebuck, Tausch, Hattie, Cornelius-White, and Teach For America have found to make a difference. These empathic qualities, coupled with good organization, goal-setting, and grit, result in significant student achievement gains.

In the past we have had some of the most ambitious studies of person-centered teaching and learning ever done. Then, in the 1980s and 1990s, drugs, and the violence that often accompanies them, began appearing in the schools. The schools' reaction against this was to tighten up, lock down the schools, bring in police, metal detectors, strict discipline, and back-to-the-basics 'reading, writing, and arithmetic, taught to the tune of a hickory stick'. Trust between teachers and students, or parents and children, invariably erodes as militaristic methods of control increase. New violent tragedies in our schools cause us to tighten up even more. There seems a large three-decade gap between that impressive person-centered research evidence of the past and the present. Now, for the first time in thirty years, we have fresh new evidence – widespread corroboration of the importance of the little-publicized, but largest and most exhaustive, field studies ever done in the 1970s and 1980s. We now have a corroborative link to the past thanks to the impressive meta-analyses of Hattie and Cornelius-White, studying all the quality research done since 1948, linked to student achievement, and showing high effect sizes for person-centered methods resulting in student achievement. Rogers has said this about this past body of research:

> The research studies reported here are among the largest and most exhaustive ever carried out in the field of education. They are based on tape recordings of thousands and thousands of hours of classroom interaction in eight countries. These came from all levels of education, many from different ethnic and national groups, and a wide spread of geographical locations. They cannot be dismissed as inconclusive.[21]

The recent meta-analysis of Cornelius-White and the huge meta-syntheses of studies by John Hattie, showing high effect sizes for person-centered teaching, goal-setting, feedback, organization of teaching, and grit, correlated with student performance and other important outcomes including less violence in schools, gives us contemporary and overwhelming evidence of the importance of person-centered methods discussed in later chapters. And now Reinhard Tausch and Renate Hüls share in their recent research on empathy in Chapter 14 the moving cries of students for more empathic teachers and that empathy can be an antidote to aggression and violence in schools.

Perhaps we have finally reached the threshold for transformation. We have overwhelming evidence about what worked in the past and what works now and over time. Student achievement is enhanced by what we broadly call person-centered methods. The government has put up the financial incentives for the first time for states to transform their requirements for rewarding teachers, not for seniority, but toward what really matters – how well their students achieve. Bipartisan organizations are springing up lobbying for reform of education.

We have the evidence to transform. But do we have the will – the intentionality and grit – to transform to a context and a world where person-centered teaching, leading, management, is widely valued and practiced? In the following chapters we explore various aspects of this and further present the research results, which, in Rogers' words, 'cannot be dismissed as inconclusive'.

Notes

1   Programme for International Student Assessment (PISA) Profiles by Country, OECD, 2009.
2   (PISA) Profiles by Country, OECD, 2009.
3   Cornelius-White, Jeffrey F. D. and A. P. Harbaugh (2010) *Learner-Centered Instruction: Building Relationships for Student Success.* Thousand Oaks, CA/London/New Delhi/Singapore: Sage Publications, p. 3.
4   Fraser, B. J., H. J. Walberg, W. W. Welch, and J. A. Hattie (1987) 'Syntheses of Educational Productivity Research'. *International Journal of Educational Research* 11: 145–252.
5   Hattie, John (2009) *Visible Learning – A Synthesis of Over 800 Meta-Analyses Relating to Achievement.* London/New York: Routledge, pp. 7–17, 118, 119, 167, 173, 182, 203–205.
6   Hattie, John (2012) *Visible Learning for Teachers – Maximizing Impact on Learning.* London/New York: Routledge.
7   Cornelius-White and Harbaugh, *Learner-Centered Instruction.*
8   Cornelius-White, J. (2007) 'Learner-Centered Teacher–Student Relationships Are Effective: A Meta-Analysis'. *Review of Educational Research* 77, no. 1 (March): 144.
9   McCombs, B.L. (2008) *The School Leader's Guide to Learner Centered Education: From Complexity to Simplicity.* Thousand Oaks, CA: Corwin Press.
10 Cornelius-White and Harbaugh, *Learner-Centered Instruction*, p. 174.
11 Aspy, David N. and Flora N. Roebuck (1975) 'The Relationship of Teacher-Offered Conditions of Meaning to Behaviors Described by Flanders Interaction Analysis'. *Education* 95, no. 3: 216–20.
12 Cornelius-White, p. 6.
13 Ibid.
14 Ibid., p. xxiii.
15 Farr, Steven (2010) *Teaching as Leadership: The Highly Effective Teacher's Guide to Closing the Achievement Gap.* San Francisco: Jossey-Bass/Wiley.
16 Kopp, Wendy (2003) *One Day, All Children: The Unlikely Triumph of Teach For America and What I Learned Along the Way.* New York: Public Affairs.
17 Kopp, Wendy. (2011) *A Chance to Make History: What Works and What Doesn't in Providing an Excellent Education for All.* New York: Public Affairs.
18 Farr, p. xiii.
19 Duckworth, A. J., P. D. Quinn, and M. E. P. Seligman (2009) 'Positive Predictors of Teacher Effectiveness'. *Journal of Positive Psychology* 4, no. 6: 545.
20 Teach For America website: http://www.teachforamerica.org/why-teach-for-america/who-we-look-for
21 Carkhuff, R. (1984) *The Productive Teacher.* Amherst, MA: Human Resource Development Press, p. 292.
22 Rogers, Carl R. (1983) *Freedom to Learn for the 80s.* Columbus, OH: Charles Merrill, pp. 197–98.

5

EDUCATING THE GIFTED AND TALENTED

Freedom to realize your potential

Harold Lyon

I'd like to invite you, the reader, to take a break and relax while reading this chapter. Don't study it or try hard to understand this chapter. Just relax and be with it. I'm going to try to be somewhat spontaneous as I write for you. One message is that to the degree that we can be spontaneous, to the degree that we can respond to one another in the moment, we have much more of our potential available for learning. And to the degree that we have a rote, fixed set of responses to life, the way we are often conditioned to in our schools, we limit our potential to a fraction of what it could be. It is estimated that we realize 5–15% of our potential in our lifetimes – a tragic waste of what we could have.

Risking being in the here-and-now

I like to think of us each having an 'ego boundary' – a particular space surrounding us. And when we're inside that space we're safe and secure. When we get out near the edge of it, we become more anxious. If you go far enough out, you can venture into what I call 'psychotic' space. But these boundaries are elastic, and by taking risks you gradually stretch your ego boundaries until you have a very large space in which to roam around freely and explore. Then it's a longer way out to the peripheral boundaries where you become anxious. And my thesis is that when you risk stretching these boundaries, you have far more of your potential available. But society tends to encourage us to restrict ourselves to very narrow ego boundaries, wanting us to be predictable. And we tend to kill off divergent thinking and creativity often before our teen years. A challenge as teachers, students and parents is to help expand those ego boundaries, to provide a safe space for that risk taking – a safety net for the freedom to fail, which is often the most indelible learning experience.

Consider that a day in your life is a precious gift to give to yourself or another. There's never another day exactly like this one. It's unique. When you are spontaneously here and now, in the moment, you have so much of your natural magnificence and potential available to share with your students, friends, and family. Consider for a moment that your doctor told you that you had only one month left to live. How would you spend those precious thirty days? What would you say to those people who are special in your life if you had only a month to live? What would you do? Where would you go? Those are the important things that we often neglect to say or do – that we're too shy or embarrassed to say. Want to discover what's important in your life? Let me suggest you soon say and do some of those things – even the outrageous ones – that you would if you had only a month left to live. Share some of these things with your loved ones, friends, and your students, and I predict that a lot more of your potential will be available to you and maybe to them as well.

Opening to miracles

It's said that aerodynamic experts have studied the bumblebee and have concluded that the bumblebee really cannot fly. It appears impossible scientifically. His body is too heavy for his small wings. The bumblebee doesn't know that, so he goes ahead and flies anyway.

I'm a believer in miracles. After miracles occur, there is always a linear or rational explanation for why they occur. But you have to have faith and intention to allow them to come about. You must create a context for miracles for them to come about. You can't predict a butterfly from a caterpillar. It is very difficult scientifically. And you don't see caterpillars running around on logs, leaping off, trying hard to achieve flight. They'd never stay still long enough to grow that cocoon and become. The effective teacher helps her students set very high goals, so high that it seems to them that a miracle is necessary for them to achieve their goals. But she helps them believe in the miracles of themselves and never gives up on them. It's these kinds of miracles that we can open to in our classrooms – in each child. The best of the Teach For America teachers do this with and for their students. They help create miracles in their classrooms every day.

Doing versus being – content versus context – finite versus infinite

There's a significant difference between 'doing' and 'being'. We need to learn 'to be' along with our great capacity 'to do'. Being is infinite – it's boundless. Doing has limits to it. It's finite, and we burn ourselves out by overdoing. The most significant doing flows as a natural extension from our being. In being one can expand to a context far beyond the content of doing and that's what we can offer students – something that many of us knew as children but have forgotten. When you expand from finite content (or doing) to infinite context (or being), miracles quite naturally occur within that infinite context. One of the first steps is to believe in such miracles. St Augustine said, 'Surely he who does not believe in miracles, will never take part in one.'

Years ago when I served in the federal government, I was driving to work in the spring and watched, each morning, a large beautiful tulip bed right across the street from the Tidal basin in Washington, DC. Every spring there's a race for glory between the cherry blossoms and these tulips. One morning I saw a sprinkling of twenty or thirty of the tulip blossoms blooming ahead of the rest, in this otherwise uniform bed of thousands of green leaves. On my way home that evening, I noticed a National Park gardener on his hands and knees clipping off these early blooming blossoms to keep uniformity in the tulip bed! I thought for a minute, 'That could only happen in the bureaucracy.' And then I realized that it happens every day in our classrooms when we clip off the blossoms of the early bloomers ... to keep uniformity in the classroom.

Thinking and being for ourselves

While participating in a New Age World Congress in Florence, Italy in 1978, the great inventor-architect-philosopher R. Buckminster Fuller, then in his twilight years, was provided the rare opportunity to freely and spontaneously talk before our small group for three hours a day for five days about his theories, his as-yet-not-fully formulated ideas, and his life. As he spoke about gifted children, he began to change that label to 'New Age Children'. I liked the term, not only because there are so many elitist concerns with the 'gifted' label, but also because by the term 'New Age Children' we were talking about a broader definition of gifted children, including those with intuitive gifts and those with spiritual and artistic gifts and divergent thinkers like Bucky Fuller.

Buckminister Fuller – a grain of sand in the oyster

Bucky shared with us that he really deserved little credit for all of his many discoveries. He claimed that the knowledge is already up there and all one has to do is break loose from institutional ways of thinking to grasp it.

What he did deserve credit for was beginning to think for himself forty years earlier, when he contemplated suicide but instead made the decision to live his life fully free from convention, come what may, as an experiment. It was then he chose to become 'a fly in the ointment' – 'a grain of sand in the oyster'. He suggested that even the slowest child in the classroom has the capacity to be as bright as the brightest ... and that the brightest child has the potential to be so far ahead of what we expect that it's almost frightening. We need to begin to free up that incredible potential that we all have to expand our ego boundaries. This means discovering ways to do this freeing work within our classrooms and our homes. This book offers person-centered research supporting such outcomes. Programs like Teach For America train young, inexperienced, person-centered teachers who open the potential for achievement for every child. Person-centered teaching fosters divergent thinking and creativity among students.

After the overly 'me-first' emphasis of the 1960s, as is often the case in social cycles, there came a backlash against a humanistic approach to education in spite of excellent, but not very visible, research which showed its benefits. It was belittled as a 'touchy-feely' approach, not relevant to hardcore student cognitive achievement. Actually the converse is true. Empirical studies show that person-centered teaching methods lead to higher achievement, less violence and absenteeism, happier teachers and learners, more creative responses, and more indelible learning.

The religious right attacked the humanistic approach to education as 'secular humanism' and even mislabeled it anti-Christian. It became the 'whipping boy' of ultra-right groups. Many of us, including David Aspy, who directed the large study presented in this book, felt we needed a better name for humanistic education – one which did not carry the stigma of being mislabeled as secular humanism. It was during this era that I personally passed through one of my own 'crucibles' and also came under attack by the radical right, partly for my book *Learning to Feel – Feeling to Learn,* which was labeled 'secular humanism' and anti-Christian, which it was not, any more than this book is.

Today we know it as person-centered teaching or, as Cornelius-White calls it, Learner Centered Instruction. As drugs and violence began increasing – especially in inner-city schools, police began being placed in schools to counter violence. A no-nonsense approach to education emphasizing discipline and law and order, in efforts to control students, forced the positive person-centered research findings into the background. But it is the very heart of person-centered philosophy, including respect and caring for persons, empathy, and genuineness, which can most effectively counter violence toward others, indifference toward learning, and help close the achievement gap.

More recently researchers have begun keeping detailed data on the performance of teachers. Teach For America 'has been tracking hundreds of thousands of kids, and looking at why some teachers can move their students three grade levels ahead in a year and others can't'.[1]

Though the most successful teachers in this data are not 'touchy-feely', they are person-centered in that they care about their students enough to set goals for them and constantly reevaluate with 'grit' how to improve their effectiveness. These studies on effective teachers corroborate the findings of the large field studies presented later in this book and the huge achievement-oriented meta-analyses of Hattie and Cornelius-White. The person-centered findings of empathy, caring for students, and genuineness, combined with the traits of frequent feedback, interactivity, organization, and goal-setting, are the hallmarks of the most successful teachers, whose students make the most dramatic performance gains.

Person-centered education – the cognitive integrated with the affective

Our classrooms tend to focus more on cognitive intellectual development where we push the student down an intellectual track with little attention paid to the affective development – to students' capacities for love, empathy, and awareness, and their communication skills. We need to integrate the affective with the cognitive and this is a part of what we call person-centered or confluent education. It's an integration of those two and, when you do that, both kinds of learning will peak and be more indelible, as we found in *Sesame Street* by injecting into each program both cognitive and affective goals for education of the whole person.

Families, churches, and society need to help foster the spiritual aspects of the child as well – another important dimension of the whole person to consider.

The psychologist Abraham Maslow said that we need to treasure 'The emotional jags of the child in the classroom' – the 'peak' experiences, as that's where real learning takes place. In my own life, as I look back over the more important learning experiences I've had, very few of them came from within academic classrooms. Rather, they came from crises – or from tragedies in my life. The Chinese character for 'crisis' is the same as the one for 'opportunity'. In the East, they understand this better than we do in the West. This is what Warren Bennis means when he says, 'Most good leaders pass through a crucible that tested them to the depths of their being and enabled the successes they realized later in life.'[2] We need to pay attention to those kinds of learning experiences, which are often the spontaneous ones – the ones we don't plan – often the unthinkables, or those our society has no system to hold or explain or accept.

The traits found in successful teachers

Carl Rogers did earlier research on the traits of the successful therapist.[3] Four other people who have contributed to this book – Reinhard Tausch, the late David Aspy and his wife, Cheryl, and the late Flora Roebuck – performed comprehensive empirical studies, over thirty-five years, taking Rogers' findings for therapists and applying them to teachers. The three traits of the successful therapist, found by Rogers, were corroborated by Tausch, Aspy, and Roebuck to exist in the successful teacher.[4] The first is genuineness or realness on the part of the teacher: the ability to be a human being with strengths and weaknesses, to be authentic with your students. This means not trying to be a perfect teacher who always knows the right answers. This trait is also called congruence. The second trait is empathic understanding, or the ability to put yourself in the student's shoes and see the world from his perspective. As you will read from their own voices in Chapter 14, Tausch and Hüls share how students who do not have an empathic teacher suffer significant damage. The third trait is prizing or caring about students, or 'unconditional positive regard' as Rogers called it. It's just the opposite of apathy. It's caring enough about the uniqueness of an individual to celebrate that student's uniqueness. When a teacher has these traits, trust is established. Students trust that the teacher is there – not to catch them up in all their faults, but to facilitate the discovery process and help them succeed in reaching their goals. Trust evolves largely from the other three traits. I add a fifth trait – competence in the subject matter – but it wasn't in the study, and I put it last on the list. It seems to be the main trait we focus on in training teachers. One might think it difficult to train people in these traits, but we have found this is not so. Tausch, Aspy, and

Roebuck's research, and our recent research in medical schools, show that teachers can be trained in these person-centered methods fairly rapidly and efficiently. The results of this research will be in chapters that follow. The data show that students with teachers with these traits have higher achievement scores, as well as many other positive outcomes – empirical data that lead to the conclusion that we must focus on the education of the whole person.

The Aspys and Flora Roebuck suggested that the governing trait of these is empathy – the teachers with high empathy tended to have the other traits as well. And so they focused on high-empathy teachers comprehensively and thoroughly in many locations and settings over many years, in the largest field study ever done on classroom teaching at all levels. They found significant evidence that the students in classrooms taught by high-empathy teachers had significantly higher achievement scores. They were also happier, as were their students. The high-empathy teachers tended to have greater influence the earlier the students were exposed to them. First grade students with high-empathy teachers achieved a ten-point IQ differential by the end of the year. And, by the end of the second grade, a further ten-point differential resulted between students with high-empathy teachers compared to low-empathy teachers largely from the effect of that first grade high-empathy teacher. So, the earlier the stimulus, the better. We've known this, but we have paid lip service to it.

The Aspys and Roebuck also found that it was easier to train elementary school teachers in empathy skills than it was high school teachers, or, for that matter, university professors. In fact, they concluded that we ought to have good school-teachers helping university professors learn how to relate better with their students.

They also found that these high-empathy teachers tended to use humor and have good physical condition. The cut-off criterion for good physical condition was they could walk or run a mile in twelve minutes or less, which is not very fast: some 70-year-old joggers are doing it faster than that. But 90% of the teachers in their studies over age 35 said they could not (I would say they *would* not) walk or run a mile in twelve minutes or less. Those teachers who were in good physical condition and had high empathy started out the week on Monday at a certain level of energy and ended up on Friday at a higher peak level of energy, synergistically drawing energy from their students, back and forth. Teachers with low empathy and low physical condition ended up exhausted on Friday. So this says something about high-empathy teachers, therapists, and people like the Teach For America teachers. As I look around at the people I respect, I find most of them have these traits.

Recent research my colleagues and I performed at two German medical universities suggests the importance of empathy in teachers and physicians and the need for empathic role models for medical students, since medical education appears to erode rather than enhance empathy in medical students.[5] This current research, in which medical teachers improve their teaching behaviors significantly along the lines of the Rogers–Aspy–Roebuck–Tausch findings, is presented in Chapter 17.

Since the time Aspy and Roebuck did their huge studies in the 1970s, the mood in education in America, followed by many other developed countries, has moved toward more rigid, behavioristic, punitive governance, and toward accountability as judged by national tests – tests teachers soon learn to teach to in order to raise their school's overall grades and save their own jobs. Teaching to the tests does not teach students how to think and solve problems. This movement has had little tolerance for the practice of person-centered approaches. The thorough studies performed by Aspy, Roebuck, and Tausch were never given the visibility they deserved. We intend to change that in this book.

In 2009, educator-researcher Dr John Hattie began publishing his life's work, which is now the largest study of effective teaching for achievement ever carried out.[6] Hattie has distilled the 'effect sizes' from over 800 meta-analyses of educational studies, which reveal some interesting surprises. This huge synthesis of meta-analyses of thousands of studies involving over 50 million students brings us back full circle to the research showing that the person-centered methods found in the Aspy–Roebuck–Tausch studies also made a real difference in student achievement. Things we thought contributed to achievement, such as small classes, homework, programmed instruction, school buildings, team-teaching, retention (holding students back a grade), and national testing don't really have much influence on achievement. Empathy, caring for and trusting students, genuineness, goal-setting, feedback, mentoring both for teachers and students, and teacher passion create high effects on student achievement. In short, Hattie's monumental studies go a long way in corroborating the findings of the past research on person-centered methods presented in this book, making them important for today and the future.

Are the same traits found in successful managers and leaders?

A study by Rensis Likert at the University of Michigan corroborated this research.[7] After looking at 5,000 organizations, he found that the high-producing managers and leaders also tend to have these person-centered traits. Low-producing managers tend to think of people as tools to get the job done, while the high producers think of people as unique individuals. This research is shared in Chapter 11.

Another way to summarize this research is to say that person-centered teachers tend to see deeper inside the student for their inner beauty. Our grading system and the focus on national testing looks at surface beauty rather than inner beauty. The effective teacher sees her students' inner beauty and is not so concerned with outer appearances but rather what do we think and feel. The whole multi-billion-dollar cosmetic industry is based on surface beauty. We need to see deeper than that, as we see our children and one another.

Robert G. Ingersoll said, 'If we had done a thousand years ago as the kings told us, we would have all been slaves. If we had done as the priests told us, we would have all been idiots. If we had done as the doctors told us, we would have all been dead. This world has been saved by our disobedience.' There's a lot of latent potential in that aliveness that sometimes seems hidden within the mischievous or darker side of the disobedient child.

Seeing versus looking

I knew a psychiatrist from California who built much of his practice on the difference between seeing and looking. He described looking as a highly cognitive 'head trip' from eyes to brain. We sort people out, judge them, and evaluate them. I evaluate children when I look at them. But seeing is a here-and-now 'groking' (to use the term from the Heinlein science fiction novel *Stranger in a Strange Land*). It's a sensing process that seems to connect mainline from eyes to heart. Seeing is accepting, right here and now. When we see children ... we can *be with* them instead of *doing to* them – this being is infinite, boundless.

Our bio-clocks

Another factor that influences our performance is our varied readiness for learning. Each of our bio-clocks is different. There are morning people and evening people. When you test a child in the evening – one who is a morning person – he might score significantly lower, and vice versa. We need to pay attention to this readiness that is unique for each child. In spite of the excellent German educational system, for example, there is no room for late bloomers, as children are branched almost indelibly at fifth grade to either the university or the technical track. Of course, their technical track leads to a superior training and a high-quality technical workforce, but the late bloomers have little chance to choose going to a university.

The motivation which triggers the readiness for learning needs to come from within the person, instead of being forced from outside. My old alma mater, West Point, was an institution for forced learning. We cadets used to say that 'It was a $100,000 education ... crammed down our throats nickel by nickel.' When I was Director of Education for the Gifted and Talented I received phone calls from parents who wanted to force their 2-year-old gifted child to learn how to read. Don't force your child to read, but help her to discover the scent of the forest, the smell of the ocean, the expressions on people's faces – body language. Then the reading of words will come as a natural way to express those feelings, much faster than it will through our linear, programmed kind of learning. We need to surround gifted children with highly conscious mentors, aware empathic teachers who will play for the long shot that the child will open to the whole universe that is within each of us.

Breaking through

We are experiencing breakthroughs in scientific discovery and levels of consciousness. At CERN, physicists have finally found the Higgs boson, the particle that could solve mysteries large and small. The work with porpoises is an example of

breakthroughs in consciousness. If you take a porpoise away from a group of porpoises, the remaining porpoises will run into one another for about a month until
they build new energy fields. Those energy fields are not unique to porpoises. We
all have them. PET scans enable us to photograph those energy fields, appearing
as auras that are different for different individuals with different feelings. When a
child leaves the home, or goes off to college, the community or family that is left is
a different one and has to adjust to new energy patterns, just as do our classrooms
as children arrive and leave.

The genetic work on DNA and RNA molecules is causing us to face complex
moral decisions about whether and how we should bring into the world incredibly
bright and gifted individuals. Work in fertilization of the human ovum promises
potential for bringing healthier, more aware, and more intelligent individuals into
society. The older work in prenatal care by Dr Leboyer ('Birth Without Violence')
was exciting in terms of what it meant to individual potential. Some African mothers
talk to their children in utero from the moment of conception, and when that child
is born it has been already learning and is nine months old, instead of starting to learn
at the moment of birth. They stimulate the unborn child with songs and by nam-
ing the child and speaking to her before birth. Research done on the 126 children
who were in Dr Leboyer's initial group showed they were incredibly intelligent,
free from most childhood diseases, and, most astonishing, 98 of them (78%) were
ambidextrous!

Using our modern technological birth procedures, including the 'saddle-block',
Joseph Chilton Pierce, who wrote *The Magical Child*, birthed 100 monkeys, 100%
of which sustained brain damage. How many humans also suffer such damage? The
African mothers that Dr Pierce studied birth their children naturally in their huts.
Then the mother puts the baby on her stomach and massages every inch of the
child, just as the mother cat licks every bit of the newborn kitten. In large litters of
twelve or more kittens, the mother cat is sometimes too tired to do the licking, and
it is these kittens that often turn out to be spastic or die prematurely. The African
mothers instinctively do this full-body massaging. The child can hear and feel the
mother's heartbeat and the mother then bites through the umbilical and puts the
child to her breast and goes out to show it to her friends. She has eye contact with
that child most of its first few months of life. Dr Pierce showed me color slides of
these tenderly birthed children holding up their heads twelve hours after birth and
smiling in a mirror, which our children (birthed through our 'normal' process)
don't do for two and a half months! These children are incredibly intelligent and
bright.

Pierce told me an interesting story. These children – diaper-less – were lined
up, with their mothers holding them to see the doctor, and he wondered why
the children were not messing on their mothers. He asked them, 'What do you
do when the child has to urinate?' They answered, 'We take them to the bushes.'
He asked, 'How do you know when the child has to go?' They laughed and said,
'How do you know when you have to go?' They are so bonded to the child that
they sense when the child needs to urinate!

Grandmother wisdom

We are finding that the beliefs of our grandmothers were often real wisdom. For example, mother's milk is the most appropriate and vital food for infants. Every minute spent at the mother's breast for an infant can have far greater significance than all the expensive private schools that the child might attend later. That nurture, that warmth, and the unknown ingredients of mother's milk, is far more significant than we know. Such discoveries, some of which are older ones we are rediscovering, offer us new opportunities in terms of nurturing children in people-centered ways.

Between 8 and 22 months, children are consumed by curiosity

Dr Burton White, a Harvard professor, found that between 8 and 22 months a child is literally consumed by curiosity. He claimed that this is the period in which the basis for creativity and curiosity is really formed. We're on the frontier of fascinating breakthroughs across the spectrum of life, the level of which we have only a glimpse.

Just before her death, Margaret Mead shared with me that she found gifted children who could hear and see ten times better than what's considered normal. She told me about one child who frequently had nightmares and was sent, with little positive result, to a psychiatrist for treatment. One night, he woke up screaming and told his parents a gruesome story about a murder. They later found out that, in the apartment building a floor above them, there was a murder. This child with extraordinary hearing had heard it in detail and even helped solve the crime by giving some of the details to the police. Imagine the assault on that child's senses that living in the inner-city had involved! We need to pay attention to some of these uncommon extraordinary gifts – gifts that we are learning exist in greater percentages than we ever thought, disguised as unexplainable phenomena and sometimes labeled as learning disabilities, neuroses, or psychoses.

In Chapter 10, I share how I taught a person-centered psychology class at Georgetown University, where the students contracted with me at the beginning of the course for the grade they wished to learn if they achieved their own suggested level of achievement. They graded themselves in how they achieved their own criteria. This is one possible model for using person-centered methods for teaching a university course in psychology.

Advocates for person-centered education are outnumbered by the apathetic. The research throughout this book underscores the importance of person-centered methods. We need to join together in mutual support groups to amass our energies, power, and creativity into that critical mass which is needed to bring about a transformation or a renaissance in education. We have that potential. Will we bury the minor differences and squabbles that invariably seem to surface between individuals, organizations, states, and nations in order to pool our considerable energies on behalf of this world's most neglected, yet valuable natural resource – our children? If we follow the recent example of the US Congress, it seems we won't make much progress. But if we create a context of person-centered transformation, miracles are possible. The difference we make makes all the difference in the world, for their realizing their potential.

Notes

1   Ripley, Amanda (2010) ' What Makes a Great Teacher'. *Atlantic* (January/February): 58–66.
2   Bennis, W. and R. J. Thomas (2002) *Geeks and Geezers: How Era, Values, and Defining Moments Shape Leaders*. Boston: Harvard Business School Press, p. 34.
3   Rogers, Carl R. (1983). *Freedom to Learn For the 80s*. Columbus, OH: Charles Merrill.
4   Aspy, D. N. and F. N. Roebuck (1977) *Kids Don't Learn from People They Don't Like*. Amherst, MA: HRD Press.
5   Newton, B. W., L. Barber, J. Clardy, E. Cleveland, and P. O'Sullivan (2008) 'Is There Hardening of the Heart During Medical School?' *Academic Medicine* 83, no. 3, pp. 244–49.
     Wilkerson, L., and D. M. Irby (1998) 'Strategies for Improving Teaching Practices: A Comprehensive Approach to Faculty Development'. *Academic Medicine* 73, no. 4: 39.
6   Hattie, John (2009) *Visible Learning – A Synthesis of over 800 Meta-Analyses Relating to Achievement*. London/New York: Routledge, pp. 7–17, 118, 119, 167, 173, 182, 203–205.
7   Likert, Rensis (1961) *New Patterns of Management*. New York: McGraw-Hill Book Co.

PART II

Person-centered learning and teaching

6

DIALOGUE BETWEEN CARL ROGERS AND HAROLD LYON

CARL: The heart of the person-centered approach to teaching and learning is that the content to be learned and the sequence in which it is to be learned both arise out of interaction. This is the interaction of the interests, needs, and curiosity of the student – with the knowledge, resources, and facilitative attitudes of the teacher. It is out of that mutual interaction that both the content and the sequence arise. I think that this approach mystifies curriculum experts because no curriculum, no lesson plans, can be firmly formulated in advance. It's a developing process rather than a careful slicing and arranging of predetermined subject matter. It's a process that can't be entirely predicted and this is often troubling to teachers and to curriculum specialists.

HAL: I would add something seemingly contradictory to your statement: that it's important for us to recognize that there is some structure in a person-centered classroom. There have been criticisms of person-centered education activities on the basis that they seem structureless, which is nonsense. There is as much structure as the teacher perceives is needed and as the students require. I think it is imperative to state clearly that structure is an individual matter in these facilitative classrooms, but it is there to the degree that it is needed for effective learning.

CARL: The structure that occurs in a person-centered classroom is an organic structure that grows out of the situation, not an imposed structure by someone who simply knows the subject matter. And the learning that takes place there is significant or experiential learning. It has a quality of personal involvement with the whole person in both his feeling and cognitive aspects being in the learning event. It is self-initiated. Even when the impetus or stimulus comes from the outside, the sense of discovery, of reaching out, of grasping and comprehending, comes from within. It is pervasive. It makes a difference in the behavior, the attitudes, perhaps even the personality of the learner. It is evaluated by the learner. He knows whether it is meeting his need, whether it leads toward what he wants to know, whether it illuminates the dark area of ignorance he is experiencing. The locus of evaluation, we might say, resides definitely in the learner. Its essence is meaning. When such learning takes place, the element of meaning-to-the-learner is built into the whole experience.

HAL: It seems to me that what you have just said is the core of what we mean when we talk about person-centered education. And it's also an integration of the affective or feelings with the cognitive or intellectual. And that integration makes the cognitive learnings, which tend to be spontaneous, more indelible. It also means that the student can incorporate his own experience as legitimate content for the classroom as your Man of Tomorrow insists. In essence the process within the classroom becomes the content. Process as content. That's when real learning takes place. You can't separate that from cognitive learning. When you integrate the two, then we have the best kind of 'back to basics' education that you can have. And to the degree you integrate the affective with the cognitive, learning is more indelible. There's no way to deny the affective process (though many attempt this) that's taking place in the classroom, because it will be going on in the students' minds anyway. I think it's important for high school graduates to have basic competencies. On the other hand, one of those competencies is interpersonal communication – an affective and intellectual skill.

I was interested in the state of Oregon's efforts, over many years, to revamp requirements for graduation from high school. They completed a major job of changing those requirements from the traditional Carnegie academic units to insisting that every high school must ensure that each graduate can do three important things. (1) They can hold a job and prove that they've earned money in some particular vocation or job. Thus, when they graduate from high school they will be able to earn income and take care of themselves and their families. (2) The basic academic requirements, traditional ones we've always had, are still expected and that's important. (3) The students must demonstrate their capacity for interpersonal relationships and communications in several ways. One of these is a summer program where the students work with other people, communicating either in writing or in person. They also have to complete a major project from which their sponsor will affirm their ability to communicate on an interpersonal level.

I think this is the kind of 'back to basics' I would like to see instead of just back to science and math or other particular 'basic' courses. I applaud a state like Oregon that was willing to move ahead in new high school requirements like this.

CARL: I don't have much to add to that. I believe that we are in the midst of a pendulum swing to the right in almost every aspect of life and I think it's natural, corrective. On some ways the attacks on you and your writing by right-wing groups are evidence of it. I'm not particularly in sympathy with a number of aspects of it, but I feel it is a natural thing that we must expect and live with.

And I see competency tests for students as being fine if they are related to adult reality. I like your stress on communication. I think that students should be able to conduct ordinary business transactions, they should know how to keep records for income tax, they should prove that they have the ability to read instructions and other skills of that nature. Those are valuable preparations for adult life. All competency tests for students should be related to adult reality. Otherwise, they have very little meaning.

On the other hand, competency measures for the teacher can be a real threat. The value of these tests for the teacher depends entirely upon the way in which they are used. They can be used in a threatening fashion or they could be used to help the teacher change to more effective teaching methods, but I do think this value depends on the purposes for which those measures are taken.

HAL: Are you saying that before we install competency tests for teachers, we need to ensure that their supervisors have some basic helping competencies?

CARL: Right. That's a very good way of putting it.

HAL: Just one more comment about the trend toward 'back to basics'. I think it's a big mistake to create a 'you or me' situation with competition between 'back to the basics' advocates and person-centered advocates. I think advocates for more person-centered education can also be in favor of good, solid, basic education. We are not on opposite poles, as we're frequently assumed to be.

CARL: I agree. I think that because we are in favor of person-centered education, we want students to learn the important tools for living. It's not very human to allow students to graduate from high school without being able to read and write. But there are also other competencies that students need, such as citizenship skills and cooperation. We tend to denigrate cooperation in most of the learning in school. If children cooperate in learning, it's seen as cheating. If all learning was cooperative between student and student or student and teacher, then this competency would be acquired naturally along the way. I think we build competition into our students while cooperation is seen as a bad thing most of the time; and then we have to devote special attention to try to develop it later. I'd like to see cooperation involved as a part of learning from the very first.

HAL: One of the problems is that we tend to establish a 'you or me' world for children as well as for adults in our society, and a 'you or me' world has little room for cooperation but lots of opportunity for competition. Competition is not bad; it's just that in a 'you or me' world competition tends to make someone win and someone lose. This isn't necessary. We can have an 'all win' situation. We can teach children to collaborate, to cooperate in a 'you and me' kind of climate. It's an environment, rather than a lesson plan or a specific curriculum which provides the opportunity for discovering these things. I also believe it begins in the home and may be far more important there than it is in school. In school we also need to provide the opportunities for the discovery of cooperation by example, by teachers working together collaboratively instead of battling with one another or against the administration. That kind of behavior sets an example of having to be against someone or trying to get ahead of them, instead of being with them or supportive of them.

We also fail to teach anything about alignment. When people can be aligned with one another, when a classroom of children can be aligned in pursuit of a goal or an objective, the whole is far greater than the sum of its parts. We really do not provide enough opportunity for children or adults to spontaneously discover this.

CARL: You mentioned the necessity for providing youngsters the opportunities to spontaneously discover a concept. I believe that's true but I also think it is incredible that we have to consider consciously about spontaneous exploration as a learning vehicle. We do so easily forget that before he or she sets foot in school, the child has been learning at an extremely rapid rate, probably a rate that he or she will never again equal. And what is the vehicle for that learning? Spontaneous exploration and play, for the most part. I hope we don't structure these and make them techniques. I just hope that we can give the child's curiosity and playful impulses free rein and I would certainly back up your notion, Hal, that parents can do a tremendous amount to see that curiosity and those searching, learning, fun impulses, are not thwarted by the home environment. When I think of educators considering 'Maybe we should use spontaneous exploration or play to help students learn', it makes me laugh. I believe they are feeling overly responsible and I would like to say to them what I tell myself when I feel I am being overly responsible. I hum the words of a song from *My Fair Lady*: 'Without you twirling it, the earth will spin.' And I would like to just modify that a little for teachers, and say, 'Without your teaching him, the child will learn.' I think if teachers were more aware of the latent curiosity and desire to learn that exists in every child, until it is squelched, they would feel less solemn responsibility for regarding play as a technique of learning.

HAL: J. McVicker Hunt was working with children in an orphanage in Iran, where he found the biggest problem was getting the attendants and teachers and others to be uninhibited enough to play with the children on their own level. They were embarrassed to make 'coo-coo' sounds or nonsense sounds, mimicking the child; they were embarrassed about playing with their toes and saying, 'This is your toe.' So he had to put them through a kind of encounter group experience for working with children. It was the only mode that he found effective in loosening up the adults so that they could play on the child's level in a spontaneous way. Perhaps our teachers need to loosen up, and that means getting rid of the burden of having to act as if they know all the answers, having to look perfect. It means expressing the genuineness that you found effective in your research with therapists, and Tausch, Aspy, and Roebuck have found in their research with teachers as being correlated with learning outcomes. It's being able to be yourself, a human being with strengths and weaknesses, instead of trying to be perfect, because that perfection is phony; it's not real. And it doesn't lead to spontaneous play and learning in the classroom. When the teacher is hiding behind her status and rank as teacher, I call that 'status authority' as opposed to the 'natural authority' that flows from spontaneously responding to the students as colleagues with whom you're learning. This is important for every child and even more so for gifted and talented children – to be able to have genuine interactions with the adults around them.

You know, we are such a crisis-oriented society that we don't pay attention to the gifted until the crises are upon us. We didn't do much until Sputnik occurred, and then, of course, we emphasized the sciences in order to catch up with the Russians in the Space Race. Then we were in crisis in the 1970s and, once again, we began to take an interest in the gifted and talented. But we must not forget, in our excitement over their potential, that these youngsters are in many ways very much like the 'average' youngster. We need to understand that they are children; they need carefree times for play, even though they might have minds like adults. We need to provide them with the opportunity still to be children so that they don't grow up at age 5 and become 'man of the house', as some of us have done when given responsibility very early.

I hope that we can maintain an emphasis on the gifted beyond the current crises. In a national study, we found that fewer than 4% of this country's most gifted youngsters were receiving services commensurate with their needs, even though these young people represent our country's most valuable and neglected natural resource. We need to pay special attention to them. We need to find better means for identifying them than just the IQ test (which is based upon such things as knowledge of middle-class nursery rhymes). We don't find many disadvantaged and minority youngsters competing well on the standard IQ test, since it's not culture-free. I worked to establish a broader definition of the gifted, one that goes beyond a 130+ IQ, to include those with leadership ability, artistic talent, and those divergent thinkers with creativity. If you take the top 5% of the IQ, you'll miss 70% of the most creative divergent thinkers, those who will come up with unique solutions to problems. But, if you take the top 20% of IQ, you will get most of the creative ones.

Some gifted children drop out of school, as they are clever enough to find more stimulating opportunities outside the school. Some drop out in order to go into business for themselves; others to deal drugs, or to explore other endeavors more stimulating and lucrative than remaining in school. Our correctional institutions are loaded with gifted people who found exciting means to their goals – means that failed to serve society or themselves. We need to maintain a national advocacy movement to recognize and nurture these youngsters. If we do anything at all for the gifted, we tend to push them down the purely intellectual or cognitive tract. We need to nurture their capacity for love, empathy, and awareness and communication skills, as well. It's a tremendous waste of talent to be realizing only 5–15% of our gifted potential. We need to find alternative ways to reach them, because they represent the possibility of such an important contribution to our entire society and our national good as well as for their own lives. The diversity of their backgrounds must not be allowed to disguise their potential.

CARL: I go along with your statement that the educating of the gifted and the talented often stresses the cognitive and I also feel that affective education certainly should have a very large place. I hope that these teachers who have gifted students are expert facilitators so that there could be intensive group experiences for the gifted. In this way, they would share their feelings and problems, they would gain insight into themselves and others, they would learn to understand and care for others. They would experience their unity with the group. These are incredibly valuable experiences for the gifted child because these are the children who will likely be tomorrow's leaders. And one final comment: I heartily endorse the special focus on the gifted. To me it would be marvelous if the gifted received as much attention, as many specially trained teachers, as many physical and technical resources, as the mentally challenged. It says something about our society that there is almost no limit to what we will do for those who are disabled in their learning abilities, and yet what we will do for the promising individuals is much less. I think it's a sad commentary on our social situation.

HAL: What we're doing for gifted and talented children is really experimental education for all our children. What we find works best for the gifted, I think, is in the forefront of what works best for all children. So it's a wonderful experimental education program; we find that it is one way to pioneer in new approaches for educating all children.

CARL: That's an exciting idea, Hal, to use these special programs for pioneering new alternatives for all education. As you know, in the vast majority of our schools, at all educational levels, we are locked into a traditional and conventional approach that makes significant learning improbable, if not impossible. But there are alternatives: alternative practical ways to handle a class or a course – alternative assumptions and hypotheses upon which education can be built – alternative goals and values for which educators and students can strive. Some of these are described later in this book, including your approach to teaching psychology at Georgetown in Chapter 10.

7

LISTENING AND BEING LISTENED TO

Carl R. Rogers

This chapter is excerpted from a taped speech that Rogers gave to the American Personnel and Guidance Association and has been modified for this book.

I realize I am much more a person who is interested in the real relationship – the actual dealing with the person on the front line – than I am in some of the more academic and scholarly sides of it, even though I've had a part in those too. Now, it's not easy for me to be here. Not only are you an awesome-looking group in number, but it's difficult to know how to make any real contact with a group like this; a group of people with diversified interests within the field. I certainly feel such contact is not achieved by a high-level scholarly kind of abstract paper, especially when you've been in meetings all day. Also I have no desire through my talk to instruct you or to persuade you to my way of thinking or to impress you with my knowledge. In short, I really have no desire to tell you what you should think or feel or do. And consequently I find myself to be in a real dilemma when I face a group like this. What can I do?

The only solution that I've come up with is that perhaps I can share something of myself, something of my experience in interpersonal relationships, something of what it has been like to be me in communication with others. This isn't too easy a thing to do, but if I can do it, if I can share something of myself, then I think you can take what I say or you can leave it alone.

You can decide whether it's relevant to your own job, your own work, your own life. You can respond to it with a reaction, 'Well, that's just what I've felt and what I've experienced and discovered.' Or, equally valuably, you may react to it, 'I feel very differently; my experience has taught me something entirely different.' In either case, it may help you to define yourself more clearly, more openly, more surely. And that I do regard as worthwhile and is something I hope I can facilitate.

So I'm going to share with you a somewhat miscellaneous bag of learnings, of satisfactions and dissatisfactions. The things I have learned or am learning about this mysterious business of relating with other human beings, about communication between persons. The reason I call it a 'mysterious business' is that interpersonal communication is almost never achieved except in part. You probably never feel fully understood by another and neither do I. And yet we find it extremely rewarding when we've been able in a particular instance truly to communicate ourselves when, for some moment in time, we have felt really close to and fully in touch with another person.

So the first very simple feeling I want to share with you is my enjoyment when I can really hear someone. I think perhaps this has been a longstanding characteristic of mine. I can remember this in my early grammar school days. A child would ask a teacher a question and the teacher would give a perfectly good answer to an entirely different question. And a feeling of pain and distress would always strike me; my reaction was 'But she didn't hear him; she didn't hear what he said.' I felt a sort of childish despair at the lack of communication which was, and I fear is, so very common. I believe I know why I'm satisfied to hear someone. When I can really hear someone, it puts me in touch with him. It enriches my life. It's through hearing people that I have learned whatever it is that I know about individuals, about personality, about psychotherapy, about interpersonal relationships.

Then there's another peculiar satisfaction in it to me. I'm not sure whether I can communicate this. When I really hear someone, I like to think it's like listening to the music of the spheres because beyond the immediate message of the person, no matter what that might be, there is the universal and the general. Hidden in all of the personal communications that I really hear, there seem to be orderly psychological laws. Aspects of the awesome order which we find in the universe as a whole. So there is both the satisfaction of hearing this person and also the satisfaction of feeling oneself in some sort of touch with what is universally true.

Now, when I say that I enjoy hearing someone, I mean, of course, hearing deeply. I mean that I hear the words, the thoughts, the feeling tones, the personal meaning, even the meaning that is below the conscious intent of the speaker. And sometimes, too, in a message, which superficially isn't very important, I hear a deep human cry. What someone has called a silent scream that lies buried and unknown, far below the surface of the person. So I've learned to ask myself, 'Can I hear the sounds and sense the shape of this other person's inner world? Can I resonate to what he is saying – resonate so deeply that I sense the meanings he's afraid of and yet would like to communicate as well as those meanings that he knows?'

I think, for example, of an interview I had with an adolescent boy, the recording of which I listened to only a short time ago. Like many an adolescent today, he was saying at the outset of the interview that he had no goals. When I questioned him on this, he made it even stronger that he had no goals whatsoever, not even one. I said, 'There isn't anything you want to do?' 'Nothing. Well, yeah, I want to keep on living.' I remember very distinctly my feeling at that moment. I resonated very deeply to this phrase; he might simply be telling me that, like everyone else, he wanted to live. On the other hand, he might be telling me, and somehow this seemed to be a possibility, that at some point the question of whether or not to live had been a real issue with him. So I tried to resonate to him at all levels.

I didn't know for certain what the message was. I simply wanted to be open to any of the meanings that this statement might have, including the possible meaning that he might have, at one time, considered suicide. I didn't respond verbally at this level; that would have frightened him. But I think that my being willing and able to listen to him at all levels is perhaps one of the things that made it possible for him to tell me, before the end of the interview, that not long before he had been on the point of blowing his brains out. Now, this little episode constitutes an example of what I mean by wanting to really hear someone at all the levels at which he is endeavoring to communicate.

I find in therapeutic interviews, in the intensive group experiences, which have come to mean a great deal to me in recent years, and even rarely in classrooms, that hearing has consequences. When I do truly hear a person and the meanings that are important to him at that moment, hearing not simply his words but him – and when I let him know that I have heard his own private personal meanings, many things happen. There's first of all a grateful look. He feels released. He wants to tell me more about his world. He surges forth with a new sense of a sort of freedom. I think he becomes more open to the process of change. I've often noticed, both in therapy interviews, in group experiences, and in classrooms that the more deeply I can hear the meanings of this person, the more there is that happens.

One thing I've come to look upon is almost universal, and that is that when a person realizes he has been deeply heard, there is a moistness in his eyes. Sometimes I thought it would be a good research project. I think in some real sense, when a person is really heard, he's weeping for joy. It's as though he were saying, 'Thank God: somebody heard me. Someone knows what it's like to be me.' In such moments I've had the fantasy of a prisoner in a dungeon tapping out day after day a Morse code message: 'Does anybody hear me? Is there anybody there? Can anyone hear me?' And finally one day he hears some faint tappings which spell out 'Yes.' And by that one simple response he's released from his loneliness, he's become a human being again.

There are many, many people in this world – young people as well as adults – living in private dungeons today. People who give no evidence of it whatever on the outside, and where you have to listen very sharply to hear the faint messages from the dungeon. Now, that may seem to you a little too sentimental or overdrawn, so I'd like to share with you an experience I had not long ago in a basic encounter group with fifteen persons in important executive posts.

Early in the very intensive sessions of the week these men were asked to write a statement of some feeling or feelings which they had, but which they were not willing to share in their groups. These were anonymous statements. One man wrote, 'I don't relate easily to people, I have an almost impenetrable facade. Nothing gets in to hurt me, but nothing gets out. I've repressed so many emotions that I'm close to emotional sterility. This situation doesn't make me happy, but I don't know what to do about it.' Well, I think this is clearly a message from a dungeon. Later in the week a member of my group identified himself as the man who had written that anonymous message. And he filled out, in much greater detail, his feelings of isolation – of complete coldness. He felt that life had been so brutal to him that he had been forced to live a life without feeling, not only at work but in social groups and, saddest of all, with his family. His gradual achievement of greater expressiveness in the group, of less fear of being hurt, of more willingness to share himself with others, was a very rewarding experience for all of us who participated.

I was both amused and pleased when, in a letter a few weeks later, he included this paragraph. He said, 'When I returned from our group I felt somewhat like a young girl who had been seduced, but I still wound up with the feeling that it was exactly what she'd been waiting for and needed.' He said, 'I'm still not quite sure who was responsible for the seduction, you or the group or whether it was a joint venture. I suspect it was the latter. At any rate, I want to thank you for what was an intensely meaningful experience.' I think it's not too much to say that, because several of us in the group were able genuinely to hear him, he was released from his dungeon and has come out, at least to some extent, into the sunnier world of warm interpersonal relationships.

Let me move on to a second learning that I'd like to share with you. *I like to be heard.* A number of times in my life I've felt myself bursting with insoluble problems or going round and round in tormented circles, or, during one period, overcome by feelings of worthlessness and despair and really quite convinced that I was going over the edge. I think I've been more lucky than most, in finding at these times individuals who have been able to hear me and receive me and thus to rescue me from the chaos of my feelings. I've been fortunate in finding individuals who've been able to hear my meanings a little more deeply than I've known them. These individuals have heard me without judging me, diagnosing me, appraising me or evaluating me. They've just listened, and clarified, and responded to me at all the levels of which I was communicating.

I can testify that when you're in psychological distress and someone really hears you without passing judgment on you, without trying to take responsibility for you, without trying to mold you, it feels damned good. At these times it has relaxed the tension in me, it has permitted me to bring out the frightening feelings, the guilt, the despair, and the confusions that have been a part of my experience. When I've been listened to and when I've been heard, I'm able to re-perceive my world in a new way and to go on. It's amazing that feelings which were completely awful become bearable when someone listens. It's astonishing how elements which seem insoluble become soluble when someone hears. How confusions, which seem just irremediable, turn into relatively clear-flowing streams when one is understood. I have deeply appreciated the times that I have experienced this sensitive, empathic, concentrated listening.

I sometimes thought that perhaps each one of us, as counselors, in developing our own style, develops into the kind of person, or the kind of manner, which he would like to meet if he went to someone for help. At least, I feel that's true in my case. But, quite unconsciously, I was building up people to whom I could go for help – who had become independent enough and sure enough and persons enough in their own right, that, when I needed them, they could give me the kind of help that I wanted. So that's been a very deep part of my experience.

I dislike it in myself when I can't hear another – when I don't understand them. If it's only a simple failure of comprehension or failure to focus my attention on what he's saying or something of that sort, then I only feel a very mild dissatisfaction in myself. But what I really dislike in myself is when I can't hear the other person because I'm so sure in advance of what he's about to say that I don't listen. It's only afterward that I realize that I have only heard what I've already decided he's saying. I have failed really to listen. This happened to me in the last encounter group I was in. I was very glad I had a co-leader, because there was one man whom I never heard, but fortunately the other leader was able to hear him and it made a great deal of difference. I think even worse are those times when I can't hear because what the other person is saying is too threatening or might even make me change my views and my behavior.

The next learning I want to share with you is that *I'm terribly frustrated and shut in to myself when I try to express something which is deeply me, which is a part of my own private inner world and the other person doesn't understand.* When I take the gamble or the risk of trying to share something that is very personal with another individual, and it is not received and not understood, this is a very deflating and a very lonely experience. I've come to believe that it's that experience which makes some individuals psychotic. They have given up hoping that anyone can understand them. Once they've lost that hope, then their own inner world, which becomes more and more bizarre, is the only place where they can live. They can no longer live in any shared human experience.

I can sympathize with them, because I know that when I try to share some feeling aspect of myself which is private, precious, and tentative, and when this communication is met by evaluation, or by reassurance, or by denial, by distortion of my meaning, I have very strongly the reaction, 'Oh, what's the use?' I think at such a time one knows what it is to be alone. So, as you can readily see from what I've said thus far, a creative, active, sensitive, accurate, empathic, non-judgmental listening is for me terribly important in a relationship. It's important for me to provide it. It's been extremely important, especially at certain times in my life, to receive it. I feel that I have grown within myself when I have been able to provide it. I'm very sure that I have grown and been released and enhanced when I have received this kind of listening.

Let me move on to another area of my learnings. *I find it very satisfying when I can be real* – when I can be close to whatever it is that's going on within me. I like it when I can listen to myself. To really know what I'm experiencing in the moment is by no means an easy thing, but I feel somewhat encouraged, because I think that over the years I have been improving at it. I'm convinced, however, that it's a lifelong task and that none of us is ever really able to be comfortably close to all that's going on within his own experience.

In place of the term 'realness', I have sometimes used the word 'congruence'. By this I mean that what is going on in my guts, if I may use that term, is present in my awareness and it's also present in my communication. Then each of these three levels matches, or is congruent. At such moments I'm integrated, or whole. I am completely in one piece. Most of the time, of course I, like everyone else I know, exhibit some degree of incongruence. I have learned, however, that realness, or genuineness, or congruence – whatever term you wish to give to it – is a fundamental basis for the best of communication and the best of relationships.

What do I mean by being real? I could give many examples from many different fields, but one meaning, one learning, is that there is basically nothing to be afraid of when I present myself as I am – when I come forth non-defensively, without armor, just me. But I can accept the fact that I have many deficiencies, many faults, make lots of mistakes, am often ignorant where I should be knowledgeable, often prejudiced where I should be open-minded, often have feelings which are not at all justified by the circumstances. Then I can be much more real. When I can come out wearing no armor, making no effort to be different from what I am, I learn so much more, even from criticism and hostility, and I'm so much more relaxed and I get so much closer to people. Besides, my willingness to be vulnerable brings forth so much more real feeling from other people who are in relationship to me that it is very rewarding. So I enjoy life much more when I'm not defensive, not hiding behind the facade, just trying to be and express the real me.

I feel a sense of satisfaction when I can dare to communicate the realness in me to another. This is far from easy, partly because what I'm experiencing keeps changing at every moment, partly because feelings are very complex. Usually there's a lag, sometimes of moments and sometimes days, and sometimes weeks, between the experiencing and the communication. In these cases I experience something, I feel something alright, but only later do I become aware of it; only later do I dare communicate it, when it has become cool enough to risk sharing it with another. Yet it's a most satisfying experience when I can communicate what is real in me at the moment that it occurs. Then I feel genuine and spontaneous and alive.

Such real feelings are not always positive. One man in a basic encounter group of which I was a member was talking about himself in ways which seemed, to me, completely false – speaking of the pride he took in maintaining his front, or his pretense, how skillful he was in deceiving others. My feeling of annoyance rose higher and higher, until finally I expressed it by saying simply, 'Oh nuts, I don't like that.' That somehow pricked the bubble. From that time on, he was a more real and genuine person, less braggadocio, and our communication improved. I felt good for having let him know my real feelings as it was occurring. I'm sorry to say that, more often, especially with feelings of anger, I'm only partly aware of this feeling in the moment, and full awareness comes later.

I only learn afterward what my feeling was. It's only when I wake up in the middle of the night and start angrily fighting with someone that I realize how angry I was at him the day before. Then I know, seemingly too late, how I might have been my real feeling self. But at least I have learned to go to him the next day to express my anger, and gradually I'm learning to be more quickly acquainted with it in myself. In the last basic encounter group in which I participated, I was, at different times, very angry with two individuals. With one I wasn't aware of it until the middle of the night. With the other, I was able to realize it and express it in the session in which it occurred. In both instances, it led to real communication, and gradually to a feeling of genuine liking for each other, but I am a slow learner in this area. I'm disappointed when I realize – and, of course, this realization also comes afterward, after a lag of time, that I've been too frightened or too threatened to let myself get close to what I am experiencing, and consequently I haven't been genuine or congruent. There immediately comes to mind an instance that I'm not too proud to reveal.

Some years ago I was invited to spend the year as a fellow at the Center for Advanced Study in the Behavioral Sciences at Stanford. The fellows are a group chosen because they're supposedly brilliant and well-informed scholars. I suppose it's inevitable that there's a certain amount of one-upmanship – of showing off one's knowledge and achievements. It seems important for each fellow to impress the others and to be a little more assured, a little more knowledgeable, than he really is. It's very subtle; it's, 'You've read so and so's, book, of course. Oh, you haven't?' Just little things like that. I found myself several times doing the same sort of thing, playing a role of greater certainty and greater competence than I really felt. I can't tell you how disgusted with myself I felt when I realized what I was doing. I wasn't being me – I was playing a part.

I regret it when I suppress my feelings too long and they burst forth in ways that are distorted, or attacking, or hurtful. I have a friend, whom I like very much, but who has one particular pattern of behavior that thoroughly annoys me. Because of the usual tendency to be nice, and polite, and pleasant, I kept this annoyance to myself for too long a time. When it finally burst its bounds, it came out, not only as annoyance, but as an attack on him. This was hurtful and it took us some time to repair the relationship.

I'm inwardly pleased when I have the strength to permit another person to be his own real self and to be separate from me. I think that's often a very threatening possibility. In some ways I have found it a sort of an ultimate test of my staff leadership with myself as a teacher, or parent, or a husband, or a therapist. Can I freely permit this staff member, or this student, or my client, or my son, or my daughter, or my grandchildren, to become a separate person, with ideas and purposes and values which may not be identical with my own?

Well, I think it's that kind of separate closeness, close separateness, which is really difficult fully to permit.

From a number of these things I've been saying, I trust it's clear that when I can permit realness in myself, or sense it, or permit it in the other, I find it very satisfying. When I can't permit it in myself, or fail to permit a separate realness in another, it is to me very distressing and regrettable. I find that when I am able to let myself be congruent and genuine, it often helps the other person. When the other person is transparently real and genuine, it often helps me. In those rare moments when a deep realness in the other meets a realness in me, then it is a memorable 'eyebrow relationship', as Buber would call it. Such a deep and mutual personal encounter doesn't happen often, but I am convinced that unless it happens occasionally we're not really human.

I now turn to another learning. *I like it when I can permit freedom to others*, and in this I think I have learned and developed considerable ability. I have frequently – not always – been able to take a group, a course, or a class of students, and to transform the whole class, including myself, into a community of learners. When I can do this, the excitement is almost beyond belief.

At first they're suspicious, sure that the freedom I'm offering is some kind of a trick. Then they bring up the question of grades. It can't be free, because at the end I will evaluate and judge them. Then, when we've worked out some solution in which we all participate – to the absurd demand of the university that learning is measured by grades – then they begin to feel that they are really free. And then curiosity is unleashed. Individuals and groups go charging off in all sorts of new directions, dictated by their own interests. Everything is open to questioning and exploration. They can try to find the meaning of their lives in the work they are doing. They work twice as hard in such a course, where nothing is required, as in courses with all kinds of required assignments (see Chapter 10 for Hal Lyon's experience with such a class of psychology graduate students at Georgetown University, who create their own goals, requirements, and grades for the course).

I can't always achieve this and when I cannot, I think it's because of some subtle holding back within myself, some unwillingness for the freedom to be complete.

But when I can achieve it, education becomes what it should be: an exciting quest, a search, and not an accumulation of facts soon to be outdated. In groups that I've been able to set free, there arise true students, real learners, creative scientists, scholars, and practitioners. The kind of persons who can live in a modern world, existing in the delicate but ever-changing balance between what is presently known, and the flowing, altering problems and facts of the future. They have become persons living in process, able to live a changing kind of life. Of all the learnings I've developed, I think the climate of freedom, which I can frequently help create, which I can often carry with me and around me, is to me one of the most precious parts of myself.

I want to move on to another area of learning in interpersonal relationships – one that has been slow and painful for me. *It is most warming and fulfilling when I can let in the fact – or permit myself to feel – that someone cares for, accepts, admires, or prizes me.* Because, I suppose, of elements in my past history, it has been difficult for me to do this. For a long time I tended almost automatically to brush aside positive feelings that were turned in my direction. I think my reaction was, 'Who, me? You couldn't possibly care for me. You might like what I've done, or my achievements, but not me.' This is one respect in which my own therapy helped me very much.

I'm not always able, even now, to let in such warm and loving feelings from others, but I find it very releasing when I can do so. I know that some people flatter me in order to gain something for themselves. I know that some people praise me because they're afraid to be hostile. Some people in recent years admire me because I'm a 'name'; I'm an authority. I've come to recognize the fact that some people genuinely appreciate me, like me, love me, and I want to sense that fact and let it in. I think I've become less aloof as I've been able really to take in and soak up those loving feelings.

I've found it to be a very enriching thing when I can truly prize, or care for, or love another person, and when I can let that feeling flow out to him. Like many others, I used to fear that I would be trapped by this. If I let myself care for him, he can control me, he can use me – worst of all, he can make demands on me. I think I've moved a long way in the direction of being less fearful in this respect. Like my clients, I, too, have slowly learned that tender, positive feelings are not dangerous, either to give or to receive. To illustrate what I mean, I'd like again to draw an example from a basic encounter group.

A mother with several children, who describes herself as a loud, prickly, hyper-active individual, whose marriage was on the rocks, felt that:

> Life was just not worth living, right? I had really buried under a layer of concrete many feelings I was afraid people were going to laugh at or stomp on, which, needless to say, was working all kinds of hell on my family and on me. I'd been looking forward to this workshop with my last few crumbs of hope. It really was a needle of trust in a huge haystack of despair.

She tells of some of her experiences in the group, and adds:

> The real turning point for me was a simple gesture on your part, of putting your arm around my shoulder one afternoon when I made some crack about you not really being a member of the group – that no one could cry on your shoulder. In my notes I had written the night before, 'There's no man in the world who loves me.' You seemed so genuinely concerned that day that I was overwhelmed. I received the gesture as one of the first feelings of acceptance, of me – just the dumb way I am, prickles and all that I have ever experienced. I felt needed, loving, competent, furious, frantic, anything and everything but just plain loved.

She continues:

> You can imagine the flood of gratitude, humility, relief, that swept over me. I wrote with considerable joy, I actually felt loved. I doubt that I shall soon forget it.

Now, in this material I have just quoted, she is, at first, speaking to me – and yet I feel within some deep sense she is also speaking for me. I too have had somewhat similar feelings. Because of having less fear of giving or receiving positive feelings, I've become more able to appreciate individuals. I've come to believe this is rather rare. So often, even with our children, we love them to control them rather than love them because we appreciate them. I've come to think that one of the most satisfying experiences I know, and also one of the most growth-promoting experiences for the other person, is just fully to appreciate this individual in the same way that I appreciate a sunset.

People are just as wonderful as sunsets, if I can let them be. In fact, perhaps the reason we can appreciate the sunset is that we can't control it. When I look at a sunset, as I did the other evening, I don't find myself saying, 'Well, it's off in the orange, a little more in that corner [*laughter*] and please, a little too intense a violet over here.' We don't think in those terms. I don't try to control a sunset; I watch it with awe as it unfolds. And I like myself best when I can experience my staff member, my client, or my son, or my daughter, or my grandchildren, in this same way. Appreciating the unfolding of a life. I believe this is a somewhat oriental attitude perhaps, but for me it's much the most satisfying one. So, in this third area – prizing or loving, being prized or loved – is experienced by me as being very growth-enhancing. A person who is loved appreciatively, not possessively, blooms and develops his own unique self. The person who loves non-possessively is himself enriched. This, at least, has been my experience.

Let me close by saying that in my experience real interpersonal communication and real interpersonal relationships are deeply growth-promoting. I enjoy facilitating growth and development in others. I am enriched when others provide a climate which makes it possible for me to grow and change. So I value it very much when I am able sensitively to hear the pain and the joy, or the fear and the anger, the confusion and the despair, or the determination and the courage to be, in another person. And I value more than I can say the times when another person has truly been able to hear those elements in me.

I prize it greatly when I'm able to move forward in the never-ending attempt to be the real me in this moment, whether it's anger or enthusiasm, or love or puzzlement, or whatever. I'm so delighted when a realness in me brings forth more realness in the other and we come closer to a mutual eyebrow relationship. I'm very grateful that I have moved in the direction of being able to take in, without rejecting it, the warmth and the caring of others, because this has so increased my own capacity for giving love, without fear of being entrapped, and without holding back. These, in my experience, are some of the elements which make communication between persons, and relationships with persons, more enriching and more enhancing. I fall far short of achieving these elements. But to find myself moving in these directions makes life a warm, exciting, upsetting, satisfying, enriching, and, above all, a worthwhile venture.

8

FACILITATING DISCOVERY

Harold Lyon

This chapter is an attempt to share with you what has been an important discovery in my own life: that learning can be enjoyable when one learns to feel deeply, savoring what one experiences. If I can interest you to take that step – experiencing and feeling some of these things for yourself – then you might not wish to return to the emptiness of the teacher-centered classroom. So in this writing I have attempted to concentrate on the first step: getting you to want to try these things yourself, knowing that, if you do, you will probably go far beyond this book in developing your own individual approach. This book is meant to be a catalyst – sharing with you our personal experiences and the empirical evidence that person-centered learning leads to student achievement.

Person-centered education is a natural outgrowth of humanistic or Third Force psychology, which grew in large part in the 1970s as a reaction against the fact that behaviorist and Freudian approaches to therapy seem inadequate in dealing with the nature of the higher human consciousness of man. We can see the influence of the behaviorists in most of our schools today, as we watch teachers trying to condition students' behavior according to the academic goals of the teacher, frequently ignoring both the goals and actualization of the individual students.

I am not suggesting that teachers become amateur therapists or that they replace counselors or school psychologists, though perhaps in a person-centered environment counselors might be freer from the rush of overwhelming anxiety problems that prevent them from helping normal children find their own productive and fulfilling place in this world. Most teachers are not professionally or legally qualified to perform the function of therapist. The argument has been that therapy should be attempted only by a professional with a Ph.D. or an MD. However, research by Rioch,[1] Carkhuff,[2] and Rogers has demonstrated that empathic laypersons such as homemakers, graduate students, and other mentors can conduct effective counseling and therapy with about six months to a year's training.

Isolating cognitive learning from affective learning makes learning much less indelible and effective. Most of the activities students enjoy about school are those highly charged with feelings and emotions and which often have little to do with the curriculum. In fact, the most indelible learning often comes from extracurricular activities. I'm talking about athletic events, romantic relationships, protests, social causes, dances, music, cars, being inspired by a stimulating teacher, and really getting to know another human being.

Anyone who has watched a class of fifth graders transform a classroom from utter chaos into one buzzing with busy children discovering things has experienced the joy of person-centered learning. For instance, a child who feels a need to ask for his own word – a particular gut feeling word of anger, joy, or fear that is gripping him that day – and has it written for him in his own word book discovers the word instantaneously and most likely never forgets it. To him, writing and reading become a natural extension of speech, as he discovers what he is actually trying to tell. How much more effective it is to facilitate a child's own discovery of words through integration of his own feelings than it is to force inane 'Dick and Jane-isms' on him day after day.

A student who has discovered something significant needs no instructor-assigned grade as a measure of his accomplishment, though acknowledging student performance is a powerful and appropriate motivator. He deeply feels the accomplishment immediately, and that's the best reward possible.

Person-centered education is present in many forms. It's really a name for a practice that some rare teachers have been practicing for generations.

An example of person-centered education and the results it can produce was made vividly clear to me while serving as a consultant to the White House Task Force on the Gifted and Talented in the late 1960s. The Task Force members toured various institutions throughout the country in an attempt to discover what it is that facilitates gifted individuals to realize their high potential while so many others fall short. One enlightening encounter took place while visiting my alma mater, the US Military Academy at West Point, to see how the military treats its gifted. The Social Science Department at West Point has always been a hotbed of gifted teachers. At the time of our visit, they had eight Rhodes Scholars on the Social Science Faculty, plus a number of other extremely gifted young officers.

The Task Force visiting team arranged to meet with a group of about twelve of these officers, including such notables as Peter Dawkins, the Rhodes Scholar, 'all-American' football player whose picture appeared on the covers of *Life, Time,* and *Newsweek* several times before he reached the age of 25.

Harold Gore, one of the Task Force members, asked the following question: 'To what predominant factor do you attribute your exceptional success and achievement?' To me, the most interesting thing was that these gifted young officers all had the same answer to this question. In each of their lives some individual had built an unusual relationship with them, either in their high school years or at West Point. In most cases the individuals had been either teachers or athletic coaches. They had put social or military status aside and had built a more intimate one-on-one relationship than tradition dictated, encouraging the students to take risks, to step out and do far more than the students thought they were capable of doing. In other words a human bond was developed between them and their mentor. The fascinating part of it was that several of these officers named the same one or two instructors, without knowing that he had also influenced the others.

Can we identify what these special mentors have that others do not and bring this into our teacher training institutions? Interestingly for me, two of the inspirational instructors mentioned by several of the young officers were also two very person-centered officers whom I recalled as being exceptional. The encouragement from their mentor to stand on tiptoe, to take risks they would not normally take, had come in endeavors such as academics, debating, or athletics, rather than in general vague encouragement. Mentorships have been found to be a highly effective mode of helping a gifted individual realize her potential.

The idea of giving students many tastes of success has important application to the classroom, especially in a child's very early years. The teacher who has cared to celebrate a child's small achievements and to encourage his feelings has the power to transform the classroom into one where children bloom rather than wilt. Robert Rosenthal's classic research on teacher expectations provides some indication of this.[3] Children who the teachers identified randomly as special achievers did far better than others in control groups, who had not been identified as gifted.

A teacher who is congruent and caring has a far greater chance of giving students indelible tastes of success than the impersonal one who stands officially behind what I call status authority rather than natural authority.

When a torpedo is shot at a submarine, the servo-mechanism in the torpedo cranks in feedback, causing the torpedo to change course, locking it on the submarine as its goal. We humans have a similar psycho–servo-mechanism within us, which can lock in on either success or failure as a goal. The more early 'success experiences', the more likely that success becomes an individual's goal. When the 'success-oriented' individual approaches one of the many obstacles or bypaths leading to failure, he consciously and unconsciously increases his energy and effort to get over bypaths to failure and stays on the path to success, his goal. The pessimist, who has made failure his goal, on the other hand, comes to one of these bypaths, takes it, fails, and says, 'I failed. I knew I would!' It's vital for us to inject, or even to contrive, as many success experiences in our children's and students' lives as we are able. The empathic teacher who uses feelings in her teaching has at her disposal so many of the attributes helpful for giving success experiences to others.

I recall providing for my brother, Bob, when he was only 6, one of these 'contrived' success experiences. We were fishing along the banks of the Shenandoah River when I caught a large 5lb channel catfish, while he was playing some distance from the river, oblivious to me. I decided to hook it on his line, which lay unattended on the riverbank. The now-recovered fish started pulling on his line and I called out to him, 'Bob! You have a fish on!' He came running and, after a thrilling battle, brought the 'monster' to my landing net. For the rest of that trip, he never left his rod and reel again … and has since become an ardent fisherman, fly-fishing guide, and outdoor writer. I have worked to provide similar successful angling experiences for my own children and grandchildren – though mostly not contrived in a such behavioristic manner – as the best ones are the genuine ones. We now have a family of eager anglers! When I eventually told my brother how I had contrived his success many years later, he was angry at being duped, but he remains an ardent angler and we love angling together. So sometimes behaviorism is effective, especially if done in a person-centered manner. Perhaps I was being quite Skinnerian, but I do not apologize for that.

I hope the chapters that follow will begin to stimulate you to make your own personal, joyful discovery of what it can mean to teach effectively in a person-centered manner.

Notes

1   Margaret J. Rioch, E. Elkes, A. A. Flint, B. S. Usdansky, R. G. Newman, and E. Sibler (1963) 'NIMH Pilot Study in Training Mental Health Counselors'. *American Journal of Orthopsychiatry* 33: 678–89.

2   Carkhuff, R. R., and B. G. Berenson (1976). *Teaching as Treatment: An Introduction to Counseling and Psychotherapy*. Human Resource Development Press, Amherst: Massachusetts.

3   Rosenthal, Robert and Lenore F. Jacobson (1968) 'Teacher Expectations for the Disadvantaged'. *Scientific American* 4 (April): 19–23.

PART III
Person-centered methods

9

DIALOGUE BETWEEN CARL ROGERS AND HAROLD LYON

The essence of intercultural education is the acquisition of empathy – the ability to see the world as others see it, and to allow for the possibility that others may see something we have failed to see, or may see it more accurately.

Senator J. William Fulbright

HAL: In the past decades many kinds of small group experiences, in many and varied disciplines, have emerged in order to meet what is apparently a need in society to help people begin inward journeys – to look within themselves for a fuller life. I think that many of those activities contribute toward people's growth and toward organizational growth. Although they may approach it differently, they quite often lead to the same place – a concept of self as free to be.

CARL: I want to comment about what you mentioned. I deal with large groups frequently and I have some reservations about some of those training programs which are highly commercialized and are sometimes unsatisfactory in other aspects. We need to think carefully about their philosophic bases. In some programs, the end justifies the means. In those programs, it seems that if the outcome is achieved, that's all that counts. For example, if contriving the success-experience for your brother fishing, as described in the last chapter, were done to condition in him something only you wanted to reinforce, without love and caring for his person, then I would pause to question the process of what you did, though it seems to have had a good end result. For me it is the process that is all-important. The process is learning to be and to become; and, for myself, I tend to discriminate between training programs on the basis of whether they stress process or whether their philosophy is that the end justifies the means. To me, this discrimination is important, because a good program, one that's based on the person in process, can make a difference in people's lives.

For example, I have found that the most rapid change in teachers' attitudes and behavior – and, I believe, the most lasting changes – occur when they can get away from the system itself in an intensive group experience. Preferably, one that is off campus, where they can really live together during the period of the group experience. There their growth as persons is paralleled by their fresh view of what it means for themselves to learn in a facilitative climate. They learn, there, to create a facilitative climate when they get back in the schoolroom. To be sure, such teachers need a support group when they return to the system if they are going to try to be innovative. By far the best means of achieving this is to have sizable groups of teachers and administrators participate in the same workshop or intensive group. Going through the experience together, they can support each other in the system when they get back home. I've found that rapid changes take place in such workshops or group experiences, and I have had a long enough experience with them to realize that many of those changes are lasting changes, particularly for the individual who is able to find some psychological support in the back-home situation. Perhaps your family provides that support for one another in your fishing.

HAL: I would agree with all that you have said – particularly the part about the support groups. And, yes, my brother and I are members of a family support group and we love angling.

We had some interesting experiences in training teams of people from every state in the country to work with gifted and talented children. We started out training isolated individuals and found that most were 'killed off' by the system when they went back to become advocates of the gifted; but when we trained five or more people from each state in leadership training institutes, they could go back and work as a mutual support group. I think such support groups are needed by any minority in education, and advocates for student-centered education tend to be a minority group, just as are advocates for the gifted and talented. We need to have mutual support groups to provide the kind of psychological 'first aid' you need to survive when you get back in the system, because the system can force you out, or kill you off, without that kind of help available to you.

It's unfortunate that in the past there has not been enough visible empirical evidence to convince others who discredit person-centered methods or don't believe such an approach offers unusual possibilities for making a difference in people. One problem is that these encounter group experiences often feel so good to people – the breaking through of the blocks and the boxes that we put around ourselves – and this is so refreshing that they don't feel they need any more data. They go back as enthusiastic and rather overassertive advocates of the experience without waiting until others can see the difference demonstrated in their lives.

It's usually those who have not experienced this kind of training who are the strongest opponents and the biggest critics of it.

With big organizations (and there aren't many larger than the US government, where I spent fourteen years), I found that without a mutual support group of other person-centered advocates, I could not be very effective. I found that I could be effective in making changes within a large system to the degree that I had a mutual support group upon which I could call – strong individuals with whom I could get together. Otherwise, I get beaten down, defeated, and burned out. I found the need for a small but strong mutual support group, when I took flack for bringing you, Moshe Feldenkrais, Bernie Gunther, George Leonard, Chris Argyris, and other leaders in the human potential movement into Washington, DC as advocates for a more humane approach toward education and management as speakers for the Congressional Staff Seminars run by my old friend, Sam Halperin, who was a strong member of my own mutual support group.

It's important not only for the teacher, but for administrators and students and members of all groups, to build those kinds of support bonds, to align with others, particularly when you want to bring about change in a large system.

CARL: I feel I don't have a great deal new to contribute to that idea. I feel very humble in the face of that question. There is plenty of evidence that we have been much more successful in facilitating change in individuals than in the large system of which they are a part. I think we have a great deal to learn in this area of changing systems.

There are a few things that I've learned from my own experience. I think it's important to include top administrators in any change process. If they're not willing to be included, then organization change is almost hopeless, in my estimation, and we better settle for individual or personal change.

Then I think it's important to tackle the procedures, the bureaucratic practices, that exist. How are decisions made? Who participates in those decisions? Why isn't there more participation? Where is the locus of power? I think this can be determined by finding out who makes the budget and how hiring and firing are done. Those two items of information provide a pretty good clue as to who really has the power in an organization. And when you have all levels of the organization included in this fact-finding and analyzing process, specific changes in procedures need to be worked out and agreed to by all concerned.

Those are just a few practical things which I feel I have learned and I would say again, that, from my own experience, I feel that my colleagues and I had much less success with bringing about change in large systems and organizations than we have in bringing about change in the personality and behavior of individuals.

HAL: I would add a couple of things from my experience, particularly in government, where I felt somewhat lonely in attempting to facilitate transformations. Changes can quite often be made. Changes are like minor adjustments, but transformations are a much bigger order of change.

The first thing I realized is that it's necessary to learn the system. Carl, you alluded to this when you said '[find] the locus of power'. You must learn the system, learn the people in it; learn how to work within it.

The second necessity is one we've already touched on – building mutual support groups. If you're going to make a change in a big system, don't try to do it all by yourself. Develop a mutual aid society with others who have different trades, different skills, different kinds of power. John Gardner, the former Secretary of Health, Education, and Welfare, and later head of Common Cause, once told me that to make change in government one needs to surround himself with many people who have different skills than the leader has. Gardner was a 'big picture' visionary and he shared with me that he needed around him the opposite kind of detailed persons in order to get new things done.

Third, when you want to change a system, don't change just for the sake of change. I'm finding many good things in even the most establishment-oriented systems that I'm in: good people, good policies, good programs. We think of the government as a place that always needs changing. I'm finding there are some good things about the way government operates that I won't have to really make any compromises from a humanistic way of being, in order to function in some aspects of that system.

Fourth, set realistic goals and set them with the help of mutual support groups, working together to bring about changes and transformations. Really, I'm saying to be patient. It takes a long time to bring about change in the trajectory of a government agency or a big university or a school system. You have to have patience to see it through, to stay with it. We need many people within our established systems who have grit and will not run away at the first backlash that swings in their direction. There were many times when I was discouraged enough to leave the federal government. I had encounters with organizations such as the John Birch Society who attacked me. I spent weeks answering the letters that came from conservative Congressmen and Senators as a result of one John Bircher newsletter. But, rather than leave then, I was able to see that through and came to consider their attacks a compliment to whatever I was able to do in government in spite of my own big mistakes. So patience is crucial in bringing about change and growth.

CARL: Let me just add that I would emphasize patience, also. I think that's one reason why perhaps I haven't been as successful as I might have been, because it has been difficult for me to have that much patience in an organization.

HAL: Though I hear what you are saying, in my opinion, and that of many, you have been incredibly successful. It sounds like you feel with more patience that you might have been able to be more successful. I think, when we really believe in something strongly, it's hard to wait until others can believe it, too, to allow them to explore their own best ways of being. I hope that the administrators, teachers, and teachers-to-be who read this book will clearly understand that what we share here is not a prescription, just a stimulator. We provoke and provide some ideas around which teachers and leaders can develop their own ideas, enhance their own creativity, and build person-centered learning with their own students in their own situations.

CARL: It is my hope, too, that the educators who find themselves motivated by the examples of person-centered learning in this book, and who want to promote such freedom among colleagues or students, will seek their own methods which might be used to facilitate such learning. This book may suggest some possible answers. It is not intended to be more than a brief survey of some of the research and many methods which a facilitator of freedom in learning may wish to choose at various levels of schooling. No more seems necessary, since every educator must choose his own style, develop his own methods.

This is for that person who wants to know 'How can I move toward becoming more encouraging of person-centered learning on the part of my colleagues or students?'

10

A COURSE IN PERSON-CENTERED PSYCHOLOGY AT GEORGETOWN UNIVERSITY

Harold Lyon

We all have our own unique styles of functioning most effectively, and these styles hopefully change and evolve as we grow through our experiencing. There is certainly no one 'best way' for all to emulate. We must make the best use of our own unique set of skills and techniques from the many that are available among the mentors and 'models' whom we may admire. I feel the need to say something more personal about this. You will be making a mistake you will learn about through experience if, after reading this book, you attempt to become a Carl Rogers, or anyone else but your self! I, for one, spent several years emulating my fellow co-author, Carl Rogers. Even though we share much of the same philosophy and some of the same values, it just didn't work to try to be him. I am different from him and from everyone, and at the same time there is a magnificent oneness about us. And I believe a one-on-one intimate relationship – a mentorship – provides one of the most effective modes for learning.

I will present a description of a course that I taught at Georgetown University. It is not really accurate to say that 'I taught' this course in Humanistic Psychology. I facilitated the course. The students did most of the teaching themselves and they learned much more than if I had tried to teach it. The course was held at Georgetown University at the undergraduate level, and at Antioch College in Columbia, Maryland, at the graduate level, where I served for two years as Abraham Maslow Professor. Interestingly, the Antioch students were much older and considerably more experienced in 'life'. One class had two widows, all but one student had been married, several were divorced or separated, and several were in second marriages. These older students were more favorably disposed toward this student-centered approach. The undergraduate students at Georgetown, on the other hand, had among them a small number who expressed in their evaluation of their course feelings of wanting more 'spoon-feeding'. The contrast between being with the less experienced and the more experienced groups of students was dramatic, and yet the sense of fulfillment that I personally experienced in the growth of individual students in both groups was profound.

Initially, most students learned about the course from the university catalog course descriptions. In later semesters, students were to learn about the course through word of mouth. The following course description gave prospective students their first clues about the course:

> *An introduction to humanistic psychology*
> This course, available on a tutorial basis to a limited number of qualified students, will explore human potential through readings in humanistic psychology. Emphasis will be on the students' personal growth and the process of interaction. Readings will include works by some of the pioneers of humanistic psychology such as Rogers, May, Perls, Maslow, Moustakas and others who have struggled to add the humanistic dimension to the discipline of psychology. Periodic experiential seminar sessions will be scheduled, and each student will be required to prepare and lead one seminar session.
> Prerequisite: permission of the instructor

Though the course was limited to only eighteen students and permission was required, I found myself deluged by hundreds of students who pre-registered for the course. Apparently the official course description (and the word of mouth!) hinted at something far more interesting than the usual lecture fare. These students then received the following letter from me, which explained a little more about the course:

> Dear Student
> You pre-registered for my course at Georgetown in Humanistic Psychology and the computer probably rejected you along with 239 others. The reason for this was that permission was required for the course.
>
> The reason for permission being required is that the course is largely experiential in nature and I feel that students should know that about the course ahead of time. For example, after we read Carl Rogers we will experience some client-centered therapy work sessions. After reading Fritz Perls, we will explore an experiential approach to Gestalt therapy work. The course will not be therapy, however. The *process* of what occurs in our classroom will be a large part of the *content* of the course. You will have the opportunity and responsibility for determining and accomplishing your own personal objectives for the course and you will grade yourself. There is space for only 18 students in the course and priority will be given to seniors and juniors.
>
> The class will meet Thursdays from 3:15–5:15 p.m. Knowing this information, if you are still interested in the course, I am interested in meeting with you personally about the course. Please come see me.
>
> Sincerely,
> Harold C. Lyon, Jr

The next step in the process was an interview with me, for those who wished to pursue farther. During this interview, I would explain a little about Humanistic Psychology, since it was a concept quite foreign to most Georgetown students, who had been exposed to a much more traditional or 'behavioristic' approach. I generally explained that 'Humanistic Psychology' was most concerned about the uniqueness of the individual – that there were no 'average' people, that we all defied averages when considered as individuals. I explained that in this course they would explore this notion both as a process for the course and as content for it. I went on to explain that each class meeting would have as a theme one of the principal contributors to Humanistic Psychology, and that a reading by that person would be assigned. The first part of the class would be devoted to a discussion of the assigned reading, such as Carl Rogers' *On Becoming a Person*. During this time I would contribute on a personal level to the discussion, as a member of the class, adding from my personal experience of the author of the assigned reading. During the last part of each class, I would lead the class through an experiential session demonstrating the techniques associated with the author of the reading for that session. For example, I would lead a 'person-centered' session after reading Rogers.

After several classes, I explained, students would begin to write out their own personal and professional objectives for this course. I would explain that I had my own objective as the professor and that each of them now had the opportunity to formulate theirs, and that, though some of them would end up having similar objectives, most would be unique and personal for them. All of these objectives, I explained, were equally valid for this course. They could vary from merely 'getting 3 credit hours', to 'learning how to communicate more effectively with someone', from 'learning more about the body of knowledge of Humanistic Psychology through the readings' to 'becoming more self confident'. They would also write, with my consultation, if desired, specific steps they would take during the semester, both within the classroom and outside, to reach each of their objectives. They were told that there would be only three requirements for the course. The first would be the writing of these objectives, which could be revised as the course progressed. The second would be a self-evaluation in writing at the end of the course of progress made toward their objectives, with a proposed grade to be recommended by the student dependent upon their own self-assessment of their accomplishments. They were, after all, the best authorities on their own personal growth. And finally, in lieu of any final exam, each student would present to the class, preferably in an experiential manner, a final project that reflected a significant learning which took place for them personally as a result of the experience of this Humanistic Psychology course. Each student was urged to keep a 'journal of the self' in which they could record daily discoveries, responses from the readings or class, significant interactions with others – in fact, any significant psychological learning that took place for them either in or out of the class. This could be shared with others in the class, with me, or kept confidential. Students were urged to attend class *unless* they felt some other experience available to them that day would be psychologically more beneficial. Attendance records indicated very few absences. Yet those absences that occurred offered serendipitous benefit to the entire class when the absent member returned and often shared with the class significant learnings that took place while absent.

In this course there was structure, in that each class meeting had an assigned theme and a book reading representing a particular author's perspective on that theme. Furthermore, each class had a general format for the process: discussion of ideas, feelings, and thoughts generated by the reading, followed by an experiential session during which the members of the class experienced the techniques of the original theme/author using their own feelings and responses as 'grist for the mill'. An entire gamut of possible responses was offered to the students, who had to formulate their own personal objectives and steps for reaching them as well as evaluating (self-grading) how well they felt they had achieved these objectives. So, within a prescribed structure, there was freedom for the students to choose and take responsibility for their own learning.

The following statement of objectives, written halfway through the course by one of my older students, is illustrative of the level of insight gained after ten class meetings:

> In the beginning of the semester I wrote down my personal goals and objectives for this course. I was trying to structure the unstructured in a way that would be most meaningful to me. I thought about why I was taking the course and what I wanted to get out of it. At first, I was really interested in group process as well as content but because the group is so diverse, with everyone having their own goals, I have thought more on an individual basis. I have revised and re-evaluated my goals since the start of the semester.

1. Main objective: to learn to take responsibility for myself and my actions, and to become a more open person – open in the sense that I can express my feelings openly and honestly and open in the sense that I can accept others' feelings and really listen and hear what they have to say.

    I feel I am making progress towards this goal. I find myself taking risks – sometimes I get negative feedback or responses but I am learning to accept these as well as the positive. I feel an inner satisfaction when I take risks for things I want to do, no matter what the outcome.

    Dr Lyon's book, *It's Me and I'm Here*, seems to have put many of my own deep down feelings and thoughts into actual words. It was refreshing and inspiring to read this book – I can think of many examples of my past experiences that could be included.

2. A second objective is: to utilize the knowledge base of humanistic psychology in my own practice of psychiatric nursing. Being in a helping role and having to communicate with people every day requires more than just knowledge and skills of the basic sciences. It requires empathy and understanding, something that I've always believed was a part of every human. I do not believe empathy can be taught but I also do not believe it can be left out when dealing with people.

    Having read the books for class has shown me that I have been dealing with the human aspects of psychology most of my life. I was taught the 'Golden Rule' when growing up and have always practiced it. I care about people. I care about the 'human' side of people, which is the reason I chose the nursing profession.

3.   Another goal I have is: to plan and present a group project that will express my feelings and will allow for others to express theirs; and that will be fun and interesting.

    I've been thinking about taking slide pictures of meaningful things in my life and setting them to music. I'm not very creative but I want my project to flow from me and to be a part of me that I can show.

Motivation came from within this student rather than from fear of failure or bad grades. Such motivation is far more powerful than any of our attempts to 'force' it. Imagine the difficulty of teaching someone how to rebuild a carburetor in a classroom. Yet, when a teenager's car is broken down, motivation from within propels him to gain this knowledge very fast indeed.

Person-centered education is not just the affective or feelings void of structure. It is an integration of the affective with the cognitive and, when this is created, both kinds of learning peak and become more indelible.

Person-centered education does have structure. It offers the individual student the opportunity to progress as fast as his capacity enables him with as much structure as he needs. It is not just affective learning as it is often labeled. It requires the element of the student taking responsibility for his own learning. My Georgetown students initially had to struggle with this. They were used to passively sitting in lectures and taking notes in preparation for exams.

This course in Humanistic Psychology contained much more freedom, which also required taking responsibility, and which made the course more difficult, challenging, and fulfilling. I will let some student evaluations speak to this. However, I must share that, for me, the professor, working and growing with these students was a uniquely rewarding experience.

One undergraduate young woman, for her class project, presented a slide show of her life from birth to the present, accompanied by selections of music played and recorded by her and by poetry she had written. During this moving presentation, we learned that she had attempted suicide only several months before the course began, which she did not reveal to me before the course began. Taking the course was, for her, the first step in taking responsibility toward living her new life. I present her vulnerable course evaluation as a final testimony to a person–centered approach toward enabling university students to take responsibility for their own learning:

> Many different things have helped me this semester to get back on my feet and to grow following my problems in December. Piecing myself, my thoughts and emotions together (or at least, starting) from my suicide attempt has been a long and difficult road, besieged by setbacks and depressions, but this course has been the most significant and meaningful time in my life thus far. When I signed out 'against medical advice' from the hospital in January, the head of psychiatry strongly 'suggested' that it was fairly probable that I'd

have a major relapse within a year. Well, it was a lonely experience for me to stand up against those 'who know best', when I thought I would make it on my own. It may have been the loneliest experience in my life, but it certainly was the wisest. Otherwise, I wouldn't be where I am now.

This class is the best thing that has happened to me academically at Georgetown, since it came at a precious time and also because I want to get my doctorate in psychology. And without this class, I never would have learned about humanistic psychology and probably would have run rats or programmed infants for the rest of my life. The class interested me academically and was emotionally supportive when I needed it most.

My objectives
Throughout the course, I have kept a journal. It reflects my growth and learning through the help and guidance of friends, lovers, this class, my doctor, movies, plays and books. I have tried to read as many outside books in conjunction with this class as time allowed. My autobiographic presentation, which I worked hard on, shows what happened before and my journal, what's happening now. A synthesis of the two is my objective. To synthesize the academic workaholic, and the lonely emotionless, cold person of the past with who I am now.

Some closing comments by Carl Rogers

I should like to add a few comments in order to make clear why the above approach of Hal's may be particularly useful to other educators.

Easily translatable

In the first place this approach could be used in any field of knowledge, in any kind of institution. It could be adapted with relative ease to the teaching of physics in a college with highly rigid standards, or to a course of literature in a college with 'liberal' leanings. It could, with a little more effort, be adapted to the teaching of high school courses. Thus it constitutes a realistic alternative to any teacher who is dissatisfied with conventional methods but who hesitates, whether because of confining circumstances or a fear of failure, to attempt something drastically different.

Non-threatening character

Related to this is the fact that these methods appear suitably academic and scholarly, that they give very adequate training in research, have a place for such standard elements as examinations, term papers, book reviews, and the like. Consequently, they are unlikely to frighten a college administrator or fellow faculty member. In spite of all these familiar externals, however, each course is built upon assumptions which are the exact opposite of the assumptions in a conventional course.

Stress upon choice and initiative

One of the most basic of these assumptions is that the course belongs fundamentally to the student, and that there will be no learning of any kind if he simply behaves in the passive manner expected of him in other courses. It is up to him to choose his goals and to continue making choices at every step, from a very wide range of alternatives. Nor are these simply consequences. There is ample encouragement given and many personal and material resources easily available, but this does not alter the fact that the student learns by making independent choices of goals and means, making these choices in terms of what will be valuable to him, and taking the initiative in implementing these choices.

A place for the instructor

When the central focus is upon learning rather than teaching, there is no doubt that some teachers fear they will be left out, that they no longer have a place on the stage. Hal Lyon has handled this, in my estimation, realistically and well. The instructor in no way denies his own interests. He recognizes his desire to instruct, to teach. Like the student, he chooses those things he wants to present, and takes the initiative in making his place in the life of the class. But he does avoid the humdrum and the routine of lecturing, and has a ready measure of the interest of the class in himself and his work, since students are free to come or stay away from class.

A rationale for evaluation and grades

Another striking element in Hal's approach is his clearly worked-out views in the realm of evaluation. Not everyone would agree with these views. Nonetheless, he has come to terms with the issue in an open, thoughtful way, which is in accord with his convictions and his personality. To me the greatest value of his approach to grading is that it shows that new ways of adapting to this perplexing problem can be worked out − ways which are both creative and realistic. He has found a way which suits him, and which helps to put grades in a perspective for the student who grades himself which maintains the student's self-respect ... and the student is the best judge in such a class as to progress he has made personally.

Desirable outcomes

The many student productions in Hal's class are evidence of outcomes very different from those of the conventional course. For two-thirds of the students to work toward definite goals for themselves, for a similar number to draw up research proposals on their own initiative, and for most of the class to present experiential seminars to the class of their learnings – clearly these are unusual outcomes. Half of the group used experiential learning to try to improve their interpersonal relationships, and an equal number undertook original experiments. Any resemblance to the usual sterile 'introductory course' in psychology is certainly coincidental. Small wonder that a surprising proportion of those who have been exposed to this kind of learning experience tend to go on for advanced degrees. Unfortunately, most of them are disappointed in what they find in the traditional graduate degree program.

Summary

A college professor, keeping himself within a conventional educational framework, has fashioned a course of a most unusual sort. While he maintains many of the external trappings of the customary course, these have been transformed by turning them over to the students to use in those ways which have meaning and significance for them. Thus the student's curiosity, his desire to learn, his ability to select and follow his own path of learning are the basis of this course. Yet this revolutionary basis is softened and made relatively non-threatening to fellow educators, by virtue of this use of such commonplace elements as text readings, term projects, presentations, and self-negotiated grades, all of which exist in a context built on the student's own objectives integrated with those of the instructor's. This is, indeed, a striking example of how a teacher is able to create a person-centered course where the teacher and the students are valued and cared about, where empathy and genuineness on the part of students and teacher are manifest, and which is highly relevant to what the students are motivated to learn.

11

PERSON-CENTERED MANAGEMENT AND LEADERSHIP

Harold Lyon

This chapter is dedicated to my West Point classmate, hero in Vietnam, and friend, Tony Nadal, who though he appeared to be tilting at windmills, made an enormous contribution helping to transform leadership throughout the U.S. Army toward being more person-centered in the tradition of General John Schofield.

If our schools and our educational systems are managed by less than people-centered managers, we cannot expect our teachers to be person-centered leaders. Accordingly, emphasis on people-oriented management must begin at the top echelons and flow down if it is to have any positive effect on workers or teachers.

An interesting study was carried out many years ago by the managerial psychologist Rensis Likert of the University of Michigan's Institute for Social Research. Likert, in a study of the management of 5,000 corporations throughout the country, focused on those managers found to be either extremely high-producing or exceptionally low-producing. He eliminated from his study managers who were of average or questionable productivity, and then isolated those personality traits or characteristics which were common to the high-producing managers as contrasted with those which were common to the low-producing managers. The traits which Likert found to be common to high and low producing managers were the following:[1]

TABLE 11.1 Traits of high- and low-producing managers

Low producers	High producers
1. Production oriented (people considered tools to get the job done)	1. People oriented (people considered to be unique individuals)
2. Little two-way personal communication (relatively inaccessible to workers)	2. Good two-way personal communication (is accessible to workers)
3. Autocratic	3. Allows subordinates to participate in decisions

(Continued)

TABLE 11.1 Continued

Low producers	High producers
4. Poor delegator	4. Good delegator
5. Punitive	5. Relatively non-punitive
6. Identifies with only his superiors or only his subordinates	6. Identifies and relates with *both* his superiors and his subordinates
7. Fails to plan ahead	7. Plans ahead effectively
8. Holds frequent formal meetings	8. Holds few formal meetings (not necessary since communications are effective)
9. In time of crisis, pitches in with workers, thereby relinquishing his role as a supervisor	9. In time of crisis, maintains supervisory role
10. Workers in his unit feel little pride toward their work groups	10. Workers in his unit feel strong pride toward their work groups
11. Workers feel their boss is ineffective in his relations with top management	11. Workers feel their manager has good communication with top management and can effectively represent their interests

Even without showing empirically (as Likert did for industry) that the character-istics of high-producing managers have relevancy for educational administrators, many of us through participation in, and observation of, real-life leadership situations, have gained enough substantial reinforcement of Likert's findings to accept them personally as being valid for most leadership situations, including those in our school systems and universities.

Take a minute and evaluate your favorite school superintendent or adminis-trator against the list of high- and low-producing managers. How does he or she stack up? How about the worst administrator you know? Now check yourself as objectively as you can. Are you on the 'high producer' or 'low producer' side of the list? Certainly it must be remembered that few high producers have all the characteristics on Likert's list of high-producing managers. They will probably have several of the high-producer traits which they emphasize and use to great advan-tage. Interestingly enough, these traits of the high producer can be clustered under the very same headings Tausch, Rogers, Aspy, Roebuck, Hattie, and Cornelius-White have found in the effective therapist and teacher.

While serving in the government, it became clearer to me every day that many of the management practices of the middle managers there closely approximated those of Likert's 'low producers'.

In the civil service bureaucracy (and also in educational bureaucracies), the feel-ing seems to prevail that bureaucrats shouldn't be expected to be motivated by their leaders – that if they have personal problems or career advancement issues they should go to the human resources office instead of to their own superior, who is sup-posed to play an impersonal, objective role rather than to develop a personal caring relationship with his subordinates. It seemed to me that even the bureaucracy could become an enjoyable place to pursue one's career if it could become more 'people oriented'. Of course, making the bureaucracy people-oriented flies in the face of Max Weber's principles of bureaucratic theory, which stipulate that the bureaucracy protects itself and the public it serves by being very impersonal and objective.

While serving in the US Office of Education, it seemed obvious to me that each leader of each unit should assume responsibility for his team of subordinates, their motivation, career development, morale, and goals rather than shifting this responsibility over to the human resources office. I felt that if this were done more pervasively, morale would rise and, along with it, motivation and productivity. It seemed to me that in an organization where most of the employees were highly educated, Likert's findings should be even more relevant.

I prepared a memo to my boss, then the US Commissioner of Education, Harold Howe II, and his deputy commissioner and other top managers, presenting Likert's findings and proposing that each manager make a self-evaluation of how he measured up on the high-producer or low-producer traits. I even prepared a little self-evaluation form, which had the traits of the high and low producers scrambled and somewhat disguised as to values. I suggested that each supervisor might wish to rate himself and then give the evaluation form to his subordinate supervisors, who could, in turn, rate him and themselves. This, I suggested, could be followed by a 'leadership discussion' hour during which the supervisor and his subordinate supervisors could discuss their ratings and each subordinate's view of how he stood on the high- and low-producer traits. The subordinate supervisors could then, in turn and in their own way, hold similar discussions with their subordinates.

I soon found out how naive I was. I received a barrage of extremely defensive memos (with copies sent to my boss) telling how I just didn't understand what a great job the managers in the office were doing under very difficult circumstances, with personnel shortages, dynamic increases in workloads, etc., etc. I was not so tactfully informed that, if I had served in the organization for a longer time, I would realize that they had made enormous strides from the place they were five years before. Recognizing that this was likely true was even more depressing, seeing how much they still needed to improve.

However, a few enlightened bureau chiefs, the Deputy Commissioner, Graham Sullivan, and my boss became interested enough to begin a few trial management development retreats. Though I had not yet met Carl Rogers at the time, I attempted to recruit him as a consultant to run these retreats, but he declined, being pessimistic about his ability to bring about change within the huge bureaucracy. Eventually we instituted a retreat for the top ten executives, run quarterly with the assistance of Chris Argyris from Yale. Many interesting 'hidden agendas' began to surface as these top executives began to slice through the communication barriers that their masks had become. Several actually began to care about each other. Another very promising out-come was that a new institutional cooperative approach to problems began to emerge. These top managers began to view themselves as something of a 'board of governors', who together had joint responsibility for our national educational programs rather than competing with one another in behalf of their own specialized program interests.

Organizations like universities or school systems are also somewhat unique in that they contain a large proportion of highly educated people. In such organizations one will find the traits characteristic of the high-producing managers to be even more relevant than in the average organization. According to Peter F. Drucker, in an organization of highly educated people:

> We will have to learn to organize, not a system of authority and responsibility or a system of command, but an information and decision system – a system of judgment, knowledge and expectations. Such people can 'only be motivated'.[2]

They must want to contribute. The supervision that we give to some workers simply cannot be applied effectively to all, especially those who have to contribute their knowledge, conceptional skill, imagination, and judgment.

The conventional bureaucratic philosophy, so often practiced in our school systems of management by 'direction and control', is inadequate in motivating today's employee, whether teacher, student, or janitor. The physiological and safety needs on which the traditional management approach relies are already reasonably well satisfied and, accordingly, unimportant motivators of behavior. Direction and control are somewhat useless in motivating people whose important needs are of the higher social and egoistic variety, such as needs for self-esteem, recognition, independence, achievement, knowledge, status, and self-fulfillment. Abraham Maslow's hierarchy of needs suggests a progression with a higher order of need emerging and motivating behavior only after the lower order is reasonably well satisfied. The characteristics which Likert has found to be common to 'high-producing managers' are conducive to creating the kind of atmosphere in which social, ego, and self-fulfillment needs can begin to be satisfied.

Douglas McGregor and Chris Argyris advocated management philosophies that parallel Maslow's and Rogers' person-centered philosophy. In McGregor's classic book *The Human Side of Enterprise*, McGregor postulates his 'Theory X' and 'Theory Y' models.[3] Theory X management is almost identical to Likert's low-producer style of management. It's based on the assumption that workers do not like responsibility or work and, hence, must be manipulated – à la Skinner's behavioristic conditioning. Under Theory X the employees are assumed to be apathetic, resist management's goals, must be rewarded and punished and persuaded with 'carrots and sticks' to accomplish the organization's goals. In educational settings, you've seen many Theory X administrators, faculty, and students. They use mainly external rewards – money or other incentives, such as grades as the carrots and punishments as the sticks. Students and teachers, however, quickly either learn how to sabotage the Theory X person or how to take advantage of him, which only tends to reinforce his belief in a stricter Theory X management philosophy.

Theory Y, on the other hand, assumes that people like responsibility when they can be self-directed, and that motivation for work or learning is natural and inherent in all people. Under Theory Y management, people-centered education flourishes. Trust and confidence develops. Student-centered learning results.

The administrator sees his task as creating the maximum opportunities possible for teachers or students to realize their potential.

McGregor felt that under both Theory X and Theory Y management everyone is still governed and motivated by unmet needs. Under Theory X managers, the motivational emphasis is usually still on the already-met lower-order bodily, social, and security needs. However, under Theory Y, there is the opportunity to meet some of the higher order ego and self-actualization needs which emerge when the lower-order needs are already satisfied. McGregor stated that the organization should be managed in such as way that people can satisfy their own personal needs best while working toward organization objectives. In this way, self-motivation is built in, as it was in my psychology class from Chapter 10. Certainly, this is the epitome of person-centered education and management. The methods used by modern management are often inconsistent with the needs of the modern-day worker. An individual will not be motivated to work for that which does not meet his most pressing needs. Most people's pressing or more motivational needs are the higher ego or self-actualization needs. Managers can learn how to integrate opportunities for satisfying the personal needs into the workday responsibility, rather than outside the job through higher pay, greater fringe benefits, longer vacations, and all the other relatively less important things today's organizations keep offering their ego-starved employees.

Application of these ideas to the educational setting is apparent. Students need more than the 'carrots and sticks' of grades. Teachers, though they badly need higher pay, really need more from their administrators. They need the opportunity to satisfy their ego needs in the school system like the highly self-motivated Teach For America teachers are doing. Likert's list of high-producing behaviors in school administrators could provide teachers with that freedom and opportunity.

How are such people-oriented managers developed? Are they born leaders? Can they be trained? I could list and describe dozens of effective techniques, such as lectures on management theory, simulations, use of process observers, the case study method, role-playing, encounter groups, or management games. As effective as these techniques may be, however, they will accomplish very little if the on-the-job managerial climate is not a fertile one.

Douglas McGregor called this approach to executive development the 'agriculture' approach, analogous to agriculture because:

> It is concerned with 'growing' talent rather than manufacturing it. The fundamental idea behind such an approach is that the individual will grow into what he is capable of becoming, provided we can create the proper conditions for that growth. Such an approach involves ... more emphasis on controlling the climate and fertility of the soil, and methods of cultivation.[4]

The most significant aspect of this philosophy is that it approaches the development of managerial skills, not so much as a program, but a state of mind – a way of life. It presupposes acceptance of the principle that developing one's subordinates is a fundamental responsibility in any management job. It requires particularly the convictions and encouragement of top management, but is dependent as well on the whole-hearted participation of all ... echelons.[5]

This approach to developing executives or teachers cannot be reduced to one plan. There are as many plans as there are teachers or faculty in the organization. Each principal is directly responsible for his own self-development and for providing challenges and opportunities to foster the self-development of his teachers in the school. If the managerial climate is conducive to growth, then 'individual managers throughout the whole organization will be involved in a process of self-development leading to the realization of their potentialities'.[6]

And the students with effective teachers will be the beneficiaries.

If the district superintendent tends to hold most of the decision making for himself and is not people centered, the structure of the organization will tend to become more centralized. Such a structure seriously limits the opportunity for growth. Peter Drucker stated that maximum decentralization of the organizational structure will 'always improve performance. It will make it possible for good men, hitherto stifled, to do a good job effectively. It will make better performers out of many mediocre men by raising their sights and demands on them.'[7]

Certainly, in a decentralized organization, an individual must take greater responsibility for his own actions and behavior. But he will receive rewards in the form of ego and self-actualization satisfaction, causing him to seek more responsibility and to grow in the process.

Teachers, principals, and superintendents at all levels should be able to make decisions without the fear that a mistake is fatal. William B. Given pointed out that giving young administrators the 'freedom to fail ... is a vital way of spreading responsibility within the organization ... Freedom to venture and take calculated risks mean nothing if failure is always punished.'[8]

Given's wise philosophy of 'freedom to fail' really says that the best investment we can make in a young teacher or administrator is to allow him enough freedom to get a few substantial failures under his belt, and still survive. How many principals or superintendents allow their new teachers this 'freedom to fail'?

A study of most of the practitioners in the field brings us always back, one way or another, to Rogers' and Likert's people-oriented high-producer management and facilitator characteristics. They work in industry. Even my early personal experience in the military taught me that the traits Likert found common to the high producer have application, as does Theory Y management. As a young army first lieutenant, I was given command of what must have been the worst rifle company in the 101st Airborne Division. The previous commander had run the company by fear of punishment (low-producer trait). Court martials were the rule rather than the exception. The unit had failed its annual army training tests, its annual general inspections, its Strategic Army Corps Readiness Tests, and every other measure of a combat unit's effectiveness and the men did not seem to care. When I took over command, I was informed that over 40% of the men were convicted felons.

The first day I took over, I removed all the little signs – 'Off limits during duty hours' – that were nailed up on the doors of every relaxing or comfortable room in the barracks, such as the poolroom, mess hall, and the lounge. I had the first sergeant call the entire group of 220 men together and I informed them that this was now their company, their community for better or worse, and that it could be as good as they wanted to make it. I told them I knew that they had the potential to be the best in the division and that I wanted us to realize that potential. I suggested that I would make arrangements for anyone who didn't want to train hard toward the company becoming the best in the division to transfer out the next day to another unit. I said that three months from then we would know and feel we were good. In six months, we would be the best in the battle group, and in a year we would be the best in the division. I began, starting with my platoon leaders, an immediate open-door policy whereby anyone with a problem could see his supervisor and know that an effort would be made to help him. I also began a weekly leadership talk with all my sergeants, during which I expressed the view that they were the most important men in the army – prizing them and empathizing with the challenges they faced. Each squad leader, after all, had direct responsibility for his eleven men – responsibility for their motivation, morale, education, development, personal problems, etc. Each man might have to be motivated in a different way by his squad leader in combat. Some would have to have their pride appealed to; others might occasionally require more confrontational means. It was a joy to see those tough old combat veterans begin to use other more positive methods of leadership than the usual kick in the ass so often practiced by them in the past.

In her excellent book on leadership *The Leader as a Mensch: Become the Kind of Person Others Want to Follow*, Bruna Martinuzzi suggests that humble leadership, even in the military leader, is what inspires more than autocratic leadership.[9] Rather than being about timidity or a lack of toughness, real humility is about who we are, our achievements, our worth but without arrogant pride, which often leads to the derailment of corporate, government, and military leaders.

I was amazed at the effect these empathic talks had on these tough soldiers who began to think of themselves as the prized elite professional soldiers they really were. In three months we had scored an 'excellent rating' on an annual equipment inspection that the unit had failed the previous year. Seven months later, we scored higher than any of the other companies in the battle group on our annual combat training tests. A year later there was no doubt in anyone's mind, with men trying to transfer into our company, that we were the best in the 101st Airborne Division. Rogers' and Likert's leadership traits, which I had never heard of at that time, became the norm in the company and, I believe, the reason for the transformation. In spite of not knowing about Likert or Rogers, when I risked this experiment in positive leadership, I had in mind something I had to memorize at West Point as a cadet. It was one quotation I had to memorize, among many useless ones, which became the most relevant to my own leadership experience. It was Major General John M. Schofield's Definition of Discipline which goes like this:

The discipline which makes the soldiers of a free country reliable in battle is not to be gained by harsh or tyrannical treatment. On the contrary, such treatment is far more likely to destroy than to make an army. It is possible to impart instruction and to give commands in such a manner and such a tone of voice to inspire in the soldier … an intense desire to obey, while the opposite manner and tone of voice cannot fail to excite strong resentment and a desire to disobey. The one mode or the other of dealing with subordinates springs from a corresponding spirit in the breast of the commander. He who feels the respect which is due to others cannot fail to inspire in them regard for himself, while he who feels, and hence manifests, disrespect toward others, especially his inferiors, cannot fail to inspire hatred against himself.[10]

So here we have it again. Likert's high-producing manager traits, McGregor's Theory Y management, and Rogers person-centered leadership methods seem to work not just in schools and classroom, but even in the bureaucracy and the military.

Though I learned from Howard Kirschenbaum's excellent biography, *The Life and Work of Carl Rogers*, that neither Rogers nor McGregor ever met or even cited each other's work, they were very much in tune with each other's people-centered management philosophies. Working with a National Training Laboratory group of top management executives, Rogers shared his own philosophy about leadership and power:

I want very much to have *influence* and impact, but I have rarely desired to, nor known how to, exercise control or power. My *influence* has always been increased when I have given away my *power or authority*. By refusing to coerce or direct, I think I have stimulated learning, creativity, and self-direction … I have found my greatest reward in being able to say 'I made it possible for this person to be and achieve something he could not have been nor achieved before'. In short I gain a great deal of satisfaction in being a facilitator of becoming. By encouraging a person's ability to evaluate him, I have stimulated autonomy, self-responsibility, and maturity. By freeing a person to 'do his thing', I have enriched his life and learning, and my own as well.[11]

This chapter has dealt with people-centered managers and leaders. Certainly, if we expect our teachers to become person-centered, we must train 'people-oriented' managers and administrators, beginning at the top echelons and on down, who will encourage and support teachers in their efforts to change their classrooms by caring about people. The early works of such managerial psychologists as Douglas McGregor, Chris Argyris, and Rensis Likert corroborate the research done by Rogers, Tausch, Aspy, and Roebuck for teachers and administrators and it is still valid today and in many diverse settings as shown by the meta-analyses of Hattie and Cornelius-White. The conclusion of one of the most successful effective teacher programs in the US, Teach For America, is that these teachers who are able to raise student achievement by two or three grade levels use the leadership skills which make any leader a successful one. This is the person–centered leadership this chapter has discussed, which a body of research shows to be the high-producing leader traits and which my own leadership experiences in the military, the university, private business, and the federal government validate for me personally. Without a fertile person-centered leadership climate – something that must be fostered by the everyday leadership of top educational administrators – humanistic growth probably will not flourish within the teachers, within classrooms, or within any organization.

The next chapter will present the important research findings of the largest field study ever done on person-centered teaching that we have been alluding to in past chapters. These studies of Aspy and Roebuck also included school leaders – principals and superintendents. Those manifesting person-centered leadership skills had more person-centered teachers, and their students, correspondingly, also showed higher achievement.

Notes

1   Likert, Rensis (1961) *New Patterns of Management*. New York: McGraw-Hill Book Co.
2   Drucker, Peter F. (1954) *The Practice of Management*. New York: Harper and Row, Publishers, p. 221.
3   McGregor, Douglas (1960) *The Human Side of Enterprise*. New York: McGraw-Hill Book Co.
4   Ibid., p. 197.
5   Appley, Lawrence A. (1958) 'Foreword'. In Harwood F. Merrill and Elizabeth Marting, eds, *Developing Executive Skills*. New York: American Management Association, p. 11.
6   McGregor, p. 197.
7   Drucker, Peter F. (1954) *The Practice of Management*. New York: Harper and Row, p. 226.
8   Given, William B., Jr. (1949) *Bottom-up Management*. New York: Hayer and Brothers, p. 6.
9   Martinuzzi, B. (2009) *The Leader as a Mensch: Become the Kind of Person Others Want to Follow*. San Francisco: Six Seconds Emotional Press.
10   Schofield, J. M. (1879) 'Address to the Corps of Cadets', US Military Academy, 11 August 1879.
11   Kirschenbaum, H. (2007) *The Life and Work of Carl Rogers*. Ross-on-Wye: PCCS Books, p. 451. [Emphasis in the original.]

12

RESEARCH ON PERSON-CENTERED METHODS

David Aspy, Flora Roebuck, and Cheryl Blalock Aspy

The National Consortium for Humanizing Education conducted training and research in forty-two states and eight foreign countries, the largest field study of effective teaching ever carried out. Its procedures were effective in discovering how effective teachers increase both emotional and academic achievement of their students.

Introduction

The National Consortium for Humanizing Education (NCHE) began as a response to widespread recognition that schools could improve their effectiveness through programs focusing on facilitative interpersonal relationships that include empathy, positive regard toward students, and genuineness. We strove to orchestrate and test some of the constructive efforts already being implemented by educators in various settings across the US. NCHE intervened in numerous school systems in an attempt to study and implement person–centered practices in education.

Establishing a research base

Educators have written widely about the value of caring for children and treating them as human beings. There is also an extensive literature describing the inadequacies of many schools' attempts to treat students humanely. In light of a somewhat unclear picture of the implementation of humane practices in schools, it became necessary for NCHE to organize some baseline data to establish the need for a more specific effort in this area.

Difficulties in collecting data

Collecting raw data from schools is difficult for a variety of reasons. Class schedules leave little time for research. Teachers are occupied with a multitude of housekeeping tasks. Parents and board members rarely ask questions that involve research of any depth. Much of the past research done in schools was either not meaningful or unused. In short, the general school climate is not research oriented. Therefore, we began our work by conducting a series of small studies of schools willing to supply data. The small studies began to form a picture that was relatively consistent and which agreed with the hypotheses of other investigators.

Technologies and instruments used to gather data

Flanders Interaction Analysis

Technologies developed by Flanders, Bloom, and Carkhuff were used to gather data. The Flanders Interaction Analysis is a procedure that describes verbal behavior in a classroom interaction (see Table 12.1).[1]

FIA categories observed and marked during teaching by the rater

Because it may be applied to either live classroom interactions or audiotape recordings of them, some of the studies involved trained observers visiting classrooms and others were completed from audio and video recordings of classroom teaching. The work showed no significant differences between the accuracy of live or recorded observations.

Teacher talk compared to student talk

The findings from these studies revealed that teachers did most of the talking (80%) in their classrooms; students did 10% of the talking, and the remainder of class time was spent in silence or confusion.[2] After four years of research, this same profile emerged from studies of verbal interaction in more than 1,000 classrooms ranging from nursery to graduate school.

TABLE 12.1 Flanders Interaction Analysis categories

Teacher talk	Indirect influence	1. Accepts feelings
		2. Praises or encourages
		3. Accepts or uses ideas of student
		4. Asks questions
	Direct influence	5. Lecturing
		6. Giving directions
		7. Criticizing or justifying authority
Student talk		8. Student talk: response
		9. Student talk: initiation
		10. Silence or confusion

The Flanders Interaction Analysis (FIA) is descriptive rather than evaluative, so NCHE did not make assessments of teaching effectiveness in the early studies. The main effort was focused on describing or diagnosing what was happening in schools. This approach put NCHE in good stead when it began its training program, because its processes allowed teachers to examine their classroom behavior without the usual argument about evaluations of good versus bad teaching.

Bloom's Taxonomy of Educational Objectives to determine various cognitive behavior in the classroom

The technology and methodology of NCHE were applicable to a second type of investigation, which explored cognitive processes in the verbal components of classroom activity. By applying Bloom's Taxonomy of Educational Objectives (BTEO)[3] it was possible to determine what types of cognitive behavior were being used by both teachers and students in their verbal interactions.

> **Bloom's Taxonomy of Educational Objectives (cognitive domain)**
> 1.00 Knowledge
> 2.00 Comprehension
> 3.00 Application
> 4.00 Analysis
> 5.00 Synthesis

A consistent pattern was found in a wide variety of studies ranging from kindergarten to graduate school. In most of the classrooms, 80% of the verbal activity was classified as memory or recall, 10% was classified as thinking, and the remaining 10% was placed in a non–cognitive category.[4]

The studies using FIA and BTEO yielded a third type of investigation that explored the relationship between type of classroom interaction and level of cognitive activity attained by teachers and students. The data indicated high positive (0.75) correlations between indirect teacher control and the cognitive levels (beyond memory) displayed by students. The inference was that teachers who elicited higher–order cognitive processes from their students tended to use less controlling behavior than those who elicited only memory.

Three trends in the typical classroom

As the correlational studies continued, the data indicated three major trends in a typical classroom:

1. Teachers tend to do most of the talking.
2. Most cognitive activity is related to memory.
3. Teacher behavior is correlated with student cognitive behavior.

No responses to feelings in most classrooms and teacher affective behavior is related to student cognitive performance

The results from FIA indicated another significant finding. There was virtually no response to students' feelings. This finding was important in and of itself, but it became even more relevant because of the findings showing that when students' feelings were recognized, their cognitive levels of performance tended to increase. The above suggested that teacher affective behavior was related to students' cognitive performance, a relationship found to be significant (p = 0.05) in a group of studies by Carkhuff.[5] Thus, it was important to begin a fourth type of study to explore the relationship between students' cognitive performance and teachers' affective behavior.

In addition to BTEO as a measure of cognitive levels, we used the Carkhuff Scales for Empathy, Congruence, and Positive Regard, used in earlier research of Rogers in the most effective therapists, to rate the levels of teachers' responses to their students' feelings.[6] Classroom relationships between the Scales and BTEO were investigated. The results of these studies indicated a positive relationship between them.

Training for empathy, congruence, and positive regard

With these results as impetus, we began an effort to explore whether or not systematic training could raise teachers' levels of empathy, congruence, and positive regard. Using the Carkhuff Scales as a basis, it was found that as many as 200 teachers could be trained simultaneously so as to raise their levels of classroom empathy, congruence, and positive regard to minimally facilitative (3.0) levels. The training lasted 15 hours and consisted of both didactic and experiential components. Changes in the teachers' levels of affective response were assessed using before and after recordings of their classroom teaching.

Further studies employing the Carkhuff Scales indicated that before training, most of the teachers offered less than minimally facilitative levels of empathy, congruence, and positive regard (2.0 average) to their students. In fact, most of the teachers offered deteriorative levels of empathy, congruence, and positive regard such that students tended to learn less than their ability measures would indicate.

The studies that related affect to cognitive gains indicated the following:

1. Most teachers do not respond to students' feelings.
2. When teachers respond appropriately to students' feelings, they enhance student achievement.
3. Teachers can be trained to respond to students' feelings.

In addition to collecting data, we also developed training procedures for each of the technologies (FIA, BTEO, Carkhuff Scales). As a result of these research and training procedures, NCHE was in a position to offer a well-documented in-service training program for improving teachers' interpersonal skills. The training program began with FIA and BTEO, which gave teachers descriptive data about their classroom teaching. When teachers received feedback from Flanders' and Bloom's scales, they were asked if they wanted to change any behaviors. If they wanted to change, they were asked to specify the behavior they wished to alter. Training was begun to accomplish the teachers' own goals.

The large field trial

NCHE had conducted research and development in over 1,000 classrooms throughout the US with virtually no financial support. It was decided that NCHE should extend its thrust by not only continuing the small studies using volunteers, but by also conducting a large field trial of its procedures.

A grant application was filed with the National Institute of Mental Health (NIMH) to implement training and research programs involving 10,000 students and 600 teachers. This proposal was initially funded for $350,000 for a three-year study. NCHE provided the training and research materials, and the schools contributed the time of their teachers and the data required for study. Essentially, NCHE was exploring the question of whether or not its training procedures could enhance student achievement by increasing the levels of person-centered skills of teachers throughout a relatively large school system. The program included the following steps:[7]

1. Gathering baseline data
2. Training of administrators
3. Training of teachers
4. Providing teacher feedback
5. Revising teachers' training according to NCHE research ratings
6. Collecting outcome data
7. Analyzing data
8. Disseminating the research results.

NCHE created an information loop with the schools. It consisted of teacher training, teacher implementation of training, evaluation of teacher implementation, feedback to teachers about implementation, revision of training based on implementation results, and training of teachers with revised procedures. This feedback loop was continued over a two-year period so that the effect of the training could be followed across an extended time period.

The small studies

In addition to the large field study, many schools and teachers throughout the nation participated in some self-selected phases of the NCHE program. The following levels of services were provided to various participants:

1. Ratings of one teacher for one or more of the scales
2. Ratings of an entire faculty for one or more of the scales
3. In-service training for an entire faculty
4. In-service training for a large city school system

5.   Consultation to a state school system
6.   Consultation to the US Office of Education
7.   Consultation to colleges and universities
8.   Consultation to schools in ten foreign countries.

The training and research efforts of NCHE were quality controlled. For example, the recordings of the classroom teaching were evaluated by raters who received extensive training prior to their participation in the research program. The raters maintained an inter-rater correlation of 0.90 throughout the three years of the major investigation. Each of the teacher trainers received extensive instruction with each training module before they offered in-service workshops to teachers. Each trainer's work was evaluated to control for the trainer effect in the research results (Table 12.2).

Research results of the large field trial

Results of the NCHE training indicated that the enhancement of empathy, congruence, and positive regard (E, C, and PR) was accomplished. The mean levels increased from 2.0 to 3.0 for these three Carkhuff Scales. Fortunately, the major thrust of enhancing student performance was also accomplished. Some of the results are listed in Tables 12.2–12.4.

TABLE 12.2 Mean difference in adjusted achievement gains

Grade level	Reading achievement	Math achievement	English achievement
1–3	+10.88★★★	No test	No test
4–6	+3.66★★	+15.44★★★	+18.66★★★
7–9	+1.96★★	+4.10★★	+11.75★★★
10–12	+1.56★	+1.94★	+0.96NS

Note: + = In favor of experimental group; NS = not significant.
★p < .05.
★★p < .01.
★★★p < .001.

TABLE 12.3 Comparisons of mean total days absent per student by grade level

Grade level	Experimental means	Control means	Significance
1–3	6.44	8.94	p < .05
4–6	4.98	8.35	p < .001
7–9	7.15	10.11	p < .05
10–12	8.30	12.13	p < .01

TABLE 12.4 Results of comparisons of adjusted treatment means from how I see myself test scores

HISM factor	Grades 3–6			Grades 7–12		
	Treatment mean	Control mean	Significance	Treatment mean	Control mean	Significance
Teacher–school	2.56	1.61	p < .05	1.52	0.53	NS
Physical appearance	1.45	−0.96	p < .01	1.81	0.01	p < .05
Interpersonal adequacy	2.87	2.20	p < .05	1.99	−0.28	p < .01
Autonomy	0.96	−1.89	p < .01	2.19	0.89	p < .01
Academic adequacy	1.25	0.02	p < .05	0.86	0.30	p < .05
Total score	8.61	1.08	p < .001	6.85	0.92	p < .001

The results in Table 12.2 indicate that the experimental group made significantly higher achievement test gains than did the control group in all grade levels except grade 10–12 students in English achievement. These results support the contention that higher person-centered functioning by teachers is related to higher academic gains by their students, especially in younger grades.

Attendance improves with person-centered teaching

The positive relationship between students' attendance and their teachers' person-centered skills is reflected in Table 12.3. When teachers relate in a person-centered manner to students, these students attend school more frequently. This result is a powerful argument for person-centered skills training for teachers because most schools receive financial support based on student attendance.

Students' self-confidence improves with person-centered teaching

Table 12.4 indicates the positive correlation between teachers' levels of interpersonal skills and their students' gains in self-concept. As their teachers used higher-order interpersonal skills, students made significant gains in most areas of self-perception as measured by the 'How I See Myself Scale'.[8]

The foregoing results are illustrations of the positive results obtained when teachers use person-centered practices in their classrooms. In general, the findings of the study revealed the following:[9]

Summary of the positive outcomes from person-centered teaching

1. There is a positive and significant relationship between teachers' gains in levels of functioning on person-centered behaviors and their participation in training programs designed to enhance these skills.
2. There is a positive and significant relationship between teachers' levels of person-centered behaviors and students' gains on achievement test scores.
3. There is a positive and significant relationship between teachers' levels of person-centered behaviors and student attendance.
4. There is a positive and significant relationship between teachers' levels of person-centered behaviors and enhanced self-concept of students.
5. There is a positive and significant relationship between principals' levels of person-centered behaviors and management and the tendency on the part of their teachers to employ interpersonal skills in their classrooms.
6. The skills of the trainers seem to be critical variables in determining the success of person-centered skills training programs.

Results of the large field study strongly supported the contention that when teachers improved their person-centered behaviors, students enhanced their classroom performances on a variety of measures. The major findings of NCHE met the test of replicability, in that a study in Germany by Reinhard and Anne-Marie Tausch reported similar results, as reported in Chapter 13. Carl Rogers recognized the value of this replicability, which is so rare in the social sciences, suggesting that the Tausch studies had replicated the NCHE field studies with 'Teutonic thoroughness'.[10]

Results of the small-scale studies

The NCHE conducted a variety of small studies before, during, and after the large field study. The findings of these investigations supported the larger one, and supplied new data in some areas. For example, these studies indicated that some teachers were able to sustain their high levels of person-centered functioning and others were not. This led to an investigation of the relationship between levels of person-centered functioning and physical fitness. The results indicated that teachers' mean scores on the Aerobics Fitness Test[11] generally placed them in the 'poor' category,[12] which corresponds to the mean score of 2.0 on the Carkhuff Scale for Empathy. This pattern was examined using 105 teachers at Northeast Louisiana University. It was found that those who maintained a physical fitness program were twice as likely to maintain person-centered functioning (3.0 and above) as those who did not do so.[13]

Physical fitness correlated with person-centered behaviors

Additional investigations of physical fitness revealed that seventy-five student teachers at three universities attained a mean score in the 'poor' category on the Aerobics Fitness Test. Furthermore, the student teachers' levels of physical fitness deteriorated significantly across one semester of student teaching. An investigation of this phenomenon was completed in an elementary school in Maryland, where a physically fit principal (a marathon runner) involved his faculty in a fitness program. In this elementary school the teachers attained a mean score of 3.5 on the Carkhuff Scales for Empathy, Congruence, and Positive Regard and maintained those levels throughout the year. Apparently an effective program for person-centered skills training requires that trainees possess a score of 'good' on the Aerobics Fitness Test.[14] In short, to attain and maintain high levels of person-centered skills, the teachers needed sound levels of physical fitness.

The efficiency of training teachers in person-centered behaviors

NCHE continued to conduct training and research in a variety of settings. The person-centered skills training has been enhanced through Carkhuff's work.[15] It is now possible to train teachers, counselors, and administrators routinely to attain minimally facilitative (3.0) levels of people-centered skills in very short times. For example, one trainer working with three different groups of twenty-five teachers recently taught all of them to make person-centered responses (3.0 on the Empathy Scale) in two hours' training per group.

Person-centered skills training or encounter groups?

Another issue addressed by NCHE was the advisability of using person-centered skills training versus encounter group processes with teachers. It is clear that teachers prefer person-centered skills training to encounter groups. The reason for this preference is that teachers generally want to see a clear relationship between their training and an instructional outcome. This relationship can be demonstrated when training proceeds systematically from person-centered skills to curriculum construction and classroom management, as in the Carkhuff training procedure.[16] Encounter group processes have been effective with some teachers, but NCHE found that their relationship to student learning is too indirect to appeal to most teachers.

The importance of demonstrating clear-cut relationships between person-centered skills and academic gains is more important today than ever. This cultural situation is reflected strongly in the text, *In Search of Excellence*.[17] In speaking of effective corporations the authors state, 'The overwhelming failure of the human relations movement was precisely its failure to be seen as a balance to the excesses of the rational model, a failure ordained by its own equally silly excesses.' This same assessment can be made of most human relations programs for schools, as most of them have failed to demonstrate their relationship to the hard-nosed performance indices that are considered the major concern of schools by most observers. This is regrettable because the relationship between academic gain and effective person-centered skills has been clearly and empirically demonstrated in our work and that of Tausch.

Summary

The intervention of NCHE has been successful in enhancing student performance. These interventions have employed technologies that developed from counseling processes. In a sense, NCHE found ways to document the efficacy of applying counseling processes to learning situations. As important as the outcomes may be, it seems equally significant that NCHE pursued a sequential path of research and development. This meant that, before large studies were begun, NCHE had accumulated considerable data to support the instructional efficacy of the processes it employed. Additionally, quality control of its training and research procedures was maintained throughout the studies. Finally, the results were transmitted to the profession through a variety of professional media, though the study did not receive the national and international visibility it merited.

The procedures of training, implementation, and feedback were essential ingredients in the NCHE program. It is difficult to see how any program can be successful without the same ingredients. Feedback is the element that is most often missing in training programs; it is critical that everyone knows the results of his or her work.

The NCHE results can be cast in a new mold, in that they reflect how we can become more productive counselors and teachers. The NCHE findings show clearly that human beings are critical variables in the learning process. Computers have dynamically grown in importance, but when people relate more effectively in a person-centered way with empathy, congruence, and positive regard toward one another, they increase the efficacy of the learning processes. Certainly, machines can enhance learning, but the most important resources for today and tomorrow are in the classroom already. People are our most important resource and, along with their people-centered skills, they are the critical variables in learning. People need human facilitation in order to sustain a prolonged learning effort. A machine, no matter how complex-looking, is the most simple of things. A man, no matter how simple-looking, is the most complex of things.

The late David Aspy was an Emeritus Professor at Texas Woman's University, and his wife, Cheryl Blalock Aspy, is a Professor at the University of Oklahoma College of Medicine. The late Flora Roebuck was Chairperson of the Department of Educational Foundations, Texas Woman's University, before she died in 2002. She had worked earlier at Johns Hopkins University. The three worked on this unique study of teacher effectiveness together for over a decade. They were close and loyal friends of mine in the 1970s and 1980s. In my current work, helping physicians become more effective teachers, part of my intervention, after diagnosing teaching using my own modified version of a Flanders Interaction Analysis, is to give each teacher this chapter and Chapter 13 (by Reinhard Tausch) to read at their leisure as references for the person-centered diagnosis I give in my feedback sessions with them, stressing that it is a diagnosis and not an evaluation, as no teacher wants to be evaluated!

HCL

Notes

1   Flanders, N. A. (1965) *Interaction Analysis in the Classroom: A Manual for Observers.* Ann Arbor: University of Michigan Press.
2   Aspy, D. N. (1972). *Toward a Technology for Humanizing Education.* Champaign, IL: Research Press.
3   Bloom, B. S., M. D. Englehart, E. J. Furst, W. H. Hill, D. R. Krathwohl (1965) *A Taxonomy of Educational Objectives: Handbook I, The Cognitive Domain.* New York: Longman.
4   Aspy.
5   Carkhuff, R. R. (1971) *The Development of Human Resources.* New York: Holt, Rinehart and Winston.
6   Carkhuff, R. R. (1969) *Helping and Human Relations.* New York: Holt, Rinehart and Winston.
7   Aspy, D. N., F. N. Roebuck, M. A. Wilson, and O. B. Adams (1974) *Interpersonal Skills Training for Teachers. Interim Report.* NIMH Grant Number 5P01 MH 19871.
8   Gordon, I. J. (1969) *Studying the Child in School.* New York: Harper and Row.
9   Aspy, D. N., and F. N. Roebuck (1977) *Kids Don't Learn from People They Don't Like.* Amherst, MA: Human Resources Development Press.
10 Rogers, C. R. (1983) *Freedom to Learn for the 80s.* Columbus, OH: Merrill.
11 Cooper, K. H. (1970) *The New Aerobics.* New York: M. Evans Co.
12 Aspy, D. N., and J. B. Buhler (1974) *Physical Health for Educators.* Denton, TX: North Texas State University Press.
13 Aspy, D. N., F. N. Roebuck, and C. B. Aspy (1983) 'Physical Fitness in Counseling and Teaching'. *Humanistic Education and Development* 21: 107.
14 Aspy, D. N., and F. N. Roebuck (1976) *A Lever Long Enough.* Dallas, TX: NCHE Press.
15 Carkhuff, R. R. (1983) *Art of Helping*, Vol. 5. Amherst, MA: Human Resources Development Press.
16 Carkhuff, R. R. (1977) *The Skills of Teaching: Interpersonal Skills.* Amherst, MA: Human Resources Development Press.
17 Peters, T. J., and R. H. Waterman (1982) *In Search of Excellence.* New York: Harper Row.

13

RESEARCH IN GERMANY ON PERSON-CENTERED METHODS

Teutonic thoroughness

Reinhard Tausch

Introduction by Harold Lyon

In Germany, Dr Anne-Marie Tausch and Dr Reinhard Tausch and their colleagues conducted a series of investigations paralleling the work of the National Consortium for Humanizing Education and corroborating the original research of Rogers, Aspy, and Roebuck. However, with what Carl Rogers refers to as 'Teutonic thoroughness', they extended their investigations to counselors, parents, athletics, textbook material, as well as researching the interactions of teachers and students. Dr Tausch's report of those studies reaffirms the exciting possibilities of a person-centered approach to learning and growing. In these days of concerns over violence in the schools, bullying, discipline, control, drug use, sexual behavior, and lack of student motivation, there is a societal movement toward more punitive and less person-centered teaching – just the opposite of what this research shows to be so productive in the classroom, in therapy, and in family relationships. Before his death, Carl expressed to me that it was a great disappointment to him that this vitally important body of research had had such little international exposure. It begs the question: Could these carefully conducted, little published, significant research findings from the past still offer society a current solution for our present problems of low achievement and violence in the schools? Meta-analyses of quality studies between 1948 and 2007, linking person-centered teaching with achievement by Cornelius-White and Hattie, confirm this with a resounding, yes.

HCL

Introduction

Some years ago, my colleagues and I carried out several research projects in order to test Rogers' assertion that the three dimensions of interpersonal conditions (empathy, congruence, and warm respect – called caring, prizing, or positive regard by Rogers) are necessary and sufficient for significant learning. Our studies have verified his statements on each point that we tested. I believe the findings indicate ways we can improve our effectiveness as facilitators whether we are counselors, teachers, or parents.

Person-centeredness in schools and effects on pupil growth

One group of our studies investigated the degree to which facilitative conditions occur in schools and the effect of those conditions on pupil growth. We began by constructing four five-point scales that could be used to rate the levels of warm respect, genuineness, empathy, and facilitative non-directive activities.[1] The non-directive activities scale includes specific teacher behaviors that arise from attitudes of genuineness, empathy, and respect (e.g. making offers, creating conditions favorable to self-determination, allowing clearing confrontations, learning together, etc.).

A scale for directive-leading was also used for rating the teacher's behavior. It measures behaviors similar to those that would be coded as Direct Instruction on the Flanders Interaction Analysis, such as lecturing, commands, criticism, and convergent questions. This dimension is not person-centered.

The scales were then applied by trained raters to audio- or videotape recordings or, in one case, to written transcripts of audio recordings of the lessons being taught in schools. Five three-minute segments from each lesson were rated. In this series, seven studies were conducted. They covered all school levels and included 6,570 students and 291 teachers. Table 13.1 shows the distribution of subjects by school level and study for these seven studies, plus two related studies to be described later.

TABLE 13.1 Distribution of teachers, pupils, and school levels investigated in nine major studies of person-centered teaching and learning in Germany

Study citation	No. of teachers or classes	No. of lessons observed	No. of pupils involved	Level/type of school	Subjects taught in classes observed
Bel-Born, Bodiker, May, Teichmann, & Tausch, 1976	32	32	889	Elementary, junior (grades 5–7)	Geography, physics, biology
Hoder, Joost, Klyne, & Tausch, 1976	21	21	530	Junior (grades 4–9)	Varied
Hoder, Tausch, & Weber, 1976	36	36	1000	Elementary (ages 7–9)	German language
Joost, 1978	96	96	2600	Secondary grammar; secondary technical; elementary (grades 6–9)	German language, sociology, mathematics

(Continued)

TABLE 13.1 Continued

Study citation	No. of teachers or classes	No. of lessons observed	No. of pupils involved	Level/type of school	Subjects taught in classes observed
Klyne, 1976	65	65	(1690)	Secondary grammar; secondary technical; vocational (ages 15 and above)	All subjects
Spanhel, Tausch, & Tonnies, 1975	18	41	(450)	Primary, elementary (grades 1–6)	7 varied subjects
Tausch, Wittern, & Albus, 1976	20	20	(300)	Kindergarten (ages 3 & 6)	varied
—	9	2 to 4 weeks per class	92	Elementary (grades 5 & 6)	sports
—	35	103	–	Grammar school (grades K–4)	varied

Notes
( ) approximate count
— students not studied individually

Prevalence of person-centered teaching in Germany

One question to which we wanted an answer was 'How much client-centered teaching is going on in the schools of Germany?' The answer we found was 'Not much!' On the average, teachers showing warm respect were uncommon; non-directive facilitative activities were rare; and few teachers expressed either empathic understanding or genuineness in the classroom. Specifically, about 11% of high school and secondary grammar, technical, and vocational school teachers[2] and about 14% of elementary school teachers were rated high on all four dimensions.[3] On the other hand, teachers with high ratings on directive-leading were very common; most teachers used autocratic educational methods, and the vast majority of lessons were clearly characterized by questions and orders of teachers.

Specifically, 86% of elementary school teachers were rated moderate to low on at least one of the conditions and evidenced incongruence, disrespect, coldness, or little empathic understanding; and 12% of teachers at all levels were medium to low in all dimensions.[4] About 15% of the secondary teachers were rated low or destructive on all dimensions. When disruptive or problem behavior occurred in the classroom, in 94% of all cases the teacher tried to motivate the student to a better behavior by autocratic educational methods. These findings were true even of the teachers of very young children. Anne-Marie Tausch and her associates found that kindergarten children (aged 3–6 years) received from their teachers only a moderate amount of respect and non-directive/encouraging activity, no sympathetic responses, a high degree of direct teaching, and a low amount of didactic skills, i.e. very little of the instruction was comprehensible to the children, easy to understand, or adapted to their age group.[5]

More direct teaching correlated with less person-centered teaching

We also found that class size had no influence on the ratings of the teachers and that teachers who had had more than twenty years of teaching experience were no different than younger teachers. Directive teaching was negatively correlated with the facilitative dimensions. That is, teachers with a high rating on directive-leading showed lower ratings on empathic understanding, warm respect, genuineness, and facilitative non-directive activities.[6] Although non-directive person-centered activities were rare, when they were present they correlated positively with warm respect and empathy and correlated negatively with directive-leading. The dimension of didactic skills was independent of the facilitative person-centered conditions, i.e. a teacher rated low on those dimensions might or might not have good didactical skills.[7]

Effects of person-centered teaching on pupils

We also wanted to know how person-centered teaching affected the growth of pupils. We measured the effects on pupils in three ways:

1. We constructed a fifteen-item questionnaire, which was administered to pupils immediately following the lesson that was tape-recorded. This questionnaire allowed pupils to state the feelings they had experienced during the lesson.
2. We developed a five-point scale for rating the quality of intellectual processes as exhibited by the pupils during the lesson, which was taped. Level 1 of the scale represented repetition of already learned material only. Level 5 was obtained when students displayed independent intellectual processes, such as combination of ideas or abstraction.
3. We also developed four categories for assessing the ways in which the pupils responded to the learning activities. The four categories were: (a) interested, eager and active pupils, (b) anxious and strained pupils, (c) inactive, indifferent pupils, and (d) restless and inattentive pupils.

Warm respect and non-direct teaching = positive outcomes

We found that a high level of warm respect accompanied by a low level of direc-tive-leading was correlated significantly with favorable processes of the pupils, i.e. with the quality of their contributions to the lessons, with independent spontane-ous behavior, with independent productive thinking and evaluation, and with the degree of decision-making and initiative of the pupil.[8] When teachers were rated high on all four dimensions (empathy, genuineness, respect, and non-directive facilitative activities), their students showed significantly enhanced intellectual pro-cesses, were more spontaneous, and more interested in the lessons, and more can-did (they said more about what they felt and thought); they were more motivated to work, had fewer feelings of anxiety, and had more communication among themselves regarding the lessons. Classes which were rated high in the proportion of interested and eager students also were rated as having teachers who were sig-nificantly genuine, more understanding, and less directive.[9] The four dimensions correlated at 0.70 to 0.77 with the quality of intellectual processes in the study while directive-leading correlated negatively (-0.68) with intellectual processes. Joost found that non-directive facilitative activities, separate from the other dimen-sions, correlated at a level of 0.40 with intellectual processes.

We also point out that the incidence of pupil-to-pupil conversation and state-ments of self-expression were very infrequent in the classes studied.[10] Eighty-nine percent of classes had no student-student expression and 91% of student statements were free from self-references ('I' statements). The remaining 9%, although includ-ing self-references, also included external references ('my book', 'you told me', 'he and I').

Person-centered teaching and positive emotional responses

Three studies were particularly concerned with the emotional responses of teach-ers and students. They compared the students of teachers who were rated high on the four facilitative dimensions to the students of teachers who were rated low in the dimensions. They found that the pupils of the high-rated teachers had more favorable emotional responses to their class, according to the statements they made themselves. For example, they made statements such as 'I like this kind of lesson' rather than 'The lessons were too difficult for me.'

Positive feelings as expressed by the pupils were generally correlated with a high degree of warm respect, non-directive activity, and intelligibility, and with a low to average degree of directive-leading. In general, the statements made by the students of the high-rated teachers indicated that they had made more personal and intellectual progress during the class, had been able to express their own thoughts and feelings more openly during the class and that they had a favorable perception of the teacher. In fact, 70% of the high-rated teachers were received favorably by their pupils, while 80% of the teachers who were low in facilitative dimensions were rated unfavorably by their pupils. My research colleague Klyne also asked the teachers to report their feelings during the class, which had been recorded and rated. More than 70% of the high-rated teachers reported positive feelings, while 70% of the low-rated teachers reported negative feelings; however, only 30% of the total teachers reported that they had felt completely comfortable during the lesson.

Reinforcing acknowledgments in sports classes = improved athletic performance

Two other studies investigated related effects on pupils but without measuring the teachers. In the first one, fifth and sixth grade boys and girls received reinforcements from the sport teachers for the athletic achievements in regular gym or sport classes. It was found that a minimum number of reinforcements resulted in significant improvements in the athletic achievements of the anxious pupils, when compared with anxious pupils who did not receive such reinforcements.

Small group learning leads to higher achievement than individual learning

The second study investigated the effect of allowing pupils to talk among themselves about the lessons while working in small groups of 3 to 6 members.[11] These small groups were compared to students who worked individually. Over 880 students took part in the study. Both the students in groups and the students working individually worked their regular problems in geography, biology, and physics, and immediately after the lesson a test was given. The test was repeated one week later. Pupils who worked in small groups showed better achievement than the students who worked alone; furthermore, the groups members also indicated more positive, emotional and social processes.

Summary: empathy, genuineness, respect, and non-directive teaching leads to higher-quality student performance outcomes

In summary, in all of the school studies, empathic understanding, genuineness, warm respect, and non-directive activities proved to significantly facilitate the quality of the pupils' intellectual contributions during the lesson, their spontaneity, their independence and initiative, their positive feelings during the lesson, and their positive perception of the teacher. Teachers who were rated high on all four dimensions felt more content with themselves and their lessons. Furthermore, all the studies indicated that low ratings on empathic understanding, genuineness, respect, and non-directive facilitation and high ratings on directive-leading accompanied lower levels of pupil intellectual performance and significantly negative emotional experiences.

If we want to diminish stress, aversion, and impairment of physical and emotional health in schools and at the same time facilitate the development of personality and the quality of intellectual performance, then we will need a different kind of teacher than we seem to produce at present. Teachers are needed who can create an atmosphere in their classes where there is empathic understanding, where pupils receive warmth and respect, where genuineness is encouraged, and where the teacher can be facilitative in non-directive ways.

Training person-centered teachers in Germany

We undertook two experiments in training person-centered teachers. In the first study, twenty-three kindergarten teachers participated in a course in helping psychology, while another twenty-eight kindergarten teachers, who were waiting to take the course, formed the control group. Before the course started, immediately after the course, and three months later, the classes of the teachers were video-taped and the recordings were rated. Both immediately and three months after the course, the trained teachers exceeded the control group in showing empathy and elaborative rather than evaluative questioning. The children of the trained teachers engaged in more constructive activity, manifested more interest, and showed more sensitivity to others than the students of the control teachers. Also, the trained teachers reported that their emotional stability was increased significantly, i.e. they felt more confident, secure, and encouraged.

In the second study, twenty-six teachers from all different types of schools took part in person-centered encounter groups for two and a half days along with other psychotherapy clients.[12] There were at least two or three teachers in each encounter group. Teachers still waiting to participate in an encounter group experience served as controls. Results of the study showed that 73% of the encounter-teachers had long-lasting positive changes in their personalities. Their self-concepts and their personal relationships improved and they decreased their negative self-communication and had fewer emotional problems. The encounter-teachers also changed their teaching behavior after having been in the group. Their school problems decreased (e.g. discipline problems, lack of time); they had a better understanding of their pupil's emotions; and considered their students' feelings more frequently during lessons. They improved their relations with their colleagues; their pupils became more trusting of the teacher and enjoyed more self-determination. And finally, 96% of the encounter-teachers thought that such person-centered encounter groups were important and helpful for their work at school.

Person-centered textbooks in Germany

There are three major sources of learning for children in school: their teachers, their peers, and the curriculum materials and activities in which they engage. The studies reported above demonstrated that, when students were allowed to interact with their peers and when they were engaged in non-directive learning activities and had person-centered teachers, their intellectual and emotional capacities were facilitated. We also investigated the remaining source of school learning, curriculum materials.

According to the behavioristic learning theory of Skinner and others, the presentation of learning materials in the form of programmed instruction is regarded as more productive of learning. Because of this, many schoolbooks had been developed which offered intellectual information in small sentences with multi-ple-choice questions. This arrangement corresponds with the rules of conditioning and reinforcement, but Carl Rogers asked as early as 1956 if this was really an appropriate form of presentation.

We believe that text material is better organized when it corresponds more to the inner world of the learner. In a number of research projects, we tested the learnings of students, children, and adults using materials which had been mod-ified from the originals to make them more person-centered. We modified the texts in four ways: (1) the language was simplified, (2) the layout of the text was organized more closely in relationship to the material presented, (3) presentation of information was short and concise but was neither terse nor redundant, and (4) additional pieces were added which contributed humor, anecdotes, questions to the reader, etc. Our research indicated that such modifications resulted in greater learning.[13]

Behavioristic programmed instruction texts compared to person-centered

In another project we compared the transmission of information in the form of pro-grammed instruction with more person-centered modified texts. Four frequently used programmed learning texts, based on Skinnerian principles, were chosen from these subjects: German language, mathematics, physics, and sociology. The con-tent of these programs was modified according to the person-centered principles laid out earlier, while the original behavioristic texts were left unmodified.

The Skinnerian programs and the modified person-centered texts were pre-sented to more than 600 students of elementary schools, vocational schools, secondary technical, and grammar schools. Half of each class was given the pro-grammed instruction; the other half received the modified texts.

Person-centered texts showed better learning and retention in shorter time

We found that students using the person-centered texts showed significantly better learning and retention. All students were examined with the tests from the pro-grammed instruction materials. The students using the person-centered texts made 14% to 29% higher scores. Furthermore, it took students using the person-centered texts over 50% less time to solve the problems than the students using programmed texts. According to their own statements, the students enjoyed the person-centered texts more and took more interest in them. They found the organization of the modified texts more intelligible and more practical to deal with.[14]

We concluded that considering the inner world of the learner and acting in a person-centered way when organizing textbook information seems to facilitate the transmission of knowledge.

Interpersonal relations at home

Since we were finding that person-centered relationships were so important in schools, we also wondered what might be the influence of facilitative dimensions on the development of family members. So we decided to study that in homes with parents.

In the one project we investigated the facilitative dimensions in the early family life of psychologically 'normal' adults with an average age of 25 years.[15] Most of these adults had not graduated from secondary school. They characterized their mothers and fathers in terms of the dimensions warmth/respect, genuineness, non-directiveness, and with less directive-leading (little directive-leading was regarded as being favorable). In addition, various personality tests were administered to the participants.

Scores assigned by the participants to their mothers, plus the scores assigned to fathers, provided eight dimensions. The persons with a favorable perception of parenting in greater than four out of eight scales were compared with those scoring their parents favorably on less than four out of eight. Adults with favorable perceptions of father and mother differed largely in key indicators of psychological health from those who had unfavorable perceptions of parents.

In the Freiburg Personality Inventory (FPI), for example, the group with favorable ratings for parents scored 4.7 in nervousness vs 7.9 for the other group and in inhibition 3.6 vs 5.7 on inhibition (or more inhibition). The favorably rated parents also showed more calmness, less aggressiveness, and a greater emotional stability.

According to the Interpersonal Communication Scale (IPK), those with favorable perceptions of parents were significantly more self-content and showed less negative psychological conditions. The groups also differed significantly in the self-respect scale of the Personal Orientation Inventory (POI).

In addition, two more groups were formed – one with favorable perceptions of parents in six out of seven dimensions, the other with favorable perceptions in only four out of five dimensions. We found a linear relationship for all four groups. The better the parents were perceived, the greater the psychological health.

The groups did not differ in their perception of their average teacher while at school. Thus the good psychological health of these persons correlated with perceiving father and mother, rather than teachers, as being warmly respectful, genuine, non-directive, and using little directive-leading.

Providing person-centered counseling to students

We were a little surprised to learn that adults' mental health was not related to the levels of the facilitative dimensions which had been provided by their teachers, but then realized that this may very well be due to the fact that only a very few teachers (about 8% to 12%) offer good levels of these person-centered conditions. Therefore, it is likely that most of the teachers experienced by the adults in the study described above had been non-facilitative. Three studies that we conducted showed that students who were psychosocially disadvantaged could profit enormously by person-centered counseling.

In one study we provided child-centered individual and group counseling for 6 or 7 weeks to 29 psycho-socially disadvantaged kindergarten children and to 30 disadvantaged primary schoolchildren.[16] The results of the pre-tests and post-tests of these children were compared with children of the same age who had not received counseling. The control children were also psycho-socially disadvantaged, while non-disadvantaged children served as a comparison group. When the counseled children were compared with the control children, they showed a significantly positive change toward a greater degree of emotional stability, social cooperation, sociability, verbal spontaneity, and easiness in a group conversation in the presence of a stranger, and perceptual accuracy on an intelligence test. In addition, some of these counseled children achieved the initial level of the non-disadvantaged comparison group students, who had started out by being much higher on all dimensions. The degree of self-exploration of the primary school children increased significantly during individual counseling and was correlated with the degree of accurate empathic understanding and positive regard offered by the psychologists.

Anxious students perform significantly better after person-centered counseling

In the second study, 116 pupils with the highest scores on scales of neuroticism and anxiety were selected from a total sample of 496 pupils in the fifth and sixth years of intermediate schools. These high-anxious students were randomly divided into two groups, one which received counseling and one which did not. Over a period of nine weeks, seventeen client-centered psychologists conducted six group and three individual meetings with the counsel group during school hours. Although the counsel group showed no psychological change in the personality tests in comparison with the control group, their teachers stated that, after the meetings, they were psychologically more stable (e.g. more self-assured and more independent) and showed improvement in their general development. Half of the pupils stated that they could now understand the problems of other pupils better. And, on the whole, the pupils rated the meetings as positive, especially when they had psychologists with higher levels of empathic understanding. Pupils who had improved in social maturity (according to test scores) showed a tendency toward more self-exploration in the individual meetings than pupils who had not improved in social maturity. In the group meetings, self-exploration was correlated with dialogues between the psychologists and the pupils.

Anxious students improve in talk-groups compared to sports groups or no groups

We also selected those 63 pupils with the highest scores in neuroticism and anxiety from all 358 fifth and sixth grade pupils in one school; but randomly assigned them to three groups: a talk-group, a sport-group, and a control group.[17] For eight weeks, the talk pupils received individual person-centered talks while the sport-group received a special program of games and gymnastics led by pupil-helpers who were specially trained youths. Almost one-third of the talk pupils showed decreases in their psychological impairments. This improvement was large enough to register on at least four out of five personality scales, but only a few sport pupils or control pupils improved. One out of ten control pupils deteriorated on two or more of the personality tests, but not one of the sport pupils or the talk pupils deteriorated. Their improvements were significantly related to the empathic understanding offered them by their pupil-helpers.

Thus, we concluded that the psychological health and social adjustment of pupils with problems could be improved, and deterioration prevented, when high levels of the facilitative dimensions were offered to them during school hours. Furthermore, the good effects of the person-centered dimensions could be attained in either individual or group settings, and the helpful conditions could be provided by either adults or youths.

Person-centered encounter groups result in significant positive outcomes

In the United States, person-centered encounter groups which are characterized by a high degree of warmth/respect, empathic understanding, and genuineness offered by the facilitators have provided favorable conditions for constructive personality change in the participants.[18] We replicated that finding in a study in which we investigated whether such groups are facilitative of the development of German clients with psychoneurotic disturbances.[19]

One hundred and thirty-two clients took part in person-centered encounter groups lasting two and a half days each. The clients were individuals who had come to our Psychological Counseling Department for psychotherapy because they felt psychological distress. The participants were mostly significantly psychologically disturbed. The range of psychological anxiety included such symptoms as tensions and muscle cramps, psychosomatic illnesses, sexual dysfunction, and other sexual difficulties. According to their scores on the Freiburg Personal inventory, 50% were 'strongly disturbed'.

There were fourteen groups in all. Each was led by a facilitator who was an experienced psychologist, trained in client-centered therapy, and one co-facilitator who was not a psychologist but who was experienced in the client-centered approach. Each group had between ten and twelve participants.

Six weeks after the encounter group experience, the clients were tested again. Some findings from this study were:

1. In their principal problem or psychological difficulty, 78% showed improvement, 15% showed no change, and 8% showed negative changes.
2. 86% of the clients regarded the encounter group experience as positive and satisfying.

3. In a series of psychological tests (FPI, IPK, Self-Concept Scale, etc.), 60% of the clients showed positive changes, 25% showed no change, and 17% showed unfavorable changes.
4. Only 7% of the clients dropped out of the experiences.
5. Verbal reports by the participants described dramatic changes. Changes most often reported were (a) increase in genuineness and openness toward themselves and others, and (b) significant increase in contract with their own feelings.
6. During the months (and, for some clients, years) after the encounter group experience, significant and positive changes continued to occur.
7. The facilitators were perceived by most participants as being respectful and warm, empathic and understanding, as well as genuine. The perception by people who did not experience positive changes was found to be less favorable.

In summary, these findings support the assumption that person–centered encounter groups, with facilitators who show real empathic understanding and genuineness and treat participants with a warm respect, are facilitative environments for the positive growth of neurotically disturbed clients.

Encounter groups result in positive growth plus cost savings

These findings are significant when the economics of psychotherapy are considered. Less than 5% of the clients who had taken part in the encounter groups desired further individual therapy. Many participants, however, took part in further encounters, meeting for a few hours only. Many groups met again: some met regularly, others irregularly, often without facilitators, and some became ongoing self-support groups.

Individual client-centered therapy

We placed less emphasis on individual therapy in our research, partly because we were more interested in groups and their power to bring about positive change and partly because our new trainee therapists were not consistently able to provide as high-level conditions of empathy, congruence, and positive regard to their clients. Because of this and other limitations, all our individual therapy is conducted by both an experienced and a trainee therapist.

However, in extensive studies the main hypotheses of Rogers regarding facilitative conditions for therapy were clearly verified.[20] Also, these experiments were encouraging for the training of therapists, as we obtained good results in training effectiveness, satisfaction of the clients, and satisfaction of the therapists.

One-hundred-twelve clients attending our counseling department received an average of eleven individual therapy contacts in four months. We compared changes in this group with a control group of people who came as clients but had to wait four months for the beginning of their therapy.

As we anticipated, most of the treated group showed constructive changes when compared with the control group. Within the treated group there were differences, however, in the degree of change. These differences were related to the therapist's behavior as perceived by the client. Clients who showed little or no changes saw their therapists as having little empathy or understanding, little warm respect, and as being less genuine. For significant changes in the client, the therapist had to be rated high on at least two of the three facilitative dimensions. Thus empathy, or warm respect, or genuineness, alone, was not enough.

When compared with clients who continued in therapy, those who dropped out after four contacts had a significantly more negative view of their therapist. Those therapists were viewed as less respectful/accepting, less empathic, less genuine, less active, less cooperative, and more passive. There was no difference in the perceived level of non-directiveness in both groups considered appropriate and effective behaviors in the process of psychotherapy. There was no significant correlation between the degree of change and the nature of the presenting problem.

Constructive changes could be predicted as early as the fourth interview. A positive outcome was correlated with early statements indicating a positive view of the therapist; for example, 'After the talks with him I realized that I felt calmer' or 'I have the impression that the talks with him really helped to make my problems clearer to me.' These kinds of emotions in the clients, as well as their perception of receiving empathic understanding, correlated significantly with the amount of self-exploration they did in their therapy sessions as evidenced by tape-recordings of the sessions.

Individual therapy works to the degree the therapist is person-centered

In summary, constructive changes in the client in person-centered therapy are significantly dependent on the personal qualities of the therapist, i.e. on his or her empathy, genuineness, and warm respect with regard to the client. It would appear that client-centered therapy affects the client's psychological processes in general, i.e. contact with emotions, expression of feeling, self-concept, ability to make good genuine contact with others. When these processes become enhanced by the therapy contact, the client then copes more effectively with his or her intra-psychic or interpersonal world, wherever the problem is.

Genuineness and other personality characteristics

In our earlier research findings, we had shown that many participants of encounter groups and client-centered psychotherapy become more genuine as persons – they rely less on facades and become more spontaneous. This is reported both by the participants themselves and by others with whom they have contact. In addition, they become more in touch with their feelings. According to Carl Rogers, these characteristics are qualities of well functioning personalities. We decided to test the relationship of genuineness to other indices of personality functioning.

We created a paper and pencil scale to measure genuineness (freedom from facades) vs not being genuine. We used such statements as 'I try not to show others what I am really like', 'I prefer to hide my thoughts and feelings', 'I often show only my polite, friendly facade', etc. This scale, genuineness vs non-genuineness, was presented together with the scales of the FPI to more than 416 persons of different ages and different professional backgrounds.

We found that 70% of people with markedly neurotic characteristics were significantly less genuine. Not being genuine (with facades) correlated 0.56 with neuroticism measured by FPI. Thus, neurotic persons tend to live more with facades than non-neurotic people.

Non-genuineness was also related to having distrust for other persons ($r = 0.45$). Persons who live behind a facade or armor seem to assume that others live the same way. On the other hand, being genuine correlated with 'openness towards the inner emotional experience' ($r = 0.28$), i.e. genuine persons seem to be in closer contact with their feelings.

These findings throw light on the processes generally described under the rather vague term of 'traditional psychological measurements'. They agree with the theoretical assumptions of what constitutes psychological health posited by Carl Rogers throughout his work and from our numerous experiences in psychotherapy and encounter groups. Persons who build up an external façade, and who present themselves differently on the outside from the way they experience themselves to be in their inner self, also experience considerable psychological stress. Specifically, they experience a high level of anxiety; they behave in incongruent ways; and they experience conflict between outer and inner worlds. All of these experiences are identifiable 'symptoms' in traditional diagnostic psychology.

It is evident, therefore, that person-centered approaches (groups, classes, therapies) are likely to provide an environment where people can become significantly less neurotic. Even more importantly, these findings also indicate that a significant contribution to the psychological health of the culture could be expected if emphasis on genuineness, understanding, and warm respect were to be encouraged in schools, families, business, and any other areas of interpersonal life.

Conclusions

The research projects summarized here represent numerous different investigations carried out or completed during a decade of the 1970s. In them, we investigated the assumptions made by Carl Rogers about the necessary and sufficient conditions for significant positive change in person-to-person contact.[21] Our findings are in agreement with Rogers and with our own observations in education.[22]

If teachers, parents, psychotherapists, members of groups, and people in general, can, to a significant extent, be genuine, empathic, and understanding, provide each other warm respect and interact in non-directive ways, the consequences would be substantial. It would facilitate constructive development of personality, lead to enhanced psychological health and promote intellectual development.

If these qualities were found in teachers, parents, psychotherapists, and group leaders, then the lives of children and adult members of groups of all kinds would be more humane and full of growth.

Unfortunately, such qualities seem relatively rare in professional helping persons at present. Our evidence indicates that less than 10% of teachers approach their classes in a person-centered way, for example. If person-centered encounter groups could be made available to teachers, teachers-in-training, therapists, and leaders of groups, then it is reasonable to assume that this would greatly influence their effectiveness in facilitating change in others.

Note: I am very much obliged to Dr Maureen Miller of the Center for Studies of the Person, La Jolla, California, for editing the English version of this manuscript–

Reinhard Tausch

Afterthoughts on our German research, by Anne–Marie and Reinhard Tausch

When I reread this article in the English language in 1980 about our research, which was so carefully edited by the late Flora Roebuck, I thought to myself: How would you, as a reader from another country than Germany, reflect on this? I imagine that you would probably come up with a few questions to which I would like to briefly give my anticipated answers:

1. Why did we do such a great amount of empirical research in regard to people-oriented situations?

    The reason for this is, we believe, that it is possible to empirically demonstrate with this type of research that it is still quite frequently inhumane the way German people relate to one another in school and at home. But we also see the possibility there for improving and humanizing interpersonal relationships. And we still have a considerable amount of additional research data not reported here.

    When I returned home after six years of serving as a soldier in the German Army in World War II, I came to realize more clearly that German National Socialism and Hitlerism were inexorably connected with the German upbringing and the social relationships in schools and within families in our country. Thus, Anne-Marie and I committed ourselves toward working hard and intensively on these research projects over decades – in order to bring about change into the sector of school and family life which showed few traces of humanity.

    We did not do this research work for the sake of our own so-called scientific careers. Whoever is familiar with the German background will realize that Anne-Marie and I often faced rejection and contempt, or scorn, when we revealed our research results and ideas. I can tell you that I received my professorships from the University of Cologne and Hamburg *in spite of* our inquiries into German methods of upbringing young people within their social climate and culture.

2. It might seem too simple and even naive that we focused only on three attitudes effective teachers should have. Are these three behaviors adequate pro-
vision for a student to become more mature mentally and also have other
positive effects on school work? And are the same three behaviors also sufficient to facilitate success for psychotherapists during their individual and group
therapy sessions as well as for parents with their families?

I would like to address these questions. Each one of these three behaviors is
very complex, although a quantitative measure for each is possible. Together,
they include a great number of particular characteristics and 'variables' which
were occasionally found to be effective in individual experiments. These three
behaviors exercise a strong influence continuously on teachers' and therapists'
behavior. For example, If a teacher is a feeling and understanding person, one
who can sense what goes on in the minds of his students, if he respects their
inner world with a little compassion, and if he is congruently open with them
and with himself, then his behavior in the classroom will have very strong
influence on his students. He will, for instance, express himself differently,
employ other ways of acting, and choose other didactive procedures that are
more in keeping with the emotional make-up and needs of his students.

3. Some readers may task, 'Are Anne-Marie and Reinhard Tausch far too enthusiastic as disciples of Carl Rogers?' Are we perhaps blind to other viewpoints
and are we really so-called objective researchers?

I would like to comment on that. I received my Ph.D. in Experimental
Psychology in the field of cognition, and I held a research appointment as
associate and full professor. This particular field was the only one forty and
fifty years ago at many German universities where one could practice any type
of scientific psychology. Thus I have had decades of experience in doing careful empirical work. And these rigorous methods were what we utilized for our
research in schools, with families, and for psychotherapy. In our research work
we have repeatedly searched to find out whether any other variables might be
of more importance than the three dimensions of Carl Rogers. I think that
we have examined and researched the people-oriented possibilities in a careful
and rigorous way. Often we over-emphasized the quantitative experimental
aspects of our empirical work more than one would expect. And yet, our
obtained research results (after laborious examination) confirm Carl Rogers'
hypotheses. These were not our own hypotheses; however, they have been
empirically examined by us and the clear findings are that empathy, warm
respect, and genuineness are the most important traits for a caretaker to have.

Before we did this work over a period of more than ten years, we did
research with families and in schools where we found repeatedly how inhu-
manely some adults quite frequently act toward children. But what we did
not find out is by what means adults can influence children and young people
significantly and promote their personal growth.

4. Another question some readers may ask: 'If I acknowledge that these research
results are pertinent, then there are consequences for me as a teacher in a

classroom situation regarding my daily conduct. In particular, I am obligated to consider the following: How can I become an understanding teacher, one who tries to comprehend the students' feelings, who respects them sincerely, who is transparent, open, and frank with himself and his students? How can my classroom conduct and actions be significantly influenced by empathy, positive regard, and genuineness?'

I think this is not a trivial goal to achieve. Intellectual capacity, formal training, and knowledge in the field of behavior modification are of little help here. I believe an intensive personal learning process is necessary. The development of our own person-centered behaviors can be more easily enhanced through the participation of teachers in people-oriented group situations or encounter groups and through close relationships with people who can personally role-model in their own lives these three person-centered traits – a person-centered role model who will let others observe him or her, showing that it is important that we learn to understand and respect ourselves and that we can be personally open and authentic. In such an open environment, we have a better chance to understand another's thoughts and feelings, to respect that person and to be vulnerable with him. Normally, acquiring these behaviors is not a quick and easy process. But I have learned that this total immersion approach, this process of becoming, is not only more satisfying for my students in our schools, but also for myself. And I am greatly encouraged by the positive changes we found by exposing teachers to training in these encounter group methods – even in short workshops and training sessions.

Conclusion to the Aspy, Roebuck, Tausch research: finding a thorough body of research which corroborates your life's work, by Flora N. Roebuck

When I finished rereading Reinhard Tausch's chapter, I felt like a baseball team that had just won a double header! And one of the games was away from home in Germany.

The field of education is replete with concepts, ideas, and models that have, at best, a handful of studies to support them. Thus, there is data to bolster many differing positions – often antagonistic ones. Furthermore, many studies are highly vulnerable to attacks on their investigative procedures. The result is that important relationships often remain unclarified. So, all those years ago, Dave Aspy and I decided that we had enough faith in the effectiveness of person-centered education to put it on the line; to subject it to the most rigorous possible tests in the toughest arena – the real world of the everyday classroom.

Since then, we've been too busy researching and training and speaking, and looking for funds to do more research, and writing up individual studies, to put all the results together in one package and take a look at it. Writing the earlier chapter has given us a chance to do that – and I am pleased with it. I think those years of effort have been well spent. The documentation that we have compiled is irrefutable. Person-centered education works – it works in the real world of schools and in the theoretical world of statistics.

In the meantime, a game away from home was also taking place, with the Drs Tausch as umpires. They conducted independent and parallel studies testing the same person-centered constructs, and some new studies in homes with parents, in counseling, and even in textbooks, and they won the game there, too! I believe that these two series of related but independent studies probably bring together the most massive collection of data ever accumulated around a humanistic theory or, perhaps, around *any* construct in the field of education. I would like to summarize in tabular form this achievement, because I believe it is unique (Table 13.2):

TABLE 13.2 Findings from independent research in the USA and Germany

Research question asked	NCHE answer (USA)	Tausch answer (Germany)
1. Do students benefit when high levels of Rogers' facilitative conditions (empathy, congruence, positive regard) are offered by their teachers?	YES. Benefits include ... • more physical movement • more problem solving • more academic achievement • more verbal initiation • more involvement in learning • more question asking by students • more verbal response to teacher • higher gains of creativity • higher scores on IQ tests • higher levels of cognition • higher self-concept scores • less absenteeism • fewer acts of vandalism	YES. Benefits include ... • more independent spontaneous behavior • more independent productive thinking • more decision making • more initiative • more interest in learning • more candid expression of self • more motivation to work • more favorable emotional response to schools • higher intellectual processes • higher perceptions of having learned • favorable perceptions of teacher • better sports achievement • fewer feelings of anxiety
2. How many teachers offer high levels of these conditions naturally (without special training)?	VERY FEW. The mean for all teachers is 2.3 (without training), slightly lower for secondary teachers, and slightly higher for elementary teachers.	VERY FEW. About 12% of all teachers were rated high on all three dimensions (11% of secondary and 14% of elementary teachers).
3. Are these dimensions related to other teacher characteristics?	NO. Levels of facilitative condition were not related to age, race, sex, years of teaching experience, or geographical location.	NO. Levels of facilitative conditions were not related to years of teaching experience, class size, or didactic teaching skills.
4. Can teachers learn to offer high levels of these conditions?	YES. Through systematic training in interpersonal skills.	YES. Through university courses and encounter group experiences.

Notes

1   Tausch, R., and A. Tausch (1998) *Experiential Psychology*. Göttingen: Hogrefe.
2   Joost, H. (1977) 'Zusammenhange zwischen Merkmalen des Leherung Schulerverhaltens'. Doctoral dissertation, University of Hamburg, Department of Psychology.
3   Hoder, J., R. Tausch, and A. Weber (1976) 'Forderliche Dimensionen des Lehrerverhaltens und ihr Zusammenhang mit der Qualitat der Unterrichsberitrage der Schuler'. In manuscript.
4   Tausch, A.-M., O. Wittern, and J. Albus (1976) 'Erzieher-Kind-Interaktionen in einer Vorschul-Lernsituation im Kindergarten'. *Psychologie in Erziehung und Unterricht* 23: S1–S10.
5   Ibid.
6   Spanhel, D., R. Tausch, and S. Tönnies (1975) 'Hauptdimensionen des Lehrerverhaltens und Zusammenhang mit konstruktivem Schülerverhalten in 41 Unterrichtsstunden'. *Psychologie in Erziehung und Unterricht* 22: 343–50.
7   Tausch et al.
8   Spanhel et al.
9   Hoder et al.
10   Hoder et al.
11   Van Bel-Born, B., M.-L. Bodiker, P. May, U. Teichmann, and R. Tausch (1976) 'Erieichterung des Lernens von Schulern durch Kleingruppenarbeit in Erdkunde, Biologie and Psysik, im Vergleich zu Einzelarbeit'. *Psychologie in Erziehung und Unterricht*, 23: 31–136.
12   Tausch et al.
13   Langer, I., Schultz, Thun, F., and R. Tausch (1974) *Verstandlichkeit*, Munich.
14   Schmerder, W., u. Tausch, R. (1977). 'Programmierte Instuktion oder personenzentrierte Informationsgestaltung? Zeitschrift f. Pad'. *Psychologie und Entwicklungspsychologie*, 9; Tausch, R., and A. Tausch (1977) *Erziehungspsychologie*, 8th ed. Göttingen.
15   Tonnies, S., and R. Tausch (1976) 'Dimensionen des Elternvserhaltens und seelische Funktionfähigkeit ihrer Kinder im Erwachsenenalter'. In manuscript.
16   Tausch, A.-M., U. Kettner, I. Steinbach, and S. E. Tönnies (1973) 'Effekte kindzentrierter Einzel- und Gruppengespräche mit unter-priviglerten Kindergarten – und Grundachulkindern'. *Psychologie in Erziehung und Unterricht*, 20: 77–88.
17   Thiel, G., I. Steinbach and A.-M. Tausch (1978) 'Schuler Fuhren hilfreiche Gesprache mit Schulern'. *Psychologie in Erziehung und Unterricht* 25: 75–81.
18   Rogers, C. (1970) *On Encounter Groups*. New York: Harper and Row.
19   Westermann, B., J. Kremer, and R. Tausch (1976) 'Unterschidiche Anderungen bei Mitliedern von personenzentierten Encountergruppen'. In manuscript.
20   Rudolph, J., I. Langer, and R. Tausch (1980) 'Prufung der psychischen Auswirkungen und Bedingungen von personenzentrierter Einzel-Psychotherapie'. *Zeitschrift fur Klinische Psychologie* 9: 23–33.
21   Rogers.
22   Tausch, R., and A. Tausch (1998) *Experiential Psychology*. Göttingen: Hogrefe.

14

STUDENTS, PATIENTS, AND EMPLOYEES CRY OUT FOR EMPATHY

Reinhard Tausch and Renate Hüls (*translated into English by Thomas Brendel and Karin Lyon*)

Introduction by Harold Lyon

Just before this book was due to the publisher, I received a call from Reinhard Tausch saying, in effect, 'Hold the press!' He told me that he and his doctoral student, Renate Hüls, had completed an important empirical study on empathy and that they should be heard in this book. This new study of Tausch and Hüls compared the highly positive feelings and reactions of participants blessed with high-empathy parents, teachers, employees, and even physicians, with participants who did not perceive empathy and cried out in despair with convincing voices. Perhaps in these voices lies one of the solutions to combat the violent outbreaks in schools, which we read about far too often in the news: the desperate need for more empathic parenting and teaching.

As I read these moving, uncensored, vulnerable, personal responses of the emotional damage teachers without empathy can cause to a child's or a student's self-confidence, performance, and well-being, I was moved and readily agreed that this summary of their research on students' perceptions of empathy was a vital addition to this book. These personal student testimonials convince us that empathy is not an option, but a necessity, for students. Lack of empathy by a teacher can lead to depression, pessimism, anger, and even violence among students, while empathic teachers can inspire, motivate, and increase student achievement and satisfaction. Please read this desperate cry for empathy on the part of learners and also see what important benefits your empathic behavior can have on others.

HCL

An empirical study showing the damaging or positively perceived effects of caretakers with and without empathy

Empathy is the center of a helpful relationship between human beings; it is beneficial and supporting for the one that is receiving empathy, but also for the one that is giving empathy. Both people are thereby in positive contact with each other and therefore are feeling connected. The ability to feel with another person is the prerequisite for developing a quality relationship. When empathy is missing, emotional injuries occur – people feel isolated and left out.

Research design and methods

We did an empirical study of 288 participants to compare the self-reported feelings and implications of persons who had empathic caretakers, including parents, teachers, professors, and physicians, to those who did not experience empathy from their care givers. We used questionnaires to sample four groups of participants, including randomized groups of adult students at the University of Hamburg, employees of large corporations, and patients concerning their physicians.

Measures

We asked them to respond on a 1 to 4 Likert scale (with 1 meaning Never; 2 meaning Seldom; 3 meaning Often; 4 meaning Always) to the following questions:

1. How often do you experience empathy with other persons?
2. Did your parents in your childhood or youth show you empathy?
3. When you experienced difficulties in your workplace, did your supervisor show empathy?
4. How often has your physician shown empathy toward you?
5. When you experienced problems in your studies in school or university, did your teacher or professor recognize that you were having difficulties?
6. Did your teachers or professors show empathy?

We encouraged the participants to include more detailed written responses and were surprised at the vulnerable, honest, and yet almost desperate responses of students who did not have empathic teachers. We report next a summary of our research results focusing mostly on these vivid student personal responses concerning both having and not having teachers with empathy.

Results and discussion

According to current research, empathy is genetically predetermined as a part of every human being. Empathy is related to mirror neurons that are the neurobiological scaffolding of spontaneous techniques of imitation. However, the genetic foundation is not a guarantee of developing the ability to feel with another person, because 'characteristics and abilities can only develop if the genetic prerequisite is addressed and activated in an appropriate way by interpersonal relationships and social interactions'.[1] This means that a child can only feel empathy towards another person, when it has the opportunity to 'make its own, personal experiences of receiving empathy' from its mother and other reference persons. We believe the basis for feeling empathy rests in these early emotional processes between mother, or closest guardian person, and her child.

What happens to the genetic prerequisite of empathy in a child through the course of his or her childhood and adolescence crucially depends on the behavior of his or her parents, but also on the role-model behavior of his or her teachers. According to Reinhard and Anne-Marie Tausch,[2]

> contacts with our fellow human beings are the essential environmental conditions for people to be empathic. Parents, teachers, and playmates define this essential environment and are the most important people for children and adolescents. They can be the source of our deepest satisfactions and emotional enrichment, but also the source of huge disturbances and suffering.

What is empathy and what are its consequences?

Empathy is the emotional and cognitive ability to feel the problems or distress of another person combined with the desire to help and to relieve his distress. It's assumed that this ability is based on a genetic prerequisite and acquired in a social process through perception learning.

The results of our study show that emotional injuries occur if teachers and professors do not treat their pupils empathically. On the other hand, sustained empathy has positive therapeutic consequences for children and young people. We will present here particular original statements from our participants to illustrate these emotional processes.

Frequency of participants feeling empathy from their teachers

How often did the participants in our study not receive empathy from their teachers? The numbers are depressing:

- Approximately 55% of our participants never or rarely received empathy from their teachers.
- Approximately 67% of our participants received empathy from none or just one of their teachers.

These results imply that more than half of our participants had to cope with difficult situations during their school days without receiving empathy from their teachers. Therefore the pupils could not expect to receive appreciation or empathy from their teachers concerning the personal or emotional difficulties they were experiencing in and outside of their classrooms.

Emotional consequences when teachers do not show empathy toward their pupils

Our participants reported that the lack of empathy by their teachers often led to very negative consequences and to serious emotional injuries. The following original statements of vulnerable feelings indicate how troublesome this was personally for the pupils in the study.

Many had these types of feelings: They felt 'very small, helpless, sometimes aggressive, sad, discouraged, without a chance, left alone, unimportant, stupid, left out, left behind, helpless, alone, and stubborn' (girls 42%, boys 20%).

They also described feelings of loneliness and inferiority, such as feeling 'lonely and lost, small, dumb and worthless, devaluated, overlooked' (girls 19%, boys 25%). Another group of our participants felt 'Rejected, small, ignorant, shabby, unwanted', by their teachers and 'a failure', or 'not accepted, misunderstood, treated unfairly, rejected!' and 'despised, neglected, and not interesting'.

This continued lack of empathy by their teachers led eventually to feelings of aggression and revenge in 29% of participants. Further vulnerable statements of the participants revealed these expressed feelings: 'angry, disappointed, questioning my whole value as a person'. The following statements show the depth of negative feelings that resulted from a teacher without empathy:

> I felt neglected, hated, longings for revenge, powerless, and at the mercy of my teachers' arbitrariness. I rejected these teachers. Their behavior triggered defiance and rage in me and prevented me from achieving the performance I usually was able to achieve.

Because of this process, the pupils in the study felt rejected, 'partially hated, and despised' their teachers. This triggered aggression on the part of these students who had teachers and/or parents without empathy, which sometimes appeared to result in purposely annoying these teachers. One reported, 'I was angry, had no trust in them and no good opinion about them.'

Individual adolescents without empathic teachers often purposely hurt teachers and fellow students at their schools. This begs the question: What are the origins of violence among teenagers? Why aren't these young people in our study able to feel empathy toward others anymore? One reason could be the lack of a secure bonding to their parents, lack of an early empathic role model, and the lack of an empathic personal relationship with their teachers.

A few participants described the deplorable environment in school and their feelings toward it:

> Since almost every pupil in class – with the exception of the best pupil – has been targeted by the teacher once or more, everybody hid or became invisible in such a situation wishing not to be the one targeted this time. Personally I felt denounced, helpless, and abandoned. For me teachers are feared persons … I never have, nor would, confide in them. That's the way the teachers are.

Albert Einstein described a serious consequence of an non-empathic teacher: 'Mental suppression and humiliation by self-absorbed teachers leads to heavy, irredeemable damage to a child's mind, which often influences the rest of its life in a fatal way.'[3]

Inghard Langer[4] found in his studies on violence in school settings that children and teenagers often feel left behind by adults. They require 'true interest and attention' by their caretakers – and therefore by their teachers. They want to be 'seen, acknowledged, and valued'. They need 'love, protection, and honesty' from people who are in contact with them. If they are denied these values of life, they can't develop normally and 'a strong inner stress or pressure emerges, as well as a feeling of threat to themselves and their security, which becomes embedded in their framework of life'. To reduce this pressure young people react with aggression. They fight to survive. This leads to reactions of relief through attacking other people that are known as 'stress-patterns'.

This disposition toward violence is probably enhanced by representation of violence in videogames and in the media. Teenagers find a role model in this inhuman, aggressive behavior and try to use it in their real-life encounters, sometimes inflicting humiliation and hurt to try to strengthen their own poor self-esteem:

> Often a lack of real role models drives teenagers to draw back from initial reference persons and look for other guiding figures whose strength is expected to flow over to them. The expectations from these new guiding figures match their own needs: To find ways out of experienced fear and helplessness.

Parents and teachers are the earliest and most important role models for children and pupils. If they set an empathic example for children, the children will recognize, learn, and emulate this empathic behavior. 'Ruthlessness is not normal, but is the result of certain learning processes. In reverse we can, if we just want to, teach our children the ability to be empathic and to help. There is no better prevention of emerging aggression.'[5]

Emotional outcomes of empathic teachers on their pupils

The student participants in this study were asked the following question: Have your teachers been empathic toward you at school? The result:

- Only 45% of our participants received empathy '*often*'.
- Only 33% of our participants received empathy by 'multiple people or most of their teachers'.

It can be assumed that most of the teachers of these students were able to feel with their pupils and expressed empathic attitudes. This assumption was confirmed: there was a small but significant correlation between the rate of empathy of teachers and the rate of the students' own empathy, regarding the male participants ($r_{sp} = 0.14$; $p = .041$) as well as the female ones ($r_{sp} = 0.15$; $p = 0.047$).

This implies that student participants who received empathy from *multiple* teachers, stated *more often* that they feel empathy toward others. Concurrently, it can be assumed that little empathic behavior on the part of teachers is also perceived by pupils and modeled and adopted as their own behavior toward other people.

Reinhard and Annemarie Tausch[6] studied these correlations between the behavior of teachers and the behavior of their pupils and found:

The type of current and future experience and behavior of children and teen-agers is influenced by the things they observe in other people. The conse-quence for educators is: they can essentially foster personal and subject-specific learning of children and teenagers, if they and other people of their environ-ment act in the same way as expected from these children and teenagers.

The majority (82%) of the student participants stated positive consequences if their teachers were empathic. They feel valued and taken seriously: 'I felt completely alright and valued whenever I am at school. Being tolerant and empathic towards others, one of my teachers really shaped my standards and values.' The pupils per-ceived empathy by their teachers as 'comfort, appreciated, you feel liked'.

Decades of research has shown that the greater the empathic understanding on the receiver, the more positive is the outcome. As Carl Rogers said, 'The more empathic and understanding a therapist or teacher is, the more constructive learn-ing and change is possible.' According to his opinion, 'empathy overrules aliena-tion. The receiver feels at least for a moment as part of mankind'.[7]

In our study approximately 12% of the participants reported a feeling of secu-rity, comfort, and hope, if teachers treated them with empathy. Consider the implications of the following personal testimonials from students in our study who had high-empathy teachers:

> You don't feel that much left alone, if teachers are interested in your worries and problems. Teachers are important reference persons over many years and it means a lot for pupils if they take a sincere interest in our lives. Teachers represent valuable support during difficult periods during which you can benefit from their wisdom. Moreover, while growing up it's helpful for young people to be taken seriously by older empathic role models.

Participants who had empathic teachers felt: in 'good hands' at school (18%): 'hav-ing the feeling of being supported; appreciation as a pupil, motivation to learn because one feels comforted and encouraged'.

Empathy by their teachers also fostered the personal academic progress of participants (9%): 'it was good for my self-confidence, built faith in myself and strengthened my capabilities'.

An empathic teacher enabled students to 'Act courageously, believe in their own strengths; avoid fearing mistakes; and talk freely about personal problems.'

> Having an empathic teacher gave me confidence in my own power and led to an improvement in my performance. I had more joy in going to school and was willing to acquire knowledge in the subjects that these teachers taught outside the classroom.

Empathy by the teachers helped one student to 'evolve my thinking and feeling freely'. Participants described in their personal testimonials such positive conse-quences of empathic teachers on their behavior at school:

They felt strengthened in classroom, had grit, and were better able to handle difficult situations (26%) when they had empathic teachers:

> I didn't give up in difficult periods, but was encouraged to go on.

> Having an empathic teacher helped me understand and cope with problems with fellow pupils – sometimes even solve these problems.

> It helped me to integrate into the class, even if I was left out by my classmates. I felt understood.

Participants (18%) were simultaneously motivated, participated more, and had more fun with their learning when receiving empathy by their teachers, as illustrated by these personal comments:

> It helped me to improve my performance in subjects I wasn't good at. And I improved my performance even more in subjects I had already excelled in earlier. I participated more willingly and relaxed in a lesson that was held by an empathic teacher.

Their teachers' empathy helped build students' grades and self-confidence: 'When I had bad marks with an empathic teacher, I became motivated within myself to learn more and better.'

Some participants of this study (9%) also felt supported in their personal problems by their teachers' empathy:

> During bad times (parents' divorce, relationship problems and so on) my teachers had been more tolerant of me during these days, but not regarding grading, which is a good thing, because dealing with these things is part of growing up. My teacher's empathy also helped when I had problems in my family, with some teachers supporting me, trying to help me to overcome my personal trauma and work actively on my issues such as an eating disorder.

This makes clear that feeling and expressing empathy towards pupils, especially in difficult situations, not only has positive effects on their behavior at school, but also on their family lives. This is especially important if children or teenagers are not getting much support at home.

Very obviously this research study should be an invitation for teachers to become aware of the significant implications of their empathy toward their pupils. Showing empathy and appreciation toward their students has many positive outcomes and is a fruitful opportunity to foster empathy in children and teenagers and to supportively accompany them on their way through life. This is evidenced by the many moving personal testimonies of the participants in this study.

Outcomes of the empathy of teachers from different disciplines on their students

The students participating in this study from different disciplines were asked to rate the empathy of their teachers and professors. The 115 student participants from the

University of Hamburg participated from the colleges of chemistry, mathematics, physics, jurisprudence, and education. The age range of students was from 18 to 42 years of age.

Results of the studies show that students at the university level received even less empathy from their professors than in their years in undergraduate schools. This outcome was multidisciplinary (true for every faculty or school). As in the Figure 14.1, students of every faculty most frequently stated that they never received empathy from a professor or docent (female 55%, male 71%).

Our study leads to the conclusion that a large percentage of the students received little emotional support from their teachers, regardless of discipline.

Psychological effects of insufficient empathy

When asked for their feelings about their teachers not showing empathy toward them, most of the students described highly negative and powerfully emotional responses. In this separate questionnaire, we collected these candid responses from students who did not have empathic teachers.

Lack of empathic teachers resulted in students (female 26%, male 17%), express-ing that they felt:

- 'Lonesome and hopeless.'
- 'I have not been given adequate consideration in solving my problems.'
- 'Distant from my teachers, anonymous, lost, helpless and left alone, in diffi-culty with no help' when important questions, anxieties and doubts came up.
- 'I felt helpless and in trouble, because not understanding makes you feel like it's your personal failure and you're alone with your problems.'

Figure 14.1 Percentages of professors with empathy toward their students in various disciplines

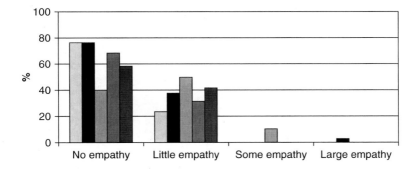

Note: Disciplines in order on chart from left to right: law, chemistry, math, physics, education.

- 'Though you're in the midst of many, there is hardly anyone to trust in school.'
- 'Though you spend much time at the school, you don't meet any real caregivers.'
- 'School does not appear familiar or homelike.'
- 'Teachers don't show empathy and they look disinterested, as if they're just doing a job and nothing more.'

Other statements emphasize that female students (25%) and male students (10%) are 'disappointed and emotionally affected'; if their professors and teachers don't show empathy, they feel 'desperate and treated unfair'.

One student said, 'I had the feeling that all my work and commitment of many months was not honored and all the nights I was working to do the work and meet the deadlines was a waste.' Without empathy from their professors and teachers, they feel, 'very uncomfortable, stranded, and misunderstood. The sad thing was that the teachers did not even try to care about me.'

Discouraging, painful feelings were experienced: 'It is painful, but I am not the only one not receiving empathy. The world is a cold hard place.'

Both female (21%) and male students (13%) felt insecure, without empathic teachers. They felt not understood and unjustly treated. In others, resentment and anger arise. They feel frustrated and rejected by their professors and are annoyed, discouraged, and sad about being unjustly treated. Some are angry, even furious, and they feel powerless. These burdensome sensations cause stress to increase.

Non-empathic teachers' influence on the course of students' studies

Several participants in the study (female 15%, male 29%) were frustrated and not motivated: 'My immense loss of motivation reduced my self-confidence.' They often gave up, and felt helpless, if their professors were non–empathic. One of the students said, 'In the short time I've been a student, I felt often left alone and lonesome. This has had a bad influence on my motivation.' For some students, this meant prolonging their studies while others planned to give up studying entirely: 'I had the thought of even giving up my studies.'

Furthermore, both female and male students had fears of failure (female = 8%, male = 8%), felt anxious and depressed, and took no pleasure in their studies (female = 5%, male = 8%). Others did not have confidence in other persons and did not respect their teachers anymore. About half the students questioned reported negative consequences toward their studies if their professors were not empathic.

Positive psychological impact on students if teachers are empathic

In contrast to the highly negative impact when caretakers show a lack of compassion, there are very positive psychological outcomes described when persons experienced empathy from their professors, teachers, and other caregivers. About 25% of the female students and 17% of the male students indicated that they felt understood, felt as they were taken seriously, felt self-secure and did not feel isolated: 'When your teacher shows empathy, you feel understood and taken seriously. I felt hope again and could hold out.' Others felt relieved and thankful (female = 19%, male = 10 %). Others commented that they felt 'Relief, motivation, and the courage not to give up.'

Empathy from their professors motivated and encouraged the students, helping them and encouraging them to master their studies. Empathic teachers 'Conveyed comfort and brought support. I got the feeling that the teacher communicated the confident feeling that there will be a solution for any kind of problem I encountered.' Empathy on the part of teachers strengthened 'motivation to pass the exam and gave me the feeling of being taken seriously'.

This study on empathy shows 91% of the female and 85% of the male students wished that their professors would show empathy for them in difficult situations. They understand that empathy by their professors is not to make their studies easier or give them better grades, or even coddle them. Instead of that, they merely want to be treated and valued as human beings.

When do students need empathy from their teachers?

Female students (44%) and male students (56%) need empathy from their teachers especially during examination time: 'In all important decisions and milestones, such as during examinations, or when doing your master's thesis, you often feel insecure and sometimes have fear of failure.'

> Also during periods of project completion or final exams or stress, or periods caused by emotional disorders like depressions, students need empathic teachers. When you feel that there is an insoluble problem you appreciate support by your professors such as their using a few encouraging words.

Students feel that the compassionate encouragements of their professors are helpful when they have personal difficulties (female = 28%, male = 22%).

> For some of us, our studies are not an easy thing, Much is demanded, so help and empathy of professors is needed. If there's something very serious happening in my life, like illness, accident, death of a family member, I need empathy from both teachers and fellow students. Students want to be valued as imperfect human beings. I am more than a matriculation number. Teachers are often the only possible reference persons for students' problems and that is why we wish to have their empathy.

As these original statements of students reveal, they have the wish for person-centered behavior from their university teachers. They describe that it is very supporting and helpful in difficult situations to get empathy from their professors and docents. Albert Einstein said:

> It is not enough to teach a person a specialty ... it is essential, that this person develops a vivid feeling for what is worth striving for. The student must develop a vivid sense for what is beautiful and morally good. He must

understand the motivation of human beings, their illusions, their pain, to gain a feeling for the individual and for the community as well. These valuable things can be passed on to the younger generation only by personal contact with the teachers and not – or at least not in the main – through textbooks.[8]

Results about findings on the empathy of students

In our surveys, educational science students indicated they often empathize with others, while also receiving empathy from most of their teachers. Students of law indicated that they rarely empathized with others and did not have individuals who showed empathy for them. It is probable that the students of educational science more often received empathy from their teachers during school time, and they, in turn, modeled and adopted it as a response to others. This was in contrast to the lack of empathy found among the law students. It's possible that the professors in educational sciences are more sympathetic as a profession and serve as more empathic models.

Results of parental empathy on participants

Mothers and fathers are the first and most important caregivers for their children. Their empathy is especially meaningful for the development of their personalities. In addressing this, the participants were asked, 'Did your parents show empathy during your childhood?'

About 20% of the participants responded 'very rarely', while another 20% responded that they only 'sometimes' received empathy from their mothers and fathers. Accordingly, 40% of the children could not count on getting support from their parents even when difficult situations appeared in their lives.

Children adopt primarily in their first years of life with their parents. Therefore it's extremely important for their future relationships to other people that there is empathic behavior in their own families as models. This is why we focused in this study on all participants (children, students, employees, patients) getting empathy from their parents and then sampled their own feelings of empathy for other people to see if this early modeling resulted in future empathic behavior. The results showed a statistical significant correlation that empathy is passed on from parents to children among male interviewees ($r_{sp} = .27$, $p = .033$) and among students of both sexes ($r_{sp} = .24$, $p = .010$).

It is important that parents are notified at an early stage how powerful an influence their own empathy has on their children becoming empathic. Often today, parents leave their children most of the day at day-care nurseries when they are only a few months old. If a little child stays by itself in an unknown environment with persons they don't know, it often feels forsaken from its mother and father. How can one think the important bonding between parents and child could ever develop?

Therefore it's very important for parents to put themselves in the child's shoes to be able to empathize. If they understand the child's feeling of desolation, they are more able to understand how extremely important it is that they care themselves for their own child, if at all possible. Are financial concerns and desires for a career more important than the emotional well-being of a child? Today, many parents fail to seriously consider this troublesome question which for some has no easy answers.

Comparing the results on perceived empathy of parents, teachers, and university professors

- About 40% of the participants in our study 'rarely or sometimes' got empathy from their parents.
- Roughly 55% of the participants 'never or rarely' received empathy from their school teachers.
- About 60% of the participants did not receive any empathy from their university professors.

The above results about empathy of parents and teachers are depressing. One wonders how a child or a young person can develop his personality if his most important caregivers never, or rarely, feel with them?

About 25% of the interviewees in our study are of the opinion that the basis for feeling empathy toward others is created by role-modeling the empathy of their parents and teachers. One of the participants describes it like this: 'A good basis for empathic living is a safe childhood and sympathetic teachers. It happened in my case and I am thankful for that.'

If the majority of the school teachers and professors have empathy for their pupils and students and provide an atmosphere of empathy between both teachers and students, then something very great is achieved. When this happens and children become adults, then empathy will have a determining influence on their lives.

How can we train empathy in teachers?

The results of this study show that stress can hinder the feelings of empathy with others. Also, empathy of teachers is influenced by stress. Reinhard and Anne-Marie Tausch found in their numerous studies in schools:

> Teachers who feel insecure in front of their class are full of tension. At the same time, students are often expecting their own achievement failures. Often classes which suffer from this constant stress, create a high level of hyper-excitability.[9]

To make it possible for teachers to be empathic and treat their students in a more relaxed manner, it would be very important, when possible, to avoid high-stress situations. In 2004, Reinhard Tausch developed patterns for stress reduction that can be learned by teachers and pupils as well:

1. Conductive (positive) thinking, appraisals, imaginings, attitude
2. Target-based action for stress-free organizing of external situations
3. Stress-reductions by physical and emotional relaxation.[10]

Furthermore, participating in person-centered discussion groups like those pioneered by Carl Rogers can be helpful to reduce mental stress of both teachers and students. In this way teachers will have a better chance to empathize and treat their students with empathy and appreciation.[11]

During the teachers' training it should be passed on to the students that their own personality and behavior as future teachers will be of highest importance for their students. Students of educational sciences who are training to be teachers should be able to see at an early stage before they begin their studies that they will pass on theoretical knowledge to pupils, but also in addition their own behavior will be a role model for their pupils. Teachers and professors must learn to see it as their key responsibility to promote the ethical and social behavior of their students. They especially need to show a good role model of empathic behavior.

In this chapter we have heard the desperate voices of participants in this study – schoolchildren, university students, employees, and patients – crying out to their parents, teachers, professors, supervisors, and physicians to be more empathic. Pessimistically, given the disturbing results of our studies, if today's caregivers do not heed these cries and become more empathic role models, there's a good likelihood these young persons will become tomorrow's non-empathic caretakers, leading to a repetitive cycle with unfortunate outcomes. But, optimistically, the opposite is true. Empathic role models today will produce empathy in tomorrow's caregivers!

Notes

1   Joachim Bauer (2009) *Warum ich fühle, was du fühlst*. Munich: Wilhelm Heyne Verlag.
2   Tausch, R., and A.-M. Tausch (1998) *Experiential Psychology*. Göttingen: Hogrefe.
3   Einstein, A. (1997) *Einstein Sagt*. Munich/Zurich: Piper Verlag.
4   Langer, I. (1994) *Überlebenskampf im Klassenzimmer*. Freiburg: Verlag Herder.
5   Ulich, D., J. Kienbaum, and C. Volland (2002). 'Wie entwickelt sich Mitgefühl?' *Augsburger Berichte zur Entwicklungspsychologie und Pädagogischen Psychologie* 87.
6   Tausch and Tausch.
7   Rogers, C. R., and R. L. Rosenberg (1980) *Die Person als Mittelpunkt der Wirklichkeit*. Stuttgart: Klett-Cotta.
8   Einstein, A. (2005) *Mein Weltbild*. Hamburg: Carl Seelig/Europäische Verlagsanstalt. GmbH & Co KG.
9   Tausch and Tausch.
10 Tausch, R. (2004) *Help with Stress and Burden*. Reinbek: Rowohlt.
11 Wittern, O, Tausch, A. (1983) 'Personzentrierte Haltungen und Aktivitäten von Lehrern und seelische Lebensqualität ihrer Schüler im Unterricht'. *Psychologie in Erziehung und Unterricht*.

PART IV

Philosophical considerations for person-centered education

15

DIALOGUE BETWEEN CARL ROGERS AND HAROLD LYON

No pessimist ever discovered the secret of the stars or sailed to an uncharted land or opened a new heaven for the human spirit.

Helen Keller

CARL: In these days of terrorism, energy crises, crime, and pollution, all of us are very aware of the destructive and deteriorative tendencies in our world. We can become discouraged and with good reason. So it's important to recognize and to feel in our bones that the universe is always creating. We are a part of that universal creativity, so we have a tremendous ally in our constructive efforts. We are creating when we are helping individuals expand their learning in their lives. In fact, when we do that, we are doing our small bit to aid in the process of human evolution. We are making it possible for individuals to surpass themselves, be more than they expected. Perhaps even to move into higher states of consciousness. We are supported not only by a network of like-minded educators, but also by a constant tendency in the universe, always developing, always incubating new forms and new ways. And I feel that that gives us certain strength to go on at times when otherwise we might well be discouraged.

HAL: I agree with you, Carl. When we can harness the energy of our intentionality with others who share that intentionality, if we believe and focus our collective energy, we can open ourselves to miracles and move mountains.

There's an interesting book by George Land, *Grow or Die,*[1] in which he postulates that everything grows or it dies. Everything – even the smallest cell – grows or it dies. Our universe either grows or it dies. He even takes the attitude that he is not upset that we're running out of coal, oil, or other natural resources. It's just a new challenge to test the creative tendency of people and the universe. Land says that this will enable us to grow in a formative way; when faced with running out of natural resources and petroleum, we will invent new ways in order to grow instead of die.

That's the challenge to us all the time. We either become creative or we become stagnant in our lives, in all of our work. Ospinski also postulated that we grow in this way; we become more evolved as a species or we face extinction. So Carl, as a natural optimist, I like your 'formative tendency' in the universe. I've always been looking in that direction. I think that children who have tastes of success early in life develop almost a natural tendency toward success very similar to the formative tendency toward creating. These youngsters unconsciously increase their energy to succeed without even thinking about it; on the other hand, those who have had big doses of disapproval or failure early in life often lock in on failure as a goal, and they'll say, 'I failed! I knew I would', as opposed to increasing their energy and getting on with succeeding.

It's almost as if we can develop a tendency toward life or toward death. By nature, we move in the formative way toward life. Unfortunately, society often tends to condition us in just the opposite way; so it's a tribute to humankind that we still move in a formative direction, toward change and growth, whenever we can.

CARL: I think the context for change occurs at a level below consciousness. It has been pointed out by many people in science that unconscious forces are at work throughout the world to bring about revolutions in technology or scientific thought. For example, in several different countries at once, similar or identical scientific discoveries are made. Just so, I see a network of people all over the globe feeling more and more strongly, at a deep level, that 'The person is worthwhile; I am worthwhile. Each of us deserves the opportunity to fulfill ourselves. Each of us deserves to be treated, first of all, as a worthwhile human being.' I think that tendency, that belief, that set of convictions is really growing, and when that sub-conscious force surfaces in many different places, education will be transformed. It won't just be changed; it will be transformed. I think industry will also be transformed and probably other social institutions. This whole context will be one in which traditional education simply has no place. As to predicting what it might be like, that would just be speculation. I've lived long enough to see the transformation of the world by flight. When education is transformed to a process built around the worth and dignity and potential of each individual child, it will be so changed from our present-day concepts that our wildest fantasies could not approach its likeness. I believe the context for that transformation is building in people throughout this planet; at all levels of awareness, we're coming ever closer to the surfacing of that context and the changes it will make in our world.

HAL: That's a beautiful statement, Carl. In saying what I want to about context, I need to acknowledge you, Werner Erhard, and James Carse for contributions to my thinking in this regard. Context is the freedom to be. Context is space. It has no form, no place, and no time, but it allows form and time. In the absence of a consciously created context, our lives are controlled by content; that is, by the forces and circumstances of the condition in which we live. This results in winners and losers, in a 'You OR I' instead of a 'You AND I' outcome; it is finite and limited. Once we create a context, however, that context then generates a process or space in which the content reorders and aligns with the context. For example, if you choose to shift the context of your life from 'I don't matter' to 'I make a difference', the circumstances in your life, though they may not have changed, take on an entirely new meaning. Then the possibilities transform from finite to infinite. This new meaning then begins to transform the circumstances themselves. Soon the situations in your life begin to reflect that you do make a difference.

Now this sounds magical; it sounds really wonderful. It is wonderful and miracles do happen; they happen when you go from content to context. That's when creativity blossoms. You move from finding a solution or a set way of doing it to a context in which it can happen; then, you provide room for all possible solutions, all possible divergent answers to contribute toward that happening. That is what President Kennedy did when he created a context of 'a man on the moon in the next decade'. Most scientists said it couldn't be done; only a few said it could; but after Kennedy created the context of 'It will be done in ten years', the people, including those who said it couldn't be done, contributed to its being done, while offering all the reasons it couldn't be done, which identified these reasons as obstacles to overcome. It was miraculous and it happened because he shifted from content to a context.

Consciously creating a context allows you to intentionally determine a new fundamental principle for your life. The fundamental life principle we often adopt as children is one of reactive, unconscious, defensive, immature kinds of boxes which we put around ourselves and which predetermine our behavior. When you choose a new context, it opens up all kinds of new possibilities that you might never have considered, like Buckey Fuller did in his life when he decided to make it an experiment. The source of context is the self. Context comes into being when an individual creates it within him- or herself. The context of oneness is ourselves in alignment with others. It's hard to grasp the idea of context because you have to open up to a bigger context of the self in order to really understand that you, yourself, can change your world. But it's quite miraculous and I'm finding it to be so in my own life more and more.

In a way, it's like the difference between being and doing. We spend our lives in this over-achieving society, participating in doing and competing; but doing has limits to it. It's finite. It's important that we do things, but doing is not nearly as interesting to me as being, which is infinite. I spent most of my life doing and not nearly enough really being with myself and others. Being is associated with the self and doing is associated with the content of your life. Being is associated with context. It's limitless, boundless, infinite. There's an interesting analogy in 'looking' versus 'seeing'. Looking is evaluating, it's almost entirely cognitive. It's finite – limited. When you look at a person, you are wondering how to classify them, you're evaluating them, how well have they done; what do they look like. On the other hand, seeing is very much like being. It's taking the other person in, just as they are. It's accepting them. It's empathic. It's being able to have prizing or unconditional positive regard. It's just being there with the person; it's accepting them for who they are – it's very Rogerian, Carl. Most of the time we look at others, we're evaluating them; we're classifying them. So looking is limited and finite; seeing is boundless and infinite. You can see all their possibilities. So, to me, doing is to being as content is to context and as finite is to infinite. It's a difference between my accomplishments (doing) and myself (being) and that's a vast difference! Out of being comes some incredibly creative doing. Doing isn't bad, but it is limited compared to being.

CARL: I would agree with you that, in our achievement-oriented society, doing things seems the primary aim. And one of these outstanding lessons from the research presented in this book is that it is important to be. When we can, within ourselves, be real and open and caring and understanding, beautiful results occur. And for any of us – parents, teachers, physicians – what we do then would be appropriate. When we really are in the process of being ourselves, then what we do will be appropriate in a situation. The most important element in person-centered learning climates is the teacher's way of being. We need to learn this truth. It has an oriental rather than a Western flavor; consequently it seems rather strange to many in our own country. But it is an important truth, I believe, and one that both research and experience support in the field of education. One thing that has been difficult for me to really learn and accept is that, on the other hand, one can learn to be sometimes by doing in a rather mechanical way. So I guess there are many channels of learning how to be and that is one of them. It is one which, for a long while, I didn't really recognize or accept, but I have come to realize that it is one channel.

HAL: I would add one other thing. In my own life, the experience of my own crises and tragedies – Warren Bennis calls them 'crucibles' – has enabled me to be more and also do more while being more. I spent most of my life doing to earn approval from others and it seemed to take these kinds of major crises and tragedies for me to break through to an inner awareness where I can earn my approval from within rather then being dependent upon others' or society's approval. These are not the kinds of things that are structured in the formal academic classroom. They are things that come along in most people's lives through the living of life, rather than formal learning, to discover our being-ness. Carl, I'm sure my family members would caution that you do not have to overdo the crises, as I seem to have done in my life!

CARL: I think that by this time, it is evident to the readers of this book that this whole approach obviously exists in a personal context, a philosophical context, a context of values, a view as to the goal of personal development. This has, I believe, been implicit throughout. But it seems only fair to the reader that these basic background elements should be made explicit also.

So, in this last portion of the book, we have intended to set forth some of our most basic beliefs about persons and the capacities they have for living and being in relationships.

Carl Rogers' idea of the 'formative tendency'

The 'formative tendency' is a basic principle that underlies all the other ideas and viewpoints which are expressed in my work in this book. This is the tendency toward higher organization – toward growth – which is apparent throughout the universe. Earlier chapters built upon and extended this basic idea as it is manifested in areas of human functioning. We have shared a line of thought and theory as to how modern man, living in his constantly changing environment, with institutions crumbling all around him, can possibly find and determine the values by which he can live, teach, and learn in this highly existential world. 'Freedom and commitment' faced an issue which is basically raised by the behavioral sciences: is there any such thing as freedom in human beings who are, according to most psychologists, completely determined by their environment? And, finally, Hal's ideas about the power of context fits well with my 'formative tendency' and takes the idea of evolutionary growth to the cutting edge, and beyond, of current explorations into man's capacities.

But what does all this have to do with education? Education, in the eyes of most, has to do with curricula, with methods, with administration, with teaching. It is our contention that tomorrow's educator, whether a parent, the humblest kindergarten teacher, or the president of a great university, must know, at the deepest personal level, the stance – the context – he takes in regard to life. Unless he has true convictions as to how his values are arrived at, what sort of an individual he hopes will emerge from his educational organization, whether he is manipulating human robots, or mentoring free individual persons, and what kind of a relationship he is striving to build with these persons, he will have failed not only his profession, but his culture. So it is without apology that tentative answers are presented to these deeply vexing questions.

You, the reader, are not asked to agree with the positions we present, for some of our thoughts are far from conventional. We ask only that you think through these issues for yourself, to the point that you know where you stand, and why, because your students and your public will increasingly be challenging you on just such issues.

Note

1   Land, George. (1973) *Grow or Die: The Unifying Principle of Transformation*. New York: John Wiley & Sons.

16

MENTORING

Harold Lyon

Research evidence on the value of mentoring

In working for nearly a decade as Director of Education for the Gifted and Talented in the US Department of Education, we discovered that one of the most effective interventions for education of this neglected target group is a mentorship. I also worked as a consultant to the White House Task Force on the Gifted and Talented in 1968, when we interviewed a sample of the country's most gifted achievers, including Nobel and Pulitzer prize winners, astronauts, famous inventors and authors of important works. We asked each this question: 'What made the biggest difference in your life?' Interestingly, most had basically the same answer. Some coach, teacher, or other respected adult had taken off their roles and rank and status and built an intimate one-on-one human relationship with them, encouraging them to step out and take risks and attempt things they would never have tried without this encouragement. These mentors had, not only exceptional capability in a particular subject matter, but also possessed certain nurturing traits.[1] Studies of exceptionally successful people reveal that those who had mentors gained a higher degree of success than those without mentors in all measures of success, including the following:

- earned more money
- achieved a higher education at a younger age
- were more likely to follow a career plan and, in turn, sponsor more protégés than those who did not have mentors
- published more works
- made greater contributions to their career fields than others
- had greater career satisfaction.

In particular, women entering professional career fields need mentors. Studies of successful women reveal that they often had several mentors (usually men) and that they, in turn, became mentors for several protégés (usually women).[2] There appears to be an interesting multiplier effect in mentorship. Those who have them tend to perpetuate the concept by becoming mentors. Certainly, this has important implications for education and all professions.

Traits of the successful mentor or teacher

The empirical research studies over a twenty-five-year period by Aspy and Roebuck, as presented in earlier chapters, concluded that certain specific traits are present in the most successful teacher-mentors.[3] These traits, when present in a mentor or teacher, correlate with the following student outcomes:

* significantly higher achievement scores
* significantly more creative (divergent thinking) responses
* lower absenteeism
* both student and teacher have higher morale and enjoy what they are doing
* young students (first and second graders) reflect significant IQ gains
* teachers with these traits have higher energy levels at the end of a week of teaching than those without these traits.

The traits occur naturally in some individuals, while others, who are willing to learn, tend to be trainable in these traits. Interestingly, elementary school teachers were found to be easier to train in these traits than university faculty.

We have found that the following traits tend to be present, not only in the most successful counselors, psychotherapists, teachers, leaders, but also in successful mentors.

* *Empathic understanding*: the ability to put oneself in the other's shoes and grasp a situation from his viewpoint – the trait Tausch and Hüls found so often missing, but which students needed.
* *Genuineness*: the ability to be somewhat 'transparent' – a congruent individual with strengths and weaknesses, instead of a 'perfect' person appearing to have all the answers. The genuine mentor has what I call 'natural authority' as opposed to 'status authority'. Natural authority is earned by sharing in a learning experience with a colleague, the student. Status authority comes from standing behind your titles, degrees, rank, or a podium, filling up the 'inferior students' with your superior knowledge.
* *Prizing*: this is high positive regard or caring about the students as unique individuals with unique feelings and experiences, each of whom may have a unique style of learning.

When these three traits are present in the mentor, something else develops: trust. The student grows to trust the mentor and knows that the mentor is not there to evaluate or catch her in her mistakes or faults, but to support her, to contribute to her with his skills and personhood, to be her advocate. Mentors with these traits foster learning significantly more (and enjoy the process) than those without these traits. These traits were found to be even more important than the mentor's competence in the subject matter.

'I'm a top notch physician. Why should I learn to be a good teacher or mentor?' Research shows that physicians spend approximately 80% of their time teaching – teaching not only medical students, but teaching colleagues plus the non-trivial job of teaching patients how to change their lifestyles. In addition to medical school faculties needing to be effective mentor/teachers in order to pass on their skills and knowledge to students and patients, there is another pressing reason for physicians to be more effective learning facilitators. You want your students and patients to live long enough and be effective enough to practice what you are teaching them. The suicide and substance abuse statistics among young people in the medical profession give stark testimony to the cost and the numbers who are lost to the profession.

An effective model for mentoring interactions

A simple and efficient interaction model I have used in mentor programs for the informal meetings between mentor and student, particularly in a busy clinical setting, is the *Get, Give, Merge, Go* model. It is applicable not only to medical mentors but to all.

Get: When meeting with your student, attend to him or her the way research shows is most effective for physician–patient interactions: eye contact, squared off face-to-face, leaning forward, listening and responding both affectively and cognitively.
Give: Communicate that you received (empathic understanding) his or her communication and genuinely give in a constructive and caring manner your best thoughts and feelings concerning the matter.
Merge: Reach consensus on your separate views in terms of what should be done – formulate a plan.
Go: Act on the plan. Do what you say you will. Follow up later to see if it meets the need.

The functions of the mentor

Teacher: to enhance the student's skills and professional development.
Sponsor: to facilitate the student's entry and advancement in the profession by opening doors through your influence and by providing opportunities for exceptional experiences.
Host and guide: to welcome the initiate into a new professional and social world and acquaint him with the values, customs, resources, and cast of characters.
Role model: to model through your own virtues, achievements, and way of living.
Counselor: to provide moral and counseling support in times of stress and crisis.
Parent analogue: to support and facilitate the realization of the 'dream', as a parent would for their child.

The traits of the successful mentor are an ideal model. In reality, no one mentor practices or has them available all the time. We do the best in our unique manner with the gifts we have. Our genuineness is expressed in our human imperfection. But we as mentors use what we have to promote, stimulate, and encourage our students.

An experiment in mentoring at Dartmouth Medical School

In 1986, I was invited by the Chair of the Dartmouth Medical School Department of OB/GYN and Pediatrics to help him address a problem. In repeated evaluations of the third year clerkship rotation in this department, the students had consistently rated the rotation significantly lower than all the other clerkships in the medical fields. He wanted to know why. I told him I'd help him find out why, but only if he'd agree to take my recommendations to improve the clerkship. He agreed, and I began to spend time with the third year students to see if I could find answers. It didn't take long.

After getting to know some of the students, it became apparent that in this clerkship students were fearful of asking faculty questions – a very poor environment for productive teaching and learning. Several faculty had a reputation of putting down students who asked questions. The students, anxious to have good ratings in the clerkship, upon which hinges their acceptance for competitive assignments as first year residents, became quickly conditioned to shut up rather than probe faculty with questions. Upon reporting my findings to the department chair, he immediately wanted to know the names of the offending faculty and take action, a request I refused. Instead I proposed a faculty development paradigm, but with a gradual introduction of a mentor program, which he approved.

In truth, there were only a few faculty members who seemed to genuinely care about medical education, most seeing the students as taking their valuable time away from their medical practice. This attitude had been reinforced by a new executive in the hospital – fresh out of Harvard Business School, and interested in maximizing profits, but ignorant of the medical field – who had decided to publish a monthly roster of faculty who had generated the most income from seeing patients. Some physician over-achievers, who were proud of being in the 'Top Ten', were competitively processing patients like cattle, but earning lots of income for the hospital, much to the delight of this new executive. After meeting with him, and finding that he would not budge from his financial incentive plan, I helped to generate a Top Ten list of the faculty who had done the most teaching and mentoring, to counteract the effect of rewarding only those who processed the most patients.

The OB/GYN clerkship director was one of the outstanding faculty members who seemed to develop excellent relationships with students. In addition two others were genuinely empathic teachers, one of whom was a nurse–midwife, low on the medical hierarchy, as was I, as a non-physician. (Non-physicians working in a medical setting often have to work hard to prove themselves to MDs.) I went to each of these three and enlisted them to be the first mentors for our experimental program. We decided each could mentor three students or a total of nine, which was 10% of the third year class. In a short one-hour mentor-training session I gave them, I cautioned, rather than to evaluate, to see their mentor role as advocate, role model, host and guide. I then randomized the students and took nine students – five female and four male – for this mentor experiment. These three faculty members became excited about this new role.

At the end of the clerkship, we were all eager to see how the students rated the OB/GYN rotation. Amazingly, those nine students with mentors rated the rotation higher than any other rotations and significantly higher than those without mentors. (Several comments from those without mentors were complaints that some students had mentors and they didn't.) The results were so encouraging that we expanded to 50% of the clerkship having mentors, though initially I had some difficulty recruiting mentors, whom I was busy training in short informal one-hour training sessions. At the end of the next rotation, the results were similar. The 50% of the students with mentors rated the rotation significantly higher than those without. I took the results to the department chair and he was ecstatic about the results and wanted to expand immediately to the entire clerkship.

Serendipity happened. The faculty were becoming excited about the mentor role in a way they had not been motivated as teachers. As I rotated some faculty in, and then out of, the mentor role – to give others a chance at this new popular challenge – faculty began coming to me to ask if they could become mentors, and those who were did not want to relinquish the role. One pediatrician whose husband had been a mentor came to me in confidence saying that her husband was so disappointed that he was not renamed a mentor and was wondering if he had not done a good job, since I had replaced him to give another faculty member a chance. I explained to her that he had done a great job and that I merely wanted to give other faculty the experience. This was my signal that all faculty who wished to be mentors should be. Most of the teaching faculty were becoming motivated to be better teachers as a result of our mentor experiment.

We put on the student evaluation form this statement: 'Name the three faculty members you feel contributed most to the quality of your learning experience in this clerkship. Give specific reasons.' Interestingly, the same three faculty mentors' names kept coming up in the student evaluations. I drafted a letter for the chair to send to these three faculty members acknowledging their excellent teaching. At first, the chair was reluctant to single out these three, as he felt this acknowledgment for a minority of three would be discouraging to the majority of the faculty. I convinced him to send the letters, and within a week two of the faculty had the letters framed and hung on their office walls along with their various diplomas. Acknowledgment of excellent teaching is powerful!

When we looked at the student evaluations of the clerkship, we were amazed that it had gone from the lowest-rated clerkship that year to the highest as a result of the mentor intervention. What's more was the new motivation among faculty to care about and work one-on-one with students! A transformation had occurred as a result of establishing a mentor program!

These results led me to design a faculty development paradigm, using a mentor program as its centerpiece. I have since implemented a similar effective teaching program in two German medical universities that are going through dynamic curricular reform, a circumstance which always generates the need for better teaching and faculty development.

Perhaps we educators have failed physicians just as we have failed our fellow educators. We now have twenty-five years, and over 200,000 teacher-hours, of solid empirical research which show what makes an effective teacher. Contemporary meta-analyses confirm the results of those older studies. We also have evidence that we can train the motivated teacher or mentor in these skills in a relatively short period of time. What we have not done well is to share this knowledge. We do this in this book.

It is also possible that teacher-physicians may fail themselves by not availing themselves of the procedures we know work for teacher training. The decision is in physicians' hands just as those of their patients are often in their hands. The stakes are high for patients if they do not avail themselves of physicians' services. But perhaps they are even higher for physicians who, as teachers of future physicians, have in their hands the health and well-being of future generations.

Notes

1   *The White House Task Force on the Education of the Gifted and Talented* (1969) US Government Printing Office.
2   Walters, Jane (1981) Unpublished study.
3   Aspy, D., and F. Roebuck (1970) *National Consortium for Humanizing Education Study*, NIMH.

17

TRAINING EFFECTIVE MEDICAL TEACHERS

Current research in person-centered methods

Harold Lyon

Much of what we share in this book comes from very significant, but not widely known, research done many years ago by five people: Carl Rogers, David Aspy, Flora Roebuck, who have long since left us, and Reinhard and the late Anne-Marie Tausch. One of the principal researchers, Reinhard Tausch, now in his nineties, is still very much alive today in Germany and still involved in person-centered research, as presented in Chapter 14. They all have left us with an amazing and convincing legacy in their research, showing that person-centered methods of teaching and facilitating can and do make significant differences in lives of patients, students, and teachers.

We are also encouraged by the comprehensive research of John Hattie, who in his book *Visible Learning – A Synthesis of Over 800 Meta-Analyses Relating to Achievement*[1] found that the 'person-centered' teaching methods presented in this book, and found to be present in the most effective teachers in the earlier research, have much power to bring about achievement – an effect size of 0.72, which is a very strong effect leading to achievement in the hundreds of thousands of studies in his mammoth meta-analysis. Jef Cornelius-White also did a large meta-analysis, including all the high-quality research studies from 1948 to 2004, focusing specifically on person-centered methods showing that these methods have significant effect, leading to achievement.

'Effect size' is merely a way to quantify the size of the difference between two groups or the strength of an intervention to cause an effect. It has many advantages over the use of tests of statistical significance by itself and is often used in meta-analyses.

> It is easy to calculate, readily understood and can be applied to any measured outcome in education or social science. It is particularly valuable for quantifying the effectiveness of a particular intervention, relative to some comparison. It allows us to move beyond the simplistic, 'Does it work or not?' to

the far more sophisticated, 'How well does it work in a range of contexts?' Moreover, by placing the emphasis on the most important aspect of an intervention – the size of the effect – rather than its statistical significance (which conflates effect size and sample size), it promotes a more scientific approach to the accumulation of knowledge. For these reasons, effect size is an important tool in reporting and interpreting effectiveness.[2]

To give you the context, an effective size of 1.0 is a full standard deviation of change equivalent to about two years of advancement in a school year. That's a powerful effect. Almost every intervention results in some change, but how much is worth the effort? Hattie decided to set an anchor point of 0.30 as the effect size above which change is significant enough to be very worthwhile.

Low effect size interventions

Hattie's work presents the effect sizes from thousands of studies comparing hundreds of interventions we have invested in for years. Among the low effect size (lower than 0.23) interventions not worth investing in are some surprises. These low influence interventions include renovating classrooms, school finances/money, programmed instruction, open vs traditional learning spaces, ability grouping, audio-visual aids, team teaching, physical attributes such as reducing class sizes (negative effect size of minus 0.05), television (negative effect size of minus 0.12), and retention in grade level or holding back a year (negative effect size of minus 0.13!), have very low effect sizes leading to achievement, and are not worth our investment. A negative effect size indicates the intervention has the opposite effect one wants to achieve.

High effect size interventions

But the following teaching approaches have high strength (effect sizes above $r = 0.60$) to bring about student achievement: feedback; developing high expectations for individual students; teacher–student relationships; caring about students; empathy; goal-setting with students; providing formative evaluation to teachers; interactivity; teaching study skills and learning strategies.

Cornelius-White's excellent large meta-analysis focused even more specifically on person-centered or Learner-Centered Instruction methods, as he calls them, showing powerful effect sizes leading to achievement.

In addition to discussing effect sizes, this chapter presents research my colleagues and I carried out in Germany at two universities in 2009–2011, the criteria for which were taken from the earlier research studies presented in this book. This work is ongoing in that we still train medical school teachers to become more person-centered using this low-cost facilitative process we developed and tested. The study was an effort to improve the teaching of faculty at two Munich, Germany, medical universities toward more effective teaching criteria based on the results of the large studies cited repeatedly in this book.

Let me back up a bit and share the context of my being in Germany to do this work. In 1988, Apple Computer sent me to the largest computer fair in the world, the CeBIT fair in Hannover, Germany, to demonstrate interactive teaching programs I was developing and evaluating with colleagues at Dartmouth Medical School. I also shared multimedia teaching programs from a consortium of fifteen other US medical schools who excelled in multimedia development. These were computer-based programs for teaching clinical reasoning and diagnosis. Working with J. Robert Beck, Edward Schultz, Frank Hirai, Jim Bell, and Joe O'Donnell and creative colleagues at Dartmouth, we conducted a large study funded by the National Library of Medicine, randomizing and stratifying the entire second year medical students in the entire Dartmouth Medical School into control and experimental groups. Students in the experimental group learned the clinical reasoning process for diagnosing anemias and for chest pain by using our multimedia teaching program, PlanAlyzer, while the controls received the exact same content and support in text form. We worked hard at extracting the algorithms from two expert clinicians – Joe O'Donnell, in diagnosing anemias, and James Bell, in chest pain. This is not a trivial task, as research has shown that 70% of an expert's embedded knowledge is unconscious knowledge, hidden from him, which he is unable to describe. In essence we were unknowingly discovering a process which now has a name, Cognitive Task Analysis, which has been shown as an effective process for extracting from an expert much of that 70% unconscious knowledge.[3]

I attempted to integrate into the interactive teaching and feedback programs of our PlanAlyzer[4] programs the same Rogerian person-centered approaches presented in this book, which was a challenge I never fully succeeded in doing to my satisfaction within our program. Instead of the computer giving the students autocratic feedback, we made it more person-centered and flavored with humor, as effective teachers do.

One major outcome of the research was that the experimental group students who had the multimedia were able to master the content in 43% less time than the controls. The experimental group didn't learn the content better; they just achieved it more efficiently – that is, in significantly less time than the controls without the computer program. But this was an important finding. We published this study, which gave us and other medical schools empirical evidence that such multimedia interventions can result in more efficiency, saving both teacher and student time, in teaching clinical diagnosis and problem solving. Luckily, we happened to control for most of the confounds Richard Clark has shown plague most computer-based teaching research.[5]

At the CeBIT fair where Apple sent me, German medical faculty loved these interactive programs and asked how they could get them. At that time, in 1988, there was not a single Macintosh computer in any German university, as computers were all purchased centrally and Apple was not the preferred brand, though many German physicians owned Macs at home. I suggested to Apple that if they donated forty Macs to one of the largest hospitals in Germany, Grosshadern Clinic in Munich, I would provide the software from the fifteen medical schools in our consortium, which was worth considerably more than the value of the Macs.

They eventually agreed, and I became a guest professor in Munich and an Apple Fellow in Germany when Apple paid my salary to Dartmouth for a year. I have worked closely over the past two decades with this unique team of enlightened German medical education pioneers, including Karl Ueberla, Florian Eitel, Joerg Hohnloser, Adolf Weindl, Heinz Mandl, Martin Fischer, Marc Batschkus, Thomas Brendel, and Matthias Holzer, each of whom was willing to take risks to try new things and to integrate the multimedia I originally brought from the US into their medical curriculum.

My young German physician colleagues, especially Martin Fischer and his team, were so clever that over the next ten years they took my US teaching programs, evaluated them pedagogically with psychologist Heinz Mandl to determine how students learn problem solving most efficiently from multimedia, and how to best create their own teaching programs. They were able to design their own medical case-based authoring system, called CASUS, which has become the most friendly and widely used in the world today. What I realized was that I could make a more meaningful contribution in working to improve teaching than I could with the technology which originally brought me there. Since the Germans were so technically skilled they soon raced way ahead of me. Their universities were in a time of dynamic curriculum reform, having reduced large lectures from 70% down to 30%. When a university experiences such dynamic curriculum reform, it invariably leads to the need for improving teaching. One of the largest innovative medical curricular reform projects, the Harvard 'New Pathway' curriculum, nearly died for the want of more effective teaching. So I decided to lend my energies to helping individual medical faculty members improve their teaching. I came to Munich for approximately six months per year with support during the early years from Apple and with a Fulbright professorship, a Fulbright Senior Specialist grant, and then a National Institutes of Health Fogarty Senior International Fellowship, plus eventually support from the German universities.

What follows is a report on our research and work to improve teaching of medical school faculty over the past years at two medical universities in Munich and our research which shows we had very high effect size power to bring about improvement in teachers toward seven person-centered criteria.

A modified Flanders Interaction Analysis diagnosis and empathic intervention at two German medical universities resulting in significant changes in teacher behavior[6]

Introduction

During the past, teaching skills were erroneously assumed to come with medical content expertise. But most physicians have had little training in pedagogy, though they actually spend a large percentage of their time teaching students, colleagues, and patients. During times of dynamic curriculum reform, faculty teaching is more important than ever before. However, as Wilkerson and Irby report in their review of strategies for improving teaching, there is little experimental research on the effects of various teaching-improvement interventions.[7] We explored in our research a low-cost method of improving teaching, combining the follow-ing: behavorial theories (individual consultation of rating results, organization of teaching) and humanistic theories (measures of empathy/prizing/genuineness) with cognitive theories (interactive learner engagement, question-asking) and more recent social learning theories (peer coaching, reflection, case-based teaching).

We chose as criteria for assessing teaching effectiveness the results of the same large research field studies on teacher effectiveness (200,000 hours of classroom anal-ysis from all levels of education in forty-two states and eight countries), the Aspy–Roebuck research presented earlier in this book.[8] This huge study was supported by the National Institutes of Mental Health (NIMH) over a ten-year period, and entitled the National Consortium for Humanizing Education (NCHE).[9] Among the most significant findings of this study, which was based on earlier research on the traits of the most successful psychotherapists by the founder of 'client-centered therapy', Carl R. Rogers, were that empathy, genuineness, and prizing (positive regard toward stu-dents) are present in the most effective teachers and that these traits in teachers result in important student motivation and achievement outcomes.[10] Other recent research by Hattie in his extensive synthesis of over 800 meta-analyses of 52,637 studies of effective teaching indicates the importance of and relatively high average effect sizes for person-centered learning methods ($r = 0.72$), including empathy, caring, and interactivity ($r = 0.56$) and question asking ($r = .46$).[11]

More specifically, Cornelius-White has done a meta-analysis of all the stud-ies since 1948 which focus on Learner-Centered Instruction (LCI) leading to student achievement, which shows high correlations between LCI and student performance.

Our feedback sessions with faculty in this study corroborate research which suggests that 'fear' is what often deters teachers from giving more interactive lec-tures – fear of losing control and possible resulting chaos, fear of not covering all the content, fear that students may either pose difficult questions or that students will fail to respond.[12]

We designed a supportive critique process to address these fears among teach-ers. We chose the Flanders Interaction Analysis (FIA), as it offers an objective measure for diagnosing teaching and was used by Aspy and Roebuck in their field studies.[13] Three other criteria were added to modify the FIA to create our seven Modified Flanders Interaction Analysis (MFIA) criteria: 1) organization of teach-ing; 2) use of case-based teaching approaches; and 3) increase in teacher empathy/genuineness/prizing.

Our research question was: Do teachers change behavior toward seven selected criteria with our MFIA-guided feedback intervention by an expert as compared with controls not receiving the intervention?

Hypothesis

Our hypothesis was that faculty receiving the intervention would change their behaviors toward our seven effective teaching criteria in their lectures in the sum-mer semester after receiving the winter semester feedback intervention, as rated by expert and student evaluations in general as well as compared to those in the control group without intervention.

Methods

Study design

Twenty-one volunteer faculty at the two medical universities were stratified by teaching experience and randomized into two matched groups: an experimental group who received a MFIA intervention feedback session from me, and a control group which had only a passive MFIA but no intervention feedback session until after the study was complete, when their results were eventually shared with them. MFIA data from the initial winter lectures from both groups before intervention were compared, to insure comparison of well-matched groups with no significant differences. Each faculty member was diagnosed while giving the same content lecture in both winter and summer semesters. All teaching was clinical lectures to third or fourth year students and the numbers of students in the lectures at both institutions varied between 31 and 162 students in each lecture for a total of 1,647 students in the study. Immediately at the end of each lecture the students did paper machine-scored evaluations. The MFIA data and student evaluations from both groups were analyzed in both winter and summer semester lectures to compare changes in behavior.

Flanders Interactive Analysis

The FIA is a tool used extensively in classroom observation studies to diagnose classroom interaction, which is descriptive or diagnostic rather than evaluative.[14] The FIA enables a diagnosis and analysis of the teaching process, including the interaction between students and teacher.[15] The rater merely sits unobtrusively in the back of the classroom, marking a check every minute or so on a matrix of ten items, as shown in Table 17.1.

TABLE 17.1 FIA categories observed and marked each minute by the rater

Teacher talk	Indirect influence	1. Accepts feelings
		2. Praises or encourages
		3. Accepts or uses ideas of student
		4. Asks questions
	Direct influence	5. Lecturing
		6. Giving directions
		7. Criticizing of justifying authority
Student talk		8. Student talk: response
		9. Student talk: initiation
		10. Silence or confusion

The percentages of each of the above behaviors for each lecture were calculated and given to the teachers in the experimental group during intervention one or two days after each of their lectures, showing the teachers how their results compared to those of the average teacher and the most effective teachers from the Aspy–Roebuck studies. This intervention feedback session with the teacher is a confidential, face-to-face, non-threatening session, giving information on the measured teaching behaviors. This includes a discussion of the Aspy–Roebuck studies, plus a portion of the manuscript for this book on this research, for the teachers to read on their own.

Effective teaching criteria

Effective teaching improvement was defined for this study as positive changes in seven teaching behaviors, including increases in: faculty question-asking; student talk; indirect (accepts, encourages, praises, asks questions) to direct (lecturing, giving directions, criticizing) teaching ratio (I/D); problem-solving teaching; teacher empathy (empathy/genuineness/prizing); organization of teaching using the ROPES (Review, Overview, Present, Exercise, and Summary) matrix, and decreases in teacher talk.[16] These criteria for effective teaching were largely based upon the results of the person-centered studies cited in this book, one of which also used the FIA:[17] 'Empathy is one of the most highly desirable professional traits that medical education should promote.'[18]

Test against bias

Recognizing a possibility of bias in that the expert doing the MFIA knew which faculty were in the experimental and control groups, we tested for this. Expert ratings of four different videotaped lectures (two from the experimental and two from the control group) were compared. Three faculty member raters, trained in the MFIA process, were blinded as to which videoed lectures were experimental and which were controls. Global Cohen's kappa for all ratings together was 83% (McNemar $p = 1.000$), indicating sufficient concordance (or no significant bias) in the ratings of the expert rater, as compared to the blinded faculty raters in terms of the expert possibly rating the experimental groups higher.

Experimental group intervention process

To design the intervention, I tested the critique process and refined it in pre-study trials using the MFIA over two prior years with faculty not in the study. Within hours of the lecture, while it is fresh in his mind, I complete a MFIA worksheet (see Appendix 1), using the data I gathered during the lecture to calculate percentages of the seven criteria. The expert then completes a 'Teacher Critique Form' (see Appendix 2) with this data, plus a narrative written critique, which is given to the teacher at the critique after reading and discussing it. This intervention process is an informal, collegial, forty-five-minute supportive, confidential coaching session between the teacher and expert, during which the teacher is assured that it is not an evaluation but rather a diagnosis, that 'process' rather then 'content' of the lecture was diagnosed, and that in one lecture it is impossible – even with a reliable instrument – to gain a fully accurate diagnosis, especially of the more subjective factors of empathy, prizing, and genuineness. The teacher and expert discuss the MFIA worksheet, with the expert presenting a summary of the results of the research studies on effective teaching. The teacher is shown how the students rated the teaching on the student evaluation forms as well as their MFIA results, comparing their results with the average teacher and the most effective teachers from the Aspy–Roebuck studies. During this process the teacher is encouraged to share her fears of being more interactive, given strategies for asking more thought-provoking questions, and is gently supported by the expert to risk moving toward the behaviors of the most effective teachers. At the end of the critique a package of materials is given to the teachers to read at their leisure. This contains information on the research on effective teaching, including the research chapters from this book. The teacher is encouraged to continue communicating with the expert with questions, as well as requesting later MFIA diagnoses, which most do.

One cannot overestimate the importance of the supportive tone in this vulnerable intervention process, which is vital toward facilitating motivation of the teacher. The traits of empathy, prizing, and genuineness, used as criteria in our study, are also essential for the expert to use during the critique intervention. Student evaluations, when combined with supportive, non-threatening individual feedback from an expert, can lead to improvements in teaching.[19] We found that a senior expert from outside the institution, such as I am, is more acceptable to the teacher being critiqued than is a local, less experienced teacher. It's difficult for a young physician in his thirties to sit own with a 60-year-old professor and give him feedback, even if well trained. But an outside expert can more easily achieve this.

Student evaluations

We created a machine-readable, anonymous student evaluation form, completed by 98% of the students, as it was immediately turned in at end of the class. This form collected on a 1–5 Likert scale most of the information also gathered by the expert using the MFIA, plus some additional information. The student evaluations asked the following questions:

1. Did the faculty member show empathy?
2. Did the faculty member prize or care for the students?
3. Did the faculty member use humor?
4. Did the faculty member ask questions?
5. Were the students actively engaged?
6. Did the faculty member use the students' ideas?
7. Did the faculty member articulate learning objectives for the students?

8. Did the faculty member summarize the teaching and integrate it into a scientific context of medicine?
9. Did the faculty member use computer-based cases?
10. Did the faculty member use live patients to teach diagnosis?
11. Did the faculty member have good learning images, videos, and learning aids?
12. Did the faculty member use problem-solving or case-based teaching?

Faculty post-intervention questionnaire

At the end of the study – after all faculty, including the controls, had been given critique feedback sessions – we sent out a questionnaire seeking evaluations and anonymous comments of the participants on how beneficial the study had been for them, as well as recommendations for the future. We were encouraged by comments submitted by faculty as shown later in this chapter.

Statistical analysis

Before randomizing the faculty from both universities into experimental and control groups, we stratified them by teaching experience based upon initial questionnaires all had completed. Data were acquired and analyzed using the Statistical Package for the Social Sciences. After determining that the data were not normally distributed, we used a non-parametrical two-tailed Wilcoxon rank sum test. An alpha level of 0.05 was used for all statistical analyses. The Hodges–Lehmann estimator and an effect size r of z/sqrt(n) were used for the difference in median location between the two groups. For inter-rater reliability and test against bias, Cohen's kappa was calculated.[20] Cronbach's alpha was used to test the reliability of student data.

Results

MFIA prior to intervention showed well-matched groups

Our data from the initial winter MFIA diagnoses for both experimental and control groups in both universities showed that both groups were well matched prior to intervention. No significant differences between the control and experimental groups existed in types or sizes of lectures or on our seven measures of teaching effectiveness prior to intervention.

Comparing pre- and post-intervention results for the experimental group

Data analysis showed that faculty in the experimental group who received the MFIA with intervention feedback after their winter lectures changed behaviors significantly in summer lectures compared to winter lectures on all seven measures: Question asking; decrease in Teacher talk; increase in Student talk; increase in Indirect to Direct teaching ratio; better Organization of the teaching; increase in Problem-solving teaching; and increase in Empathy, Caring, Genuineness.

Post-intervention improvement in teacher effectiveness criteria comparing experimental with control group

Changes in behavior in the experimental group were significantly higher compared to the control group for all but one criteria (ROPES: organization of teaching).

Effect sizes of intervention comparing control and experimental groups

Effect sizes of our intervention's power to bring about change in the experimental group's teaching as compared to the controls were calculated, showing very strong effects of the intervention received by the experimental group:

- Question asking: $d = 0.97$
- Decrease in teacher talk: $d = -1.12$ (indicates that more teacher talk has a negative effect)
- Increase in student talk: $d = 1.00$
- Indirect to direct teaching ratio: $d = 1.27$
- Organization of teaching (ROPES): $d = 0.56$
- Problem-solving teaching: $d = 1.28$
- Empathy: $d = 1.12$

As stated in Chapter 16, Hattie suggests that effect sizes of those shown above indicate real-world change in judging strength of an intervention, which 'is typically associated with advancing achievement by two to three years, improving the rate of learning by 50%'.[21] The effect sizes we found were far beyond our expectations.

Our data show that the faculty in the control group, who were passively diagnosed with the MFIA in both winter and summer semesters, but did not receive any intervention feedback session until the study was over, did not change behaviors significantly on any of the seven measures.

Student evaluations

The student questionnaire evaluation data (n = 1,647 with 98% completion compliance) show that the students evaluated the experimental group faculty significantly higher than the controls in the four composite behaviors. Cronbach's alpha showed the reliability of the following composite sub-scale findings for Empathy, Interactivity, Organization, and Problem-solving teaching, as in the results summarized below:

1. *Empathy*: resulted in significant increase in experimental group and significant decrease in control group. Effect size: $d = 0.80$.
2. *Interactivity*: resulted in significant changes in the experimental group and no change in the control group. Effect size: $d = 0.88$.

3. *Organization*: resulted in no significant changes in either group. Effect size: $d = 0.49$.

4. *Problem-solving teaching*: resulted in significant positive changes in experimental group and significant negative changes in control group. Effect size: $d = 0.38$.

Discussion

Our hypotheses, that our intervention with the experimental group in the form of a supportive forty-five-minute feedback session about the MFIA results had strong power to create more interactivity and positive changes in faculty lecturing, were suggested from earlier years of experience in both universities. During two years of pre-trials, I had observed faculty who, after being diagnosed with the MFIA and given non-threatening feedback, would invite me back to diagnose their next lecture after our feedback session. And I was always impressed at how much improvement toward the person-centered criteria I observed. This encouraged me to do this controlled study to learn just how powerful this process was in bringing about improvement in teaching.

This current controlled study was a process study rather than a process-outcome study. A process-outcome study would attempt to correlate the intervention with student performance such as Hattie and Cornelius-White did – which involves many possible confounding factors outside the scope of this study. We chose to obtain more objective data about these observed possible changes between two balanced groups – one with our intervention and one without. We chose to bring out of 'mothballs', so to speak, an old but reliable and validated instrument, the FIA, as it was also the vehicle used in the Aspy–Roebuck studies of effective teaching behavior as well as in other medical education settings.[22] Additionally, it is relatively easy to train a person to use the FIA and it has high inter-rater reliability.[23] The experimental group changed behaviors significantly after intervention compared to the control group on all of these criteria except ROPES: organization of teaching.

Empathy, prizing, genuineness

The Aspy–Roebuck studies found that teachers with empathy, prizing (caring about students), and genuineness (or congruence), plus the FIA interactive criteria discussed above, had significantly higher desirable outcomes from their students, including the following:

1. increased standard achievement scores
2. less absenteeism
3. fewer discipline problems
4. increased IQ scores (if the students were young children)
5. increased self-concept scores

6. improved attitudes toward learning
7. increased levels of cognitive functioning (more thinking)
8. increased creative responses
9. increases in teacher energy and satisfaction levels
10. these teachers also tended to integrate humor into the classroom and be in better physical condition than average teachers.

We diagnosed humor in this study, gave faculty feedback about it, but did not use it as one of our seven criteria, as it had only a small significance in the large research studies upon which we based our study. Other studies using various measures of empathy have found a positive relationship between teacher empathy and student cognitive gains as measured by standardized achievement scores.[24] There is also evidence that empathy is a teachable skill.[25] Hattie's synthesis of the 800 meta-analyses also showed that person–centered learning overall has a strong effect size ($d = 0.72$).[26] Our study results corroborated results of the earlier studies and also suggested that even a short intervention can cause faculty to be significantly more empathic as well as interactive in their teaching.

ROPES: organization of the teaching

Carkhuff found that the more effective teachers organized their teaching in a way which:

1. reviewed the content to access learners' abilities
2. overviewed the content with the students, motivating them and showing why it will be important to them
3. presented the content in small simple steps, asking questions while doing this
4. exercised the content to provide learners time to practice the skills
5. summarized to obtain a follow-up after learning. ('What have you learned this hour?').[27]

Effective teachers integrate these steps in multi-sensory Tell–Show–Do steps, as in the matrix shown below:

ROPES	TELL	SHOW	DO
REVIEW			
OVERVIEW			
PRESENT			
EXERCISE			
SUMMARY			

The average teacher uses only two or three of these steps. More effective teachers tend to use more steps. We found the effect size for ROPES for the experimental groups' influence on this was $d = 0.56$. Many of the components involved in the ROPES organizational process, such as the motivational overview, the exercising of the content by students, and the summary with Tell, Show, and Do, coincide largely with what Hattie describes as behavioral objectives/advanced organizers ($d = 0.41$), direct instruction ($d = 0.59$) (which has a different meaning than our use of direct feedback) ($d = 0 .73$), and instructional quality ($d = 1.00$).[28] Our findings show that the control group without intervention also improved significantly on only this one criterion: 'organization of teaching'. One explanation for this improvement could have been a 'Hawthorne effect' resulting from the faculty in the control group knowing that they were in a study on effective teaching and, being volunteers, they might have been motivated to improve the organization of their teaching from winter to summer semesters in spite of receiving no feedback intervention. Our post-study questionnaires and feedback sessions with the controls after the study showed that some voiced their disappointment in not being randomized into the experimental group. Indicative of the Hawthorne effect is this comment from the post-study questionnaire of a teacher:

> I had somehow heard – even though I was assigned to the control group – that one of the topics of the study concerned how the teacher is organized and if the teacher is asking questions during his lecture. Obviously this was thought-provoking to me and I think I was more organized and asked more questions in my second lecture even though I had no feedback since I was a control group member.

Interactivity

Our study had several measures with high effect sizes that could be described as Interactivity, including: students answering questions ($d = 1.03$), teacher asking questions ($d = 0.97$), student talk ($d = 1.00$), and the indirect to direct teaching ratio ($d = 1.27$). These are impressive effect sizes given the context Hattie describes, in which an effect size of $d = 1.0$ equals change of one standard deviation or the equivalent of two to three years of schooling. Any effect size of over $d = 0.40$ is a significant educational intervention toward achievement. Hattie's meta-analyses found a high effect size ($d = 0.93$) from question-asking and -answering.[29]

During the feedback interventions, we gently encourage teachers that taking the risk to overcome their fears to teach more interactively by asking questions is worthwhile, as it enhances student motivation and thinking. We share with them that faculty who involve their students by asking more questions are perceived more favorably by students than those who merely lecture.[30] We also suggested to them to pare down their content, focusing on only the most important objectives, and to use handouts or eLearning cases to supplement their other teaching objectives outside of the classroom. We counsel that they be patient in preparing their students to gradually assume more active roles in their learning than the passive roles most lecturers expect from lectures.

Since lectures are not comparable with problem-based learning (PBL), and being aware of the difficulties inherent in PBL research which contain multiple complex variables, which 'will invariably confound attempts to seek cause-effect relationships',[31] we studied only lectures to avoid many of these potential confounds. However, we recommend that future research replicate ours with small seminar and PBL teaching.

Problem-solving teaching approaches

In our study, the expert (and students) assessed the teacher's use of 'problem-solving teaching approaches', which we defined broadly as the quality of visual material such as images, video clips, PowerPoint slides, simulated cases and problems, eLearning cases, and especially the use of live patients. A Likert scale score from 1 to 5 was assigned by the expert in each lecture to reach an overall subjective case-based teaching (CBT) score. Our research corroborates other studies showing that active participation of learners in large groups is facilitated by clinical examples and cases presented with frequent relevant question-asking.[32,33] Our expert MFIA and student ratings showed significant increases in this CBT criterion in the experimental group with an effect size of $d = 1.28$.

Student evaluations

Student evaluations of teaching at both universities have been conducted for the past seven years. However, these evaluations are done by students online and later at the end of the block of instruction and, consequently, have a poor return rate of approximately only 20%, compared to our return rate of 98%, which we achieved by requiring students to complete and turn in a questionnaire at the end of each lecture.

We view our student data with some caution, as such feedback was interesting to the teachers during critique sessions and they are as a measure of student satisfaction. This study was not concerned with content or content learned, but rather the teaching process.

Faculty participant post-study questionnaire

The post-study questionnaire completed by eighteen faculty indicated the following about the MFIA faculty development process on a Likert scale of 1 to 5.

1. Faculty motivation to improve teaching was increased (rating: 5 out of possible 5).
2. The MFIA process helped them as teachers (4.9 out of 5).
3. The MFIA process should be continued with other faculty (5 out of 5).

Illustrative faculty comments about the study from the post-study questionnaires

Illustrative comments and suggestions to improve the process about important learnings were:

Teacher 1

I learned to pay more attention to the structure of my lectures and some new skills to intensify and enhance my interaction with students. The precise analysis/diagnosis of my teaching by Prof Lyon and the personal feedback given me, against the background of the basic research on medical didactics, pointed out for the first time to me what I have been doing wrong or right for many years of teaching until now. What I learned in this project is helpful for me far beyond my lecturing including for my academic speeches and interaction with colleagues in different venues as I realize I am actually often teaching as a leader of an academic department and as a dean and the teaching principles I learned in this Flanders project apply to much of my academic career and life.

Teacher 2

Even if one thinks, he is teaching an interactive class, I learned from this Flanders diagnosis of my teaching that through the use of question asking and other skills, my teaching can become much more interactive and gain much greater student participation. The positive encouragement I received led to a great increase in my motivation to teach classes than I had before ... and much more effectively. As a chairman of my department I will encourage others to participate in this process

Teacher 3

A pivotal learning from this project for me is to work to gain active participation of the students, which can be enhanced with several methods. I had the opportunity to do this when I reorganized my second lecture after receiving the Flanders feedback. The more I include student participation in the lecture, the more active is their participation and also acceptance and perception gains. The friendly, sensitive, and cooperative feedback sessions after the analysis of my first lecture were exceedingly helpful. I am even more motivated for my second lecture and will try to make more of the suggested improvements in future lectures. I would like to continue working with Flanders diagnoses to be able to achieve more improvement. This Flanders diagnosis process should be given to all teachers in the university to create a critical mass of effective teaching faculty. I am motivated to recruit and motivate other faculty and will do so.

Limitations of this study

• Though our findings are encouraging in providing evidence that our intervention has power to change teachers' behavior on our criteria for effective teaching, our study focused on process and not on process outcomes (student performance). Though the large studies upon which we based our study found that teachers with the same criteria we used had desirable student performance outcomes, we did not test for performance outcomes. As difficult as it is to control for confounds in performance studies, further research controlling for the usual confounds is recommended to see if our modified MFIA interventions with faculty might also improve student performance in clinical reasoning or diagnostic ability, such as some research on Problem-Based Learning (PBL) seems to suggest.[34]

- The student evaluations reinforce earlier evidence that teaching with these seven criteria improves student satisfaction. Future research should replicate the findings of this study controlling more for the variances, confounds, and weaknesses of student evaluations.
- We found it important to use as critiquing expert, a senior, highly experienced professional who had recognized credibility with senior teaching faculty rather than younger inexperienced faculty, which restricts replication and might limit the speed of infusion of this process at other institutions.
- Our study was limited to improving lectures and did not focus on small-group teaching.
- Our MFIA process is limited to those volunteering to be diagnosed. Those not volunteering or fearful of being diagnosed are more than likely to be those who need the most to improve their teaching, while those who volunteer are those who need the help least.

Conclusions and recommendations

1. The MFIA is a reliable, effective instrument for diagnosing teaching and, when used as a feedback intervention as in this study, a powerful low-cost vehicle to positively change teaching behavior toward more person-centered criteria, transforming passive lectures into more interactive seminar-types of teaching.
2. Our study found significant behavior changes in teachers, resulting from our low-cost MFIA intervention in the following six teaching behaviors:
   - increases in faculty question-asking
   - increases in student talk
   - decreases in faculty talk
   - increases in the indirect to direct teaching ratio (I/D)
   - increases in use of case-based teaching
   - increases in teacher empathy.
3. It is possible for one or two trained, senior 'change agents' to diagnose teaching and change faculty teaching behavior using this low-cost procedure and intervention. Though other studies show that teacher behavior can change with longer and more costly faculty development workshops or more structured comprehensive 'Education Scholars Programs',[35] this study shows our MFIA process to be a low-cost, efficient alternative for some institutions. Now that our MFIA process has been developed and tested, it takes the expert an average investment of four to five hours per teacher: two hours of expert

diagnosing the lecture with MFIA, plus one to two hours of expert preparing results and report for teacher, and one hour feedback intervention with expert and teacher.

4. Our seven modified Flanders criteria embody many of the same criteria and concepts found to be present in effective PBL tutors: 'empathy; indirect teaching; organization; interactive; elaboration; constructive; self-directed; collaborative; and contextual'.[36] It can be argued that our process of reinforcing empathic interactivity, more pupil talk and less teacher talk, more questioning, indirect teaching, and problem-solving teaching – all hallmarks of effective PBL – is a process for encouraging teachers of traditional lectures to move their teaching process in the direction of more interactive PBL learning.

Other serendipitous results came from this study, including a 'Hawthorne Effect' leading to an increase in the control group faculty in organization (ROPES) of faculty teaching. However, the subjective finding of high motivation to become better teachers, as evidenced in our post-study questionnaires and in our feedback interventions, is one of the most encouraging outcomes of the study. The faculty interest in more effective person-centered teaching has spread beyond the confines of the study as a result of this work. Over 125 Flanders diagnostic and intervention sessions have now been done at the two universities, and more continue. This study seems to have created a 'grain of sand' in the medical school's 'oyster' which is gradually leading to additional faculty volunteering to change their teaching toward a more person-centered approach through our MFIA process, a faculty development process continued with volunteers now that the study is over. We see this successful test of our MFIA faculty development intervention as a viable possibility for replication through low-cost training of additional person-centered 'change agents' at other medical education institutions.

So we have yet another carefully controlled study, this time at two contemporary medical universities in Germany, where we find that we are able efficiently and at low cost to train medical school professors in the very same person-centered traits that Rogers, Aspy, Roebuck, Tausch, Hattie, and Cornelius-White show lead to higher achievement and that the unique, most effective Teach For America teachers also possess.

Notes

1   Hattie, John A. C. (2009) *Visible Learning – A Synthesis of Over 800 Meta-Analyses Relating to Achievement* London/New York: Routledge.
2   Coe, Robert (2002) 'It's the Effect Size Stupid – What Effect Size is and Why it is Important'. Paper presented at the Annual Conference of the British Educational Research Association, University of Exeter, England, 12–14 September.
3   Clark, R. E., and J. Elen (2006) 'When Less is More: Research and Theory Insights About Instruction for Complex Learning'. In J. Elen and R. E. Clark, eds, *Handling Complexity in Learning Environments: Research and Theory*. Oxford: Elsevier Science, pp. 283–97.
4   Lyon, H. C., et al. (1992) 'PlanAlyzer, an Interactive Computer-Assisted Program to teach Clinical Problem-Solving in Diagnosing Anemia and Coronary Artery Disease'. *Academic Medicine* 67, no. 12: 823.

5   Clark, R. E. (1992) 'Dangers in the Evaluation of Instructional Media' (critiquing H. Lyon's PlanAlyzer article and discussing the usual confounds in evaluation studies of instructional media and how PlanAlyzer controlled for them). *Academic Medicine* 67, no. 12). 819–20. See: http://journals.lww.com/academicmedicine/Abstract/1992/12000/Dangers_in_the_evaluati on_of_instructional_media.4.aspx

6   Lyon, H. C., M. Reincke, T. Brendel, A. Hesse, J. Ring, M. Holzer, and M. Fischer (2009) *Improvement of Faculty Lecturing by a Modified Flanders Interaction Analysis.* Published Proceedings of the International Association of Medical Science Education (IAMSE) Annual Meeting. University of Leiden, Netherlands, 29 June.

7   Wilkerson, L., and D. M. Irby (1998) 'Strategies for Improving Teaching Practices: A Comprehensive Approach to Faculty Development'. *Academic Medicine* 73, no. 4: 390.

8   Aspy, D. N., and F. N. Roebuck (1974) *Research Summary: Effects of Training in Interpersonal Skills. Interim Report.* NIMH Grant Number 5P01 MH 19871. ERIC Document ED 106733.

9   Aspy, D. N., and F. N. Roebuck (1977) *Kids Don't Learn from People They Don't Like.* Amherst, MA: Human Resources Development Press.

10   Lyon, H. C. (1974) *Learning to Feel – Feeling to Learn.* Columbus, OH: Merrill. Rogers C. R. (1983) *Freedom to Learn for the 80s.* Columbus, OH: Merrill.

11   Hattie, pp. 119, 182.

12   Steinert, Y., and L. S. Snell (1999) 'Interactive Lecturing: Strategies for Increasing Participation in Large Group Presentations'. *Medical Teacher* 21, no. 1: 37.

13   Campbell, J. R., and C. W. Barnes (1969) 'Interaction Analysis – A Breakthrough?' *PHI DELTA KAPPAN* (June): 589.

14   Wragg, E. C. (1999) *An Introduction to Classroom Observation,* 2nd ed. London: Routledge.

15   Kishi, K. I. (1983) 'Communication Patterns of Health Teaching and Information Recall'. *Nursing Research* 32, no. 4 (July/August): 230.

16   Carkhuff, R. R., and B. G. Berenson (1967) *Beyond Counseling and Therapy.* New York: Holt, Rinehart, and Winston.

17   Aspy, David N. and Flora N. Roebuck (1975) 'The Relationship of Teacher-Offered Conditions of Meaning to Behaviors Described by Flanders Interaction Analysis'. *Education* 95, no. 3: 216–20.

18   Newton, B. W., L. Barber, J. Clardy, E. Cleveland, and P. O'Sullivan (2008) 'Is There Hardening of the Heart During Medical School?' *Academic Medicine* 83, no. 3: 244–49.

19   Cohen, P. A. (1989) 'Effectiveness of Student-Rating Feedback for Improving College Instruction: A Meta-Analysis of Findings'. *Research in Higher Education* 13: 321–41.

20   Cohen, J. (1988). *Statistical Power Analysis for the Behavioral Sciences.* New York City: Lawrence Erlbaum.

21   Hattie, pp. 7–17.

22   Davis, W., R. Nairn, M. Paine, R. Anderson, and M. Oh (1992) 'Effects of Expert and Non-Expert Facilitators on the Small Group Process and on Student Performance'. *Academic Medicine* 67, no. 7: 470–74.

23   Wragg.

24   Aspy and Roebuck.

25   Blatner, A. (2002) 'Using Role Playing in Teaching Empathy'. *Proceedings of the Symposium on the Arts in Medicine* at American Psychiatric Association Annual Meeting, September.

26   Hattie, p. 118.

27   Carkhuff, R. (1984) *The Productive Teacher.* Amherst, MA: Human Resource Development Press, Inc, p. 292.

28   Hattie, pp. 167, 173, 205.

29   Hattie, p. 203.

30   Papp, K. K., and F. Miller (1996) 'The Answer to Stimulating Lectures is the Question'. *Medical Teacher* 18, no. 2: 147–49.

31 Norman, G. R., and H. G. Schmidt (2000) 'Effectiveness of Problem-Based Learning Curricula: Theory, Practice, and Paper Darts'. *Medical Education* 34: 725.

32 Nierenberg, D. W. (1998) 'The Challenge of Teaching Large Groups of Learners: Strategies to Increase Active Participation and Learning'. *International Journal of Psychiatric Medicine* 28, no. 1: 115–22.

33 Irby, D. M. (1994) 'What Clinical Teachers in Medicine Need to Know'. *Academic Medicine* 69, no. 5: 333–42.

34 Norman and Schmidt, 721.

35 Frohna, A. Z., S. J. Hamstra, P. B. Mullan, and L. D. Gruppen (2006) 'Teaching Medical Education Principles and Methods to Faculty Using an Active Learning Approach: The University of Michigan Medical School Education Scholars Program'. *Academic Medicine* 81, no. 11: 975–78.

36 Dolmans, D. H. J. M., W. De Grave, I. H. A. P. Wolfhagen, and C. P. M. van der Vleuten (2005) 'Problem-Based Learning: Future Challenges for Educational Practice and Research'. *Medical Education* 39: 732–41.

18

A FINAL DIALOGUE

Carl Rogers and Harold Lyon

HAL: Where do you think education is going, Carl? What do you think it will be like in the year 2020?

CARL: I see a bifurcation in education which makes it hard to predict. If reduced budgets and the generally traditional mood persists, then I think education will continue to produce conforming individuals, who have almost never been encouraged to think for themselves while in school. The result will be that education will be a factor in the further decline in our culture that I think is taking place, possibly leading to a catastrophic ending. Humane education may be an idea whose time has not come. But that isn't all that's going on in education. There's another trend in education that is supported and encouraged by this book. If education moves toward becoming more person-centered, if it has that as its vision, and context, as you put it, if it appreciates and stimulates the creative potential that exists in each individual, if it stands for both the uniqueness and diversity in and among persons, then I believe it can aid our culture. We will have those students who can find innovative solutions to the critical problems of our time. My contacts with education are not sufficiently wide for me to predict which trend will predominate, but I certainly hope with all my heart for the latter.

HAL: There's an old Chinese proverb that says, 'If we do not change our direction, we are likely to end up where we're headed', and I'm enough of a believer in your formative tendency to support what you have said about teaching becoming more person-centered. I hope, and even go beyond hope, to open a context of a more humane education where children can see that they can make a difference in the world. Children naturally want to make a difference in the world. But they have the will extinguished out of them very early in the system. We have to move toward a transformation which enables miracles, which requires a context of the world working in a 'you and me' way. I hope we'll go in that direction, even though our schools are currently facing many serious problems, such as violence, and a declining student population.

That smaller student population means we're going to have to focus on quality rather than quantity. During the next few decades a smaller population of young people in our classrooms will be nurtured, or not nurtured, to fill all the leadership positions of the future. One of the big problems is that the growing older population tends not to vote in favor of child-oriented issues, but in favor of security and other kinds of issues that are their own concerns. One big question for society is, 'As older people become the dominant population, will they be aware of the needs for child-oriented programs, and be willing to implement them, to vote money for them, to approve them?' This is one crisis we're facing and I believe that as we become the 'older people', we're going to have to take responsibility for nourishing our youth as the leaders of the future. Our own survival as older people in the future will depend on these younger people.

CARL: I think that part of the fear about a declining school population is that it also means a decrease in funding, in fewer teachers, in lessened resources. I think those fears are realistic, but they also can be seen as a challenge. The issues seem to me to be much the same as those we have faced in our dialogue here. Can the teachers create a facilitative climate? If so, the learning in the classroom will be of a better quality. Then, one other thing, can teachers permit students to teach students? To my mind, this is a little-used resource and yet a very important one. It has great advantage to the student who is helping another student. I'm sure we all have experienced the fact that to know a subject you have to teach it; then you really learn it. The student who is trying to help another student understand really begins to learn that topic himself or herself. Then I think there are also advantages to the student being helped; he has the individual attention of a peer who is less threatening than the teacher, the adult. The big advantage to the teacher is that he or she has more time free for high-priority activities. I deplore the fact that funding and numbers of teachers and resources will probably decline. Yet I do believe that if declining enrollments are seen as a challenge, contributing to the context, as you put it, we can develop ingenious ways of meeting the difficulties that are presented.

You mentioned another difficulty our schools are facing: the problem of violence. I have an unusual perspective on that. I think that we are paying a fearful price for making education compulsory. Suppose the only children admitted to school were those who wanted to learn and no one above the age of 10 or 12 had to go to school. It would work a miracle in lessening the amount of vandalism and the number of assaults on teachers and students. I realize this will be regarded as a totally unrealistic or radical suggestion. Supervised recreation, work programs, or other alternative programs would have to be provided for these children who decided not to go to school, but it would be no more costly than keeping them in school. Then I am certain that many who dropped out would later wish to return to school to learn – and could do so, would do so, and would come back with a totally different attitude.

I can't begin to describe how important I think this is. It would again make school an opportunity, which it once was, and not a jail for great numbers of students that it now is. When there is compulsory education, teachers are viewed as jailers, and jailers are going to be attacked. Also students who are in school against their will are a frustrated, alienated group and, to my mind, it's not so surprising that they attack other students and teachers. I think it's deplorable, but I can understand it. I think it goes back to something which was a splendid idea when it started – compulsory education so that children couldn't be exploited as child laborers – but now compulsory education has become a millstone around the neck of education.

HAL: I want to add an example your discussion on compulsory education brings to mind that is so disturbing to me that I have trouble every time I think about it. A black woman contacted me around Christmas time some years ago because she said her gifted child was not being served – he was being placed in a special education class for the learning disabled, but she had him tested and he was gifted. She said that since the school wouldn't place him in the gifted program, she had decided to take him out of school and teach him herself because he was a brilliant, young, 7-year-old. The school had taken legal action against her and the only reason she wasn't in jail over Christmas time was that her attorney had been able to free her long enough to take her child to Johns Hopkins at her own expense to get him tested there.

There was very little that I could do about this issue. I contacted the state department officials and talked with them and they said that the law is that the child had to go to school and that parents cannot teach the child at home if there is an appropriate school. I received a letter from this lady about a month after I talked with her. She was back in jail and had already spent almost a month there for resisting the court order to take her child to school. I felt helpless and saddened that a school would send a mother to jail for a month because she felt that her child deserved a better education, which she could give him at home – better than he would have in school. I had told her in our first conversation that her going to jail might cause more damage to her child than sending him to school, but she felt so strongly that she could do a better job that she was willing to go to jail. This is such an extreme example, I know, but it's where compulsory miseducation does more damage than good.

It's also an illustration of what happens when we fail to take into account the individual needs or abilities of students. It's one of the reasons why I'm glad to see laws requiring an individually prescribed program for children with special needs or gifted and talented children. Unfortunately there is little funding for some of these programs. One of the crucial steps for teachers to take, busy as they are, is to match that student's own individual needs with appropriate materials in the classroom instead of blindly moving forward in a lock-step curriculum.

One of the problems that we find in person-centered education is a notion among some people that there should be no structure. Some children flourish with more organization and more structure. They need a teacher who is flexible enough to give that. Other children need the teacher to get out of their way and provide a great deal of freedom and space for them to grow and develop in their own way. The key is the teacher's ability to match, empathically, his or her style with the student's needs. This doesn't mean we ignore the teacher's own style and the teacher's own specific skills and agendas. In the name of person-centered education, some educators make learning so student-centered that the teachers feel almost apologetic about their own agendas. This is a mistake. It's alright for the teacher to have an agenda, just as the students have agendas. The teacher as the leader of the classroom needs to provide sufficient structure, but also must provide opportunities for students to learn in the style that is most effective for them. I think this is one of the challenges we face to enable individually prescribed learning to become a real and vital process in education.

CARL: I like that. I would go along with all of that. I think I have just one general comment: that the research shows the importance of the teacher's understanding the meaning of the school experience to the student and the importance of the extent to which the teacher cares for the student. So it's a matter of matching the resources and the options that are known to the teacher with the needs and interests expressed by the student and understood by the teacher. I would heartily concur in your statement that some students want and need structure and guidance; they should be matched with the teacher for whom that is a natural and acceptable approach. Other students want a lot of freedom, want to guide themselves, want to be self-directing, and they should be matched to the teacher who believes in that direction for learning. I think that I'm simply talking about a psychological matching that to me is very important.

HAL: I wonder what your reaction might be to another of those big problems for education – the need to do something to help young people deal with the epidemic of unplanned teenage pregnancies that can have such negative consequences on the health of mother and infant and on the long-term quality-of-life consequences for society as well as the mother, the father, and the child.

CARL: I think that we have a very hard time recognizing that, in our Western culture and particularly in the United States, with its continuous sexual stimulation in every medium, children mature physically and sexually at a very early age. That early sexual maturity is a cultural phenomenon. In China, by contrast, men and women marry at ages 26 to 28. There is almost no premarital sex and an astonishingly small number of illegitimate pregnancies, and even those few occur mostly among mothers who are 22 years old or older. I didn't believe those statements until I went to China, visited the hospitals, talked to the doctors and talked to other people. I realized that their culture simply develops a very different attitude toward sex than ours. So the results are also very different. In our culture, we do everything possible to stimulate early sexual consciousness and maturation, usually in the name of commerce to promote sales.

I think as far as the schools are concerned, what we need are not only courses in parenting for teenagers, but education in sexual matters, generally, and especially education in birth control. I know that's a controversial topic and probably a controversial statement, but we are not going to stop adolescent sexual intercourse by withholding contraceptive information. In my estimation, courses in contraception could be made voluntary, but they are vitally necessary if we're to avoid this flood of younger and younger mothers having unwanted pregnancies. That's a real tragedy for the young girl – she is not a woman yet, but has the responsibility of caring for a child. I feel it's a tragedy for them and I feel it's a tragedy for society. The schools and other agencies bear a responsibility for that unless they, at a very early age, provide contraceptive information.

HAL: I agree. Furthermore, even though it's difficult and controversial, the teenager's parents must be involved in this process of family education for two reasons. First, students spend about half of their waking hours in the non-school environment, much of that time at home. Second, usually parents can best provide the teenager with support and guidance for contraception, as well as model a value system about sexuality and about lovingness, in being with other people in a supportive way that needs to go along with basic family planning and contraceptive information.

I think it ought to be mandatory to teach young people in high school and junior high about parenting, nutrition, and nurturing. Then, as a result of being concerned about their own future offspring, they might be somewhat more concerned about what they are putting into their own bodies – what they're smoking, what they might be taking in the way of drugs – knowing what effect that will have on their own children as well as on themselves.

CARL: That's very true. I think another thing needs to be stressed in high school, and could be stressed in grammar school as well. When a child is born, the parent is taking on at least an eighteen-year responsibility. Somehow, in the flow of visioning pregnancy, and childbirth and the creation of a new life, I think young people have no concept whatsoever of the fact that after the birth they are going to be responsible for a young person for at least eighteen years; they are not undertaking something that will be all over in two or three years. That is, I think that the current attitude among many young people, a kind of unconscious attitude, is 'It would be nice to have a baby and to take care of it.' Yes, but babyhood is followed by childhood, and then adolescence, and illnesses and other problems as well as the need for financial support – the whole gamut of responsibility over a long period of time. Young people need to recognize that.

HAL: I think that's very important. And there are other things our schools need to teach young people about being parents, such as the fact that the period from 8 to 22 months in the infant's life is critical to the person's ability later to be creative and inquiring. Also, teenagers need to be taught the realities of the birth process

– not just an idealized version – but what it is and what it means to them, including up-to-date findings about the impact of health practices, diet, and so forth. If we're going to stop this epidemic of unplanned teenage pregnancies, school and parents have a big job ahead of them – and one they need to undertake cooperatively, not competitively nor selfishly.

CARL: I would agree with that.

HAL: Earlier, you said that you saw a trend toward a more positive, a more human kind of education. Were you thinking about alternative schools?

CARL: Alternative or charter schools seem to me to be a very exciting and promising development. I think that the more alternatives there are, the more parents and students and school administrators will have to think deeply about education and what they want in the way of education. If there are wide choices among alternative schools available, parents and students will have to choose, individually or together, what kind of education, what kind of schooling they want. That will raise their consciousness in regard to the educational process and educational philosophy. In turn, school administrators will begin to wonder why the enrollment at school 'X' is increasing, while 'mine' is decreasing and that will, in my estimation, raise educators' consciousness. I see it as a healthy competition, which should improve all schools. I even wish the voucher system could become viable in which parents and students would be given vouchers and could take those to the school of their choice and then that school would be repaid by a central organization. I'm sorry that the voucher system is opposed by so many teachers and administrators, because it could be a healthy thing. Of course, we have to face the fact, and I certainly face it, that some alternative schools are going to be poor and students may not learn very much in some of them. But I guess my reaction to that is, 'So, what else is new?' There are plenty of poor schools today, plenty of schools in which students learn very little, so that I don't regard it as a danger. I regard it as a promising and hopeful way of causing all of us to think more deeply about what we do want in education and how learning can take place effectively. I think any kind of experimentation is helpful because it makes people think.

HAL: I agree; I believe it's high time that parents and families had a consumer's choice about schools. Schooling is one of the most important decisions a family makes and a good deal of their tax money goes to schools. Yet, parents and the community currently have no choice other than to take their child out of the public school and pay an exorbitant amount for a private school which may, or may not, be any better than the public school. My experience is that many of them are not any better and are certainly very costly. So I think that alternative schools, competition coming on the scene, is a healthy movement for education.

In the area of gifted and talented education from the national level, we've been encouraging mentorships for gifted children as a supplement to the regular classroom experience. So gifted and talented programs have been establishing in communities, or helping communities to establish, their own community mentor program as an alternative to the regular school program. But we did not set it up in competition with the regular school program; instead, by involving teachers in it, we made it a part of the school program, even though it was an alternative.

The community can inventory its human and non-human resources. The non-human resources may be anything from a fish hatchery, to a library, to a museum or a business. Human resources might be, perhaps, a retired author of a history book who works well with youngsters, or an artist or musician in their twilight years, who have a lot to contribute to young persons, or a businessman who would let gifted children who are interested in business work with him on a Friday afternoon. The program can establish a booking agent who might be a librarian or a volunteer parent who would have a roster of these mentors. Teachers would send the children that need to go faster than the average to the booking agent, who would make a linkage between the mentor and the youngster. Then the students could pursue in depth, with that mentor, a subject that really excites them. Even though they miss school for a couple of days a week, we found that they usually leapfrog over whatever it is they miss when they were allowed to explore something they find exciting. When they come back to school, they can lead a segment of instruction in the particular topic in which they were interested or assist the teacher in presenting a block of instruction.

We found, also, an interesting serendipity occurring in these communities. Bond levies were passed that didn't pass before. The community became more interested in that community's most valuable resource – their young people – and older people found exciting possibilities in their lives that weren't happening before. It can be good for them as well as for the young people. It can expand the walls of the classroom out into the community and this can make a significant difference. We need to be willing to look at such alternatives because if we're going to have a transformation in education, it's not going to happen by the small changes or gestures we make year to year. It's going to take a major transformation – which is much bigger than change. Such alternatives offer some opportunity for that level of breakthrough.

CARL: Hal, I think that's marvelous, and it reminds me of a story from long ago. A good many years ago, I had a chance to talk with René Dubos, who at that time, was very active in the Rockefeller Institute, which I think has since become Rockefeller University. Anyway, it was a center for research and medicine. I asked him, 'If you had your choice, how would you like to see people educated to work in your institution?' He replied, 'Well, I would like to take them right out of high school and have them work with me and my staff and add other resources for their learning, but the main impetus to the learning would be the mentor relationship with me and with other members of my staff at the institute.' And that was a rather surprising answer so many years ago.

HAL: It seems to me we're talking about developing ways to help each individual student become a fully functioning person, Carl. Just suppose schools were to adopt that as the overall goal of education! How do you imagine they could set about doing it?

CARL: That's a topic for a book, Hal, but they'd probably have to approach it through some intermediate goals that they could operationalize. I've thought about some intermediate or personal goals that might help the student to become more fully functioning. I'll just try to go through those rather briefly.

Rogers' educational goals for the fully functioning student

Opening to experience from without and within

One goal would be to provide opportunity for the student to become realistically open to experience and by that I mean experience coming from without and experience coming from within. It could be done in several different ways to make sure that differing values and differing perspectives on many subjects are presented in the classroom. These presentations would come through the students or from books. That exposure to sharply differing points of view would help students learn both to take their own stances in regard to those issues and to become more independent and more thoughtful choosers of ways of being. Another way of obtaining that goal might be to emphasize field trips that would acquaint the students with different socioeconomic levels, different kinds of organizations, varied lifestyles. Again the locus of evaluation would be within the student, like in your psychology course at Georgetown, being open to the evidence from all sources. A third way to get closer to inner experience would be open discussion by students and the teacher of social problems, personal problems, and controversial issues. Some of those need mentioning: birth control, abortion, premarital sex, use of drugs, problems with parents, the generation gap, things of that sort. These would help the student to become more aware of what he is experiencing within himself. These are just a sample of the ways in which the student would learn to evaluate a wide range of stimuli, to develop his own changing way of being in relation to his world.

Freedom with responsibility

A second goal for a school system would be to provide freedom with responsibility. In the way I would like to see it, decision making would be participatory. There is a marvelous example of that in children with reading disabilities to whom the teacher gave freedom with responsibility. They explained that they didn't want to read aloud in class; they wanted to read privately to her so that their deficiencies wouldn't show up. They made a number of other good suggestions and, together, through mutual decision making, students and teacher worked out a very fine pattern of learning which helped all of them – teacher and students alike. Another aspect of that, one that we're often afraid of, is that when decisions are made people must live with the consequences. That's a part of the responsibility of having freedom and often we're reluctant to see the child suffer because of a bad decision. The time–worn example is the first time a child gets an allowance, it is all spent on the first day. Alright, the child has to live with the consequences of that. If we provide extra money to meet wants or needs during the week, we do the child a terrible injustice – we prevent the child from learning through experiencing his/her own choices. In general, what I'm saying is that the opportunity and the freedom to make mistakes would be a large part of the curriculum – the freedom to fail, as you described it in an earlier chapter on management. I think that we have this terrible notion that mistakes are not to be made. Yet mistakes provide our most valuable learning experiences and, in a way, they should be treasured. The opportunity to make mistakes and to learn from them should not be neglected or put down as wrong.

Living with expectations

The third goal would be to help students live with their expectations. This would involve a recognition that, in any vital life, there is changing-ness. When I wonder how it could be implemented, I think of periodic self-evaluation. What have I learned, how have I grown and changed, how have I become different? If students were given the opportunity to make such periodic self-evaluations, like in your psychology class at Georgetown, I think they would recognize within themselves the changes that have and are occurring which can be of some value to themselves.

Encouraging creativity

Another goal would be to encourage creativity in every field. I think we are lacking in imagination on that, encouraging students to look to art, to writing, to expressive movement, to sculpture, to use of materials, to dance, to theater, and to drama, as ways of expressing their own uniquenesses. There are all kinds of ways in which creativity can be expressed. But I don't mean to limit it to art because I think that creativity can be exercised in mathematics or the learning of language. How can I solve this mathematics problem in a new way? How can we be creative in learning this foreign language? Some students have achieved some remarkably creative learning in thinking along these lines.

Develop self-esteem, confidence, and trust in self

Then, an important final goal would be to develop self-esteem, self-confidence, trust in one's self. I think one of the most important questions for teachers and administrators to ask themselves is: Does every student have ample opportunity to gain in self-esteem and self-confidence? That is a question that should be asked every day, not just once a year. People need reinforcing experiences to help develop their trust in themselves. We need to ask: How can we encourage the experiences of self-worth in every grade from kindergarten to high school? How can we encourage it in every kind of activity?

So, those are a few of the special goals which I think could be operationalized at every grade level; thus each student could move toward becoming a more fully functioning person in this school which I have idealistically described. Reinhard Tausch's research presents solid evidence that person-centered teachers do stimulate higher self-confidence in their students.

HAL: Excellent! I would just add that I think those kinds of goals would create the 'You and Me' as opposed to the 'You or Me' world-view which I would like to see our schools hold as a context for students. It would be a context in which students could make a difference in the world. I think that, with the goals that you have specified, we could move in that direction. Carl, is there any last thing you want to say to the parents, teachers, therapists, managers, and educators for whom this book is intended?

Carl Rogers' final thoughts

CARL: Let me see if I can really try to pretend that I'm talking to a group of educators and that perhaps I wouldn't have an opportunity to speak to them again. I probably would say something like this. I realize that you as educators have difficult pressures. Parents, new federal demands and regulations, boards of education, all of these pressures drive you away from teacher–student interaction in the classroom. They also tempt you to play it safe, to keep from rocking the boat, to stick to the traditional ways that are not so likely to be criticized. I feel very sympathetic to you in your difficult situation.

Yet this is a critical time in our history, a time when education can have great social impact. I know that some of you will have the courage to empower the person, to empower yourselves first of all, or to empower your teachers if you are an administrator; and, most of all, to empower your students.

If you trust them, they will respond to that trust. If you can openly be your real self, they will respond to you as a person. If you nourish their exploring, they will grow. If you feed their curiosity, they will learn. If you care for them as persons, they will return that caring. If you can understand their feelings, it will expand and blossom and bloom, and then they will learn more in reading and math, in all the subjects. They will learn to think for themselves, they'll find ways of solving problems, they will speak for themselves as independent persons, they will respond with hard, disciplined work to the climate you have created. They will begin to discover the enormous strength and potential that resides within each one of themselves.

It has been shown that being fully human in the classroom works. The facts – the research evidence – coincide with your most idealistic aims. I hope that when you are tempted to despair, you will remember that, and it will help you have the courage to actualize the best of you as a human person, to bring out the best in your students, the best work, the best learning, the most personal growth. You will be releasing enormous constructive powers. I'm not just talking about a new technique or methods, a patch to be added to an already over-patched education system. I'm talking about a fresh approach in which, by being fully human yourself, you nourish the learning person in the student and help them toward being their own full person. I wish you well in your exceedingly important and difficult task.

Harold Lyon's final thoughts

As I read back through these dialogues I was privileged to share with Carl, I realize just how fortunate I was to have my path cross in such interesting ways with this warm, brilliant, and special man. Similarly, in just completing the fascinating little book *Carl Rogers – The China Diary*, I was thrilled to see glimpses into the future from the young Carl's perspective nearly a century ago! This fresh perspective from Carl gives a wondrous snapshot into the uncensored thinking of the curious, but already passionate, person-centered 20-year-old. Carl writes:

> I wish I knew why I am always so lucky. It seems as if I were always on the inside, by some hook or crook, or accident, whenever there is anything of real interest going on. I am having opportunities that competent men would give a year's pay to have. Yet they just fall into my hands. It means a big responsibility.[1]

In a similar vein, I myself feel very 'lucky' in having been so touched by these extraordinary two men, Rogers and Tausch, and for the opportunity of sharing more of their person-centered philosophy in this book.

Coming from the vastly different polarity of my macho West Point, Ranger background, Carl and his way of being has had a strong influence on my becoming the man I am today. He helped free me from a driven man, 'doing' to succeed and earn the approval (and disapproval) of society, to a man, still doing lots, but gradually becoming more of a man of 'being', who gets more of his approval from within.

In the 1970s, it seemed to me Carl had a vicarious curiosity about my confessions of free experimentation in life and love. He was grounded in the safety of more puritanical mores than I, but he seemed to envy my willingness to adventure out more recklessly. One time he told me that he saw me as one of the courageous pioneers of what marriage and relationships might be like in the future. Carl was as imperfect as the rest of us and was sometimes just wrong. I'm certainly far from a good role model for marriage and have made more tragic mistakes than most!

At the Association for Humanistic Psychology meeting in Hawaii in 1972, I vulnerably shared with Carl that I had fallen hopelessly in love with a young woman and was torn about whether or not to tell my partner about this new love. Drawing more from his experiences in encounter groups than his own personal life, Carl said he felt whether to take the risk of opening up the painful truth to my partner or not was a difficult decision. It was a huge risk, as it would lead to either the end of that relationship or to a positive new level of honesty and fulfillment the relationship had never known. Carl did not prescribe, but helped me in true Rogerian fashion to see my own options.

The total honesty option was based more upon his *theory* for repairing a damaged love relationship, if possible, than it was from his own *real experience*. He would not experience the pain of this decision personally in his own marriage until a few years later. I chose the more painful option and I emerged with a new, seemingly non-Rogerian, belief. Sometimes opening one's self honestly is a selfish cathartic act – more helpful to the one opening than for the one it is dumped upon in the name of honesty. We need not always open every detail of our lives to our partners, as it sometimes selfishly shifts a burden and pain from us to them.

Shelly Kopp used to tell me that it's time to end therapy when you realize you know more of your own truth than the therapist does. And Carl always said the patient has the important answers within and that it's the therapist's role to facilitate the patient's discovery of his own answers. This was my time to end my 'therapy' with Carl and just be a friend. As Leonard Cohen sang, 'Have I carved enough, my Lord?' 'Child, you are a bone'.[2]

What does this self-disclosure have to do with becoming an effective teacher or facilitator of any sort? I leave that to you, the reader, but I suggest that compassion, grit, vulnerability, and self-discovery may have something to do with it.

More than three decades later, and having survived more than my share of crucible-learning experiences, I'm hopefully a bit wiser. I now believe that the rest of my life is about living within a context of love – not just the Eros of those earlier years, but a much broader context, including Eros, Agape, and loving my partner just as she is. This broader context of love includes loving myself, family, precious friends, work, students, nature, and the amazing universe all around me.

In my twilight years, I'm discovering something magical about love: the more love I give, the more I have to give. We never run out of love. Love is not something scarce we need to save up in a 'bank' for that future person or time. Love is all around us and we need to live deeply in it, to give it away freely to others, and risk opening ourselves to receiving it as well. In this life, we only get to keep what we give away. Yes, there's the risk of pain in losing a love, but love is worth the risks. Tennyson was right. ''Tis better to have loved and lost than never to have loved at all'.[3]

Person-centeredness – authenticity, empathy, and caring – is a way to express love. Teachers, and we're all teachers, have unique opportunities to give love and receive it as well. This is the context for the works and lives of Carl Rogers, the Aspys, Flora Roebuck, and Reinhard Tausch. Love is that person-centered ingredient, revealing itself within the meta-analyses of John Hattie and Jef Cornelius-White. This is the secret ingredient often hidden within those dedicated Teach For America teachers who create a context of love for their students with enough grit and commitment to facilitate the raising of their students' grade levels two or three years in one year. Love is truly what person-centeredness is all about. I thank Carl Rogers for helping me to open to this transforming context for life, which was always within me just waiting for me to discover it.

Victor Hugo said, 'Nothing in the world can stop an idea whose time has come.' Is person-centered teaching an idea whose time has come? We have all the empirical evidence we need that person-centered methods work. Do we have the intentionality to create the transformation toward person-centered teaching throughout the world? This is entirely up to you – to each of us individually – to create a context of person-centered teaching in the world.

St Augustine said, 'Surely he who does not believe in miracles will never participate in one.' We need a context – your personal context – and a critical mass of teachers, administrators, and parents in alignment who believe in the evidence we have presented ... and in miracles.

It is important to realize that opposing positions actually contribute toward establishing such a context. The nay-sayers in 1961 who objected to President Kennedy's context of 'A man on the moon in the next decade' actually contributed to it happening. In the civil rights movement in America during the 1960s, all those who opposed civil rights for blacks actually contributed to creating a national dialogue that demonstrated to the country that the issue could no longer be ignored. Let me share my firsthand experience in the context for an idea whose time had come.

I served as the aide-de-camp to Charles Billingslea, the commanding general of the 2nd Infantry Division, which was ordered to go to Oxford, Mississippi in September, 1962 to enforce the Federal Court order to integrate an outstanding black veteran, James Meredith, into the University of Mississippi. We put up roadblocks around 'Ol' Miss' and stopped hundreds of cars from neighboring states and communities carrying people with guns, knives, and explosives coming to defend the 'honor of the South' against us 'Federal invaders'. We were shot at and a Federal Marshal was killed, yet because of good leadership we never fired a shot against an American citizen in the midst of these violent riots.

We were later ordered to enforce the integration of the University of Alabama in Birmingham, blocked by Governor Wallace in what became known as 'The Stand in the Schoolhouse Door'. I was deeply immersed in the midst of this context of the end of segregation in our schools. On June 10, 1963, in Birmingham, Alabama, Governor George Wallace secretly met with us and offered a solution he believed would lead to his own political gain. But his solution was to bring about the end of segregation in America as an idea whose time had come. He said he would stand in the door of the University of Alabama the next morning. If our troops agreed to carry him off before full network television coverage, there would be no more bloodshed, he promised. Nicholas Katzenbach, the Deputy US Attorney General, immediately called the White House and told Bobby Kennedy, who got President Kennedy on the phone, who told my boss, General Charles Billingslea, 'Take that deal.'

All those people, every government official in the South who stood cruelly in the doorway of schools and prevented black children from entering, had been a cause, a part, of the persistence of the problem of the injustices to black citizens. After the creation of the context, 'equal rights and dignity for blacks', the very same inhumane actions that had been a part of the problem's persistence were transformed into actions contributing to the end of legal discrimination against minorities. Every such action contributed to an increased awareness of the issue, to the passage of civil rights legislation, and to the gradual change in attitude that ultimately evidenced itself in the recognition that civil rights was an idea whose time had come. This was now something that all the biased forces in the world could not stop, and in fact helped to bring to fruition.

I have one last thing I want to say, which is sensitive and delicate. Each time some child has his creativity killed off as a consequence of inhumane teaching, that destructive act is further evidence of the need for person-centered teaching. The students crying out in despair for more empathy in Reinhard Tausch's and Renate Hüls research is further moving evidence of the destructiveness of inhumane education. Disturbing as they are, these cries for empathy contribute to people-centered teaching becoming an idea whose time has come. The instant you, the reader, personally create a context for yourself to bring the end of inhumane behavior in your home, your classes, your offices, and on the planet – then such destruction resulting from inhumane behavior occurs within the context of its ending. Suddenly the same destruction that had been a manifestation of the persistence of the inhumanity of it contributes to the end of the problem. This opens the context of person-centered education to become an idea whose time has come … which, as Victor Hugo said, all the forces in the world cannot prevent. Are you willing to open to the miracle – the powerful context of person-centeredness in your life and work?

HCL

Notes

1   Cornelius-White, J. H. D. (ed.) (2012) *Carl Rogers: China Diary*. Ross-on-Wye: PCCS Books, p. 135.
2   Leonard Cohen lyrics from the song 'Teachers'. Available from http://www.song-meanings.net/songs/view/61018/
3   Tennyson, A. L. (1849) *In Memoriam A.H.H.*, canto 27.

THE DEFINITIVE BIBLIOGRAPHY ON PERSON-CENTERED PHILOSOPHY AND CARL ROGERS

This bibliography is modified and printed with the permission of Natalie Rogers from her website: http://www.nrogers.com/carlrogersbiblio.html

It also contains excerpts from *Carl Rogers The Quiet Revolutionary: An Oral History*, Carl R. Rogers and David E. Russell (Penmarin Books, 2002. www.penmarin.com)

The bibliography is divided into four sections:

1. Books by Carl Rogers, listed chronologically
2. Articles by Carl Rogers, listed chronologically
3. Books about Carl Rogers and the person-centered approach, listed alphabetically
4. Articles about Carl Rogers and the person-centered approach, listed alphabetically.

Acknowledgments

This bibliography has been compiled from bibliographies collected by the following authors and editors whose contributions to the person-centered approach have been extensive over the years. With gratitude, we wish to acknowledge:

Tom Greening, professor at Saybrook Graduate School, San Francisco, and editor of the *Journal of Humanistic Psychology*, which has devoted several entire issues to Carl Rogers and the person-centered approach, as well as numerous articles by and about Carl over its forty-year span.

Howard Kirschenbaum, author of the definitive biography on Carl Rogers, *The Life and Works of Carl R. Rogers*, and *On Becoming Carl Rogers*, coeditor of the *Carl Rogers Reader* and the *Carl Rogers Dialogues*, and many other books. He is chairman of the Department of Counseling and Human Development at the Warner Graduate School of Education, University of Rochester, Rochester, New York.

Germain Lietaer, professor at the Catholic University of Leuven, where he teaches client-centered/experiential psychotherapy and process research in psychotherapy and is a staff member of their postgraduate training. His extensive bibliographical collection of client-centered/experiential psychotherapy, ranging over sixty years, includes works in five languages. His survey of books from 1939 to 2001 is published in the May 2002 issue of the *Journal of Humanistic Psychology*.

David Mearns, Professor of Counseling at the University of Strathclyde, Glasgow, Scotland. He is the author of several books on person-centered counseling.

David Russell, director of the Davidson Library Oral History Program at the University of California, Santa Barbara, where the Carl Rogers Archives are located. He interviewed Carl Rogers, as well as transcribed, compiled, and edited the material for this oral history.

Peter Schmid, associate professor at the University of Graz, visiting professor at the Hochschule, St Gabriel, and teacher at several universities in Austria and Europe. He is in private practice and is a trainer at the Academy for Counseling and Psychotherapy at the Institute for Person-Centered Studies, Austria. He is the founder of Person-Centered Training in Austria and the author of many books. His website has bibliographical entries in nine languages: http://www.pfs-online.at/rogers.htm.

Alberto Segrera, professor in the Department of Education and Human Development at Universidad Iberoamericana, Mexico City. As a colleague of Carl Rogers, he organized and facilitated many international person-centered forums. His website has bibliographical entries in seven languages: http://aiecp.bib.uia.mx/aiecp.

Brian Thorne, professor emeritus and former director of counseling at the University of East Anglia, Norwich, England, and a founding member of the Norwich Center for Personal and Professional Development. He has authored several books on the person-centered approach and Carl Rogers.

The Department of Special Collections at the Davidson Library, University of California, Santa Barbara, contains selected papers, photographs, audio and videotapes of Carl Rogers. The papers include records from his association with the Center for Studies of the Person (a group he cofounded), reprint articles from the Carl Rogers Memorial Library (now extinct), diaries, University of Chicago Counseling Center discussion papers, correspondence and his China diary. The audio- and videotapes include outstanding works, such as 'The Steel Shutter' and 'The Journey into Self'.

To access any papers or audiovisual materials, visit the Carl Rogers Archives website at http://www.oac.cdlib.org/cgi-bin/oac/ucsb/rogers. On the left side of the opening page, you will find audiovisual materials and a list of papers under 'Container List'. For a description of the listed papers, go to 'Series Descriptions'. The Archives can make copies of any item listed there. Their reproduction policy is detailed on their webpage at http://www.library.ucsb.edu/speccoll/copies.html.

Natalie Rogers

Books by Carl R. Rogers

Rogers, Carl R. *Measuring Personality Adjustment in Children Nine to Thirteen Years of Age*. New York: Teachers College, Columbia University, 1931.

Rogers, Carl R. *The Clinical Treatment of the Problem Child*. Boston: Houghton Mifflin, 1939.

Rogers, Carl R. *Counseling and Psychotherapy: Newer Concepts in Practice*. Boston: Houghton Mifflin, 1942.

Rogers, Carl R., and John L. Wallen. *Counseling with Returned Servicemen*. New York: McGraw-Hill, 1946.

Rogers, Carl R. *Client-Centered Therapy: Its Current Practice, Implications, and Theory*. Boston: Houghton Mifflin, 1951.

Rogers, Carl R., and Rosalind F. Dymond, eds, *Psychotherapy and Personality Change: Coordinated Research Studies in the Client-Centered Approach*. Chicago: University of Chicago Press, 1954.

Rogers, Carl R. Chapter in H. Greenwald, ed., *Great Cases in Psychoanalysis*. New York: Ballantine Books, 1959.

Rogers, Carl R. 'A Therapist's View of Personal Goals'. *Pendle Hill Pamphlet 108*, Wallingford, PA, 1960.

Rogers, Carl R. *On Becoming a Person: A Therapist's View of Psychotherapy*. Boston: Houghton Mifflin, 1961. Also published in 1965 with a new introduction by Peter Kramer.

Rogers, Carl R. *Personal Adjustment Inventory: A Series of Character and Personality Tests: A Manual of Directions*. New York: Associated Press, 1961.

Rogers, Carl R., and Barry Stevens. *Person to Person: The Problem of Being Human: A New Trend in Psychology*. Walnut Creek, CA: Real People Press, 1967.

Rogers, Carl R., E. T. Gendlin, D. J. Kiesler, and C. B. Truax, eds, *The Therapeutic Relationship and Its Impact: A Study of Psychotherapy with Schizophrenics*. Madison, WI: University of Wisconsin Press, 1967.

Rogers, Carl R., and William R. Coulson, eds, *Man and the Science of Man*. Columbus, OH: Charles E. Merrill, 1968.

Rogers, Carl R. *Freedom to Learn: A View of What Education Might Become*. Columbus, OH: Charles E. Merrill, 1969.

Rogers, Carl R. *Carl Rogers on Encounter Groups*. New York: Harper and Row, 1970.

Rogers, Carl R. *Becoming Partners: Marriage and Its Alternatives*. New York: Delacorte Press, 1972.

Rogers, Carl R. *Carl Rogers on Personal Power: Inner Strength and Its Revolutionary Impact*. New York: Delacorte Press, 1977.

Rogers, Carl R. *A Way of Being*. Boston: Houghton Mifflin, 1980. Also published in 1995 with a new introduction by Irvin Yalom.

Rogers, Carl R. *Freedom to Learn for the '80s*. Columbus, Ohio: Charles E. Merrill, 1983.

Rogers, Carl R. *Carl Rogers Dialogues: Conversations with Martin Buber, Paul Tillich, B. F. Skinner, Gregory Bateson, Michael Polanyi, Rollo May, and Others*, ed. Howard Kirschenbaum and Valerie Land Henderson. Boston: Houghton Mifflin, 1989.

Rogers, Carl R. *The Carl Rogers Reader*, ed. Howard Kirschenbaum and Valerie Land Henderson. Boston: Houghton Mifflin, 1989.

Rogers, Carl R., and H. J. Freiberg. *Freedom to Learn*. Columbus, OH: Charles E. Merrill, 1994.

Rogers, Carl R. *Carl Rogers: Student-Centered Learning*. Project Innovation. Chula Vista, CA, 1996.

Articles by Carl R. Rogers

Rogers, Carl R. 'An Experiment in Christian Internationalism'. *Intercollegian (YMCA)* 39, no. 9 (1922).

Rogers, Carl, with C. W. Carson. 'Intelligence as a Factor in Camping Activities'. *Camping Magazine* 3, no. 3 (1930): 8–11.

Rogers, Carl R. 'A Test of Personality Adjustment'. New York: Association Press, 1931.

Rogers, Carl R. 'Personality Adjustment Inventory'. New York: Association Press, 1931. Slightly revised form of 'A Test of Personality Adjustment', 1931.

Rogers, Carl R., and Mitchell E. Rappaport. 'We Pay for the Smiths'. *Survey Graphic* 19 (1931): 508.

Rogers, Carl R. 'A Good Foster Home: Its Achievements and Limitations'. *Mental Hygiene* 17 (1933): 21–40. Also published in F. Lowry, ed., *Readings in Social Case Work*. New York: Columbia University Press, 1933.

Rogers, Carl R. 'Social Workers and Legislation'. *New York State Conference on Social Work Quarterly Bulletin, Syracuse* (1936): 48–54.

Rogers, Carl R. 'The Clinical Psychologist's Approach to Personality Problems'. *Family* (1937): 18, 233, 243.

Rogers, Carl R. 'Three Surveys of Treatment Measures Used with Children'. *American Journal of Orthopsychiatry* 7, no. 1 (1937): 48–57.

Rogers, Carl R. 'A Diagnostic Study of Rochester Youth'. *New York State Conference on Social Work Quarterly Bulletin, Syracuse* (1938): 48–54.

Rogers, Carl R. 'Authority and Case Work – Are They Compatible?' *New York State Conference on Social Work Quarterly Bulletin, Albany* (1939): 16–24.

Rogers, Carl R. 'Needed Emphasis in the Training of Clinical Psychologists'. *Journal of Consulting Psychology* 3 (1939): 141–43.

Rogers, Carl R. 'The Process of Therapy'. *Journal of Consulting Psychology* 4, no. 5 (1940): 61–64.

Rogers, Carl R. 'Psychology in Clinical Practice'. In J. S. Gray, ed., *Psychology in Use*. New York: American Book Company, 1941.

Rogers, Carl R., and Chester C. Bennett. 'The Clinical Significance of Problem Syndromes'. *American Journal of Orthopsychiatry* 11, no. 2 (April 1941): 222–29.

Rogers, Carl R. 'Predicting the Outcomes of Treatment'. *American Journal of Orthopsychiatry* 11, no. 2 (April 1941): 210–21.

Rogers, Carl R. 'Mental Health Problems in Three Elementary Schools'. *Educational Research Bulletin* 21 (1942): 69–79.

Rogers, Carl R. 'The Psychologist's Contributions to Parent, Child, and Community Problems'. *Journal of Consulting Psychology* 6, no. 1 (1942): 8–18.

Rogers, Carl R. 'The Use of Electrically Recorded Interviews in Improving Psychotherapeutic Techniques'. *American Journal of Orthopsychiatry* 12, no. 3 (1942): 429–34.

Rogers, Carl R., and T. C. Holy, et al. 'A Study of the Mental Health Problems in Three Representative Elementary Schools'. In *A Study of Health and Physical Education in Columbus Public Schools*. Ohio State University Bureau of Education Research Monograph 25, 1942: 130–61.

Rogers, Carl R. 'Therapy in Guidance Clinics'. *Journal of Abnormal Social Psychology* 38 (1943): 284–89. Also published in R. Watson, ed., *Readings in Clinical Psychology*. New York: Harper and Row, 1943.

Rogers, Carl R. 'The Development of Insight in a Counseling Relationship'. *Journal of Consulting Psychology* 8, no. 6 (1944): 331–41.

Rogers, Carl R. 'Psychological Adjustments of Discharged Service Personnel'. *Psychological Bulletin* 41, no. 10 (1944): 689–96.

Rogers, Carl R. 'Wartime Issues in Family Counseling'. *Journal of Home Economics* 36 no. 7 (1944): 390–93.

Rogers, Carl R. 'Counseling'. *Review of Educational Research* 15 (1945): 155–63.

Rogers, Carl R. 'A Counseling Viewpoint for the USO Worker'. *USO Program Services Bulletin* (1945).

Rogers, Carl R. 'Dealing with Individuals in USO'. *USO Program Services Bulletin* (1945).

Rogers, Carl R. 'The Non-Directive Method as a Technique for Social Research'. *American Journal of Sociology* 50 (1945): 279–83.

Rogers, Carl R., R. Dicks, and S. B. Wortis. 'Current Trends in Counseling: A Symposium'. *Marriage and Family Living* 7, no. 4 (1945).

Rogers, Carl R., and V. M. Axline. 'Teacher–Therapist Deals with a Handicapped Child'. *Journal of Abnormal and Social Psychology* 40, no. 2 (1945): 119–42.

Rogers, Carl R. 'Psychometric Tests and Client-Centered Counseling'. *Educational Psychological Measurement* 6 (1946): 139–44.

Rogers, Carl R. 'Recent Research in Nondirective Therapy and Its Implications'. *American Journal of Orthopsychiatry* 16 (1946): 581–88.

Rogers, Carl R. 'Significant Aspects of Client-Centered Therapy'. *American Psychologist* 1, no. 10 (1946): 415–22.

Rogers, Carl R., and G. A. Muench. 'Counseling of Emotional Blocking in an Aviator'. *Journal of Abnormal and Social Psychology* 41 (1946): 207–16.

Rogers, Carl R. 'The Case of Mary Jane Tilden'. In W. U. Snyder, ed., *Casebook of Nondirective Counseling*. Boston: Houghton Mifflin, 1947.

Rogers, Carl R. 'Current Trends in Psychotherapy'. In W. Dennis, ed., *Current Trends in Psychology*. Pittsburgh, PA: University of Pittsburgh Press, 1947.

Rogers, Carl R. 'Research in Psychotherapy: Round Table'. *American Journal of Orthopsychiatry* 18 (1947): 96–100.

Rogers, Carl R. 'Some Observations on the Organization of Personality'. *American Psychologist* 2 (1947): 358–68. Also published in A. Kuenzli, ed., *The Phenomenological Problem*. New York: Harper and Row.

Rogers, Carl R. 'Dealing with Social Tensions: A Presentation of Client-Centered Counseling as a Means of Handling Interpersonal Conflict'. *Pastoral Psychology* 3, no. 28 (1948): 14–20; 3, no. 29 (1948): 37–44.

Rogers, Carl R. 'Divergent Trends in Methods of Improving Adjustment'. *Harvard Educational Review* 18, no. 4 (1948): 209–19.

Rogers, Carl R. 'Some Implications of Client-Centered Counseling for College Personnel Work', part 2. *Educational and Psychological Measurement* 8, no. 3 (1948): 540–49.

Rogers, Carl, Bill L. Kell, and Helen McNeil. 'The Role of Self-Understanding in the Prediction of Behavior'. *Journal of Consulting Psychology* 12 (1948): 174–86.

Rogers, Carl R. 'The Attitude and Orientation of the Counselor in Client-Centered Therapy'. *Journal of Consulting Psychology* (1949): 82–94.

Rogers, Carl R. 'A Coordinated Research in Psychotherapy: A Non-Objective Introduction'. *Journal of Consulting Psychology* 13 (1949): 149–53.

Rogers, Carl R. 'Client-Centered Therapy: A Helping Process'. *University of Chicago Round Table* 698 (1950): 12–21.

Rogers, Carl R. 'A Current Formulation of Client-Centered Therapy, A'. *Social Science Review* 24, no. 4 (1950): 442–50.

Rogers, Carl R. 'The Significance of the Self-Regarding Attitudes and Perceptions'. In M. L. Reymert, ed., *Feelings and Emotions*. New York: McGraw-Hill, 1950. Also published in L. Gorlow and W. Katkovsky, eds, *Readings in the Psychology of Adjustment*. New York: McGraw-Hill, 1959.

Rogers, Carl R. 'What Is to Be Our Basic Professional Relationship?' *Annals of Allergy* 8 (1950): 234–39, 286. Also published in M. H. Krout, ed., *Psychology, Psychiatry, and the Public Interest*. Minneapolis: University of Minnesota Press, 1956.

Rogers, Carl R., D. G. Marquis, and E. R. Hilgard. 'ABEPP Policies and Procedures'. *American Psychologist* 5 (1950): 407–408.

Rogers, Carl R., and R. Becker. 'A Basic Orientation for Counseling'. *Pastoral Psychology* 1, no. 1 (1950): 26–34.

Rogers, Carl R. 'Perceptual Reorganization in Client-Centered Therapy'. In R. R. Blake and G. V. Ramsey, eds, *Perception: An Approach to Personality*. New York: Ronald Press, 1951.

Rogers, Carl R. 'Through the Eyes of a Client'. *Pastoral Psychology* 2, no. 16 (1951): 32–40; no. 17 (1951): 45–50; no. 18 (1951): 26–32.

Rogers, Carl R. 'Where Are We Going in Clinical Psychology?' *Journal of Consulting Psychology* 15 (1951): 171–77.

Rogers, Carl R. 'Client-Centered Psychotherapy'. *Scientific American* 187 (1952): 1–7.

Rogers, Carl R. 'Communication: Its Blocking and Its Facilitation'. *Northwestern University Information* 20, no. 25 (1952): 9–15.

Rogers, Carl R. 'A Personal Formulation of Client-Centered Therapy'. *Marriage and Family Living* 14, no. 4 (1952): 341–61. Also published in C. E. Vincent, ed., *Readings in Marriage Counseling*. New York: T. Y. Crowell, 1957.

Rogers, Carl R., and F. J. Roethlisberger. 'Barriers and Gateways to Communication'. *Harvard Business Review* (July/August 1952): 28–34. Also published in *Harvard Business Review* (1988): 19–25.

Rogers, Carl R. 'The Interest in the Practice of Psychotherapy'. *American Psychologist* 8 (1953): 48–50.

Rogers, Carl R. 'A Research Program in Client-Centered Therapy'. *Psychiatric Treatment, Proceedings of the Association for Research in Nervous and Mental Disease* 21 (1953): 106–13.

Rogers, Carl R. 'Some Directions and End Points in Therapy'. In O. H. Mowrer, ed., *Psychotherapy: Theory and Research*. New York: Ronald Press, 1953.

Rogers, Carl R., et al. 'Removing the Obstacles to Good Employee Communications'. *Management Record* 15, no. 1 (1953): 9–11, 32–40.

Rogers, Carl R. 'Becoming a Person. Two Lectures Delivered on the Nellie Heldt Lecture Fund'. *Oberlin College Nellie Heldt Lecture Series*. Oberlin, OH: Oberlin Printing, 1954.

Rogers, Carl R. 'Studies in Client-Centered Psychotherapy III: The Case of Mrs. Oak – A Research Analysis'. *Psychological Service Center Journal* 3 (1954): 47–165. Also published in C. R. Rogers and R. F. Dymond, eds, *Psychotherapy and Personality Change*. Chicago: University of Chicago Press, 1954.

Rogers, Carl R. 'Towards a Theory of Creativity'. *ETC: A Review of General Semantics* 11 (1954): 249–60.

Rogers, Carl R., et al. 'Studies in Client-Centered Psychotherapy I: Developing a Program of Research in Psychotherapy'. *Psychological Service Center Journal* 3 (1951): 3–28. Also published in C. R. Rogers and R. F. Dymond, eds, *Psychotherapy and Personality Change*. Chicago: University of Chicago Press, 1954.

Rogers, Carl R. 'Facilitation of Personal Growth'. *The School Counselor* 2, no. 1 (January 1955).

Rogers, Carl R. 'A Personal View of Some Issues Facing Psychologists'. *American Psychologist* 10, no. 6 (1955): 1–12. 'Personality Change in Psychotherapy'. *The International Journal of Social Psychiatry* 1 (1955): 31–41.

Rogers, Carl R. 'Persons or Science? A Philosophical Question'. *American Psychologist* 10, no. 7 (1955): 267–78.

Rogers, Carl R. 'Client-Centered Theory'. *Journal of Counseling Psychology* 3, no. 2 (1956): 115–20.

Rogers, Carl R. 'Client-Centered Therapy: A Current View'. In Frieda Fromm-Reichmann and Jacob Levi Moreno, eds, *Progress in Psychotherapy*. New York: Grune and Stratton, 1956.

Rogers, Carl R. 'Counseling Approach to Human Problems, A'. *American Journal of Nursing* 56 (1956): 994–97.

Rogers, Carl R. 'Implications of Recent Advances in the Prediction and Control of Behavior'. *Teachers College Record* 57 (1956): 316–22.

Rogers, Carl R. 'Intellectualized Psychotherapy: Review of George Kelly's "The Psychology of Personal Constructs"'. *Psychology of Personal Constructs, Contemporary Psychology* 1, no. 12 (1956): 357f.

Rogers, Carl R. 'Review of Reinhold Niebuhr's "The Self and the Dramas of History"'. *Chicago Theological Seminary Register* 46 (1956): 13–14.

Rogers, Carl R. 'What It Means to Become a Person'. In C. E. Moustakes, ed., *The Self*. New York: Harper and Brothers, 1956.

Rogers, Carl R., and Burrhus F. Skinner. 'Some Issues Concerning the Control of Human Behavior: A Symposium'. *Science* 124, no. 3231 (1956): 1057–66. Also published in L. Gorlow and W. Katkovsky, eds, *Readings in the Psychology of Adjustment*. New York: McGraw-Hill, 1959; and in R. I. Evans, *Carl Rogers – The Man and His Ideas*. New York: Dutton, 1975.

Rogers, Carl R., et al. 'Behavior Theories and a Counseling Case'. *Journal of Counseling Psychology* 3 (1956): 107–24.

Rogers, Carl R. 'Becoming a Person'. In S. Doniger, ed., *Healing Human and Divine*. New York: Association Press, 1957. Reprinted from 'Becoming a Person', *Oberlin College Nellie Heldt Lecture Series*. Oberlin, OH: Oberlin Printing, 1954.

Rogers, Carl R. 'The Necessary and Sufficient Conditions of Therapeutic Personality Change'. *Journal of Consulting Psychology* 21, no. 2 (1957): 95–103.

Rogers, Carl R. 'A Note on the Nature of Man'. *Journal of Counseling Psychology* 4 (1957): 199–203.

Rogers, Carl R. 'Personal Thoughts on Teaching and Learning'. *Merrill Palmer Quarterly* 3 (1957): 241–43. Also published in Howard Kirschenbaum and Valerie Land Henderson, eds, *The Carl Rogers Reader*. Boston: Houghton Mifflin, 1989.

Rogers, Carl R. 'A Therapist's View of the Good Life'. *Humanist* no. 5 (1957): 291–300. Also published in Howard Kirschenbaum and Valerie Land Henderson, eds, *The Carl Rogers Reader*. Boston: Houghton Mifflin, 1989; also expanded and published in Carl R. Rogers, *On Becoming a Person: A Therapist's View of Psychotherapy*. Boston: Houghton Mifflin, 1961.

Rogers, Carl R. 'Training Individuals to Engage in the Therapeutic Process'. In C. R. Strother, ed., *Psychology and Mental Health*. Washington, DC: American Psychological Association, 1957.

Rogers, Carl R. 'The Characteristics of a Helping Relationship'. *Personnel and Guidance Journal* 37, no. 1 (1958): 6–16.

Rogers, Carl R. 'Concluding Comment of Discussion of R. Niebuhr's "The Self and the Dramas of History"'. *Pastoral Psychology* 9, no. 85 (1958): 15–17.

Rogers, Carl R. 'Listening and Understanding'. *Friend* 116, no. 40 (October 1958): 1248–51.

Rogers, Carl R. 'A Process Conception of Psychotherapy'. *American Psychologist* 13 (1958): 142–49.

Rogers, Carl R. 'The Way to Do Is to Be. Review of "Existence: A New Dimension in Psychiatry and Psychology"'. In Rollo May, Ernest Angel, and Henri F. Ellenberger, eds, *Contemporary Psychology*. New York: Basic Books, 1958: 196–97. Also published in Howard Kirschenbaum and Valerie Land Henderson, eds, *Carl Rogers: Dialogues*. Boston: Houghton Mifflin, 1989.

Rogers, Carl R. 'Client-Centered Therapy'. In Silvano Arieti, ed., *American Handbook of Psychiatry*. Vol. 3. New York: Basic Books, 1959. Also published in Howard Kirschenbaum and Valerie Land Henderson, eds, *Carl Rogers: Dialogues*. Boston: Houghton Mifflin, 1989.

Rogers, Carl R. 'Comments on Cases'. In S. Standal and R. Corsini, eds, *Critical Incidents in Psychotherapy*. New York: Prentice Hall, 1959.

Rogers, Carl R. 'The Essence of Psychotherapy: A Client-Centered View'. *Annals of Psychotherapy* 1 (1959): 51–57.

Rogers, Carl R. 'Lessons I Have Learned in Counseling with Individuals'. In W. E. Dugan, ed., *Modern School Practices, Series 3, Counseling Points of View*. Minneapolis: University of Minnesota Press, 1959: 14–26.

Rogers, Carl R. 'Significant Learning in Therapy and in Education'. *Educational Leadership* 16 (1959): 232–42.

Rogers, Carl R. 'A Tentative Scale for the Measurement of Process in Psychotherapy'. In E. Rubinstein and M. B. Parloff, eds, *Research in Psychotherapy*. Washington, DC: American Psychological Association, 1959: 96–107.

Rogers, Carl R. 'A Theory of Therapy, Personality, and Interpersonal Relationships, as Developed in the Client-Centered Framework'. In Sigmund Koch, ed., *Psychology, a Study of a Science,* Vol. 3, *Formulations of the Person and the Social Context*. New York: McGraw-Hill, 1959.

Rogers, Carl, Madge K. Lewis, and John M. Shlien. 'Time Limited Client-Centered Psychotherapy: Two Cases'. In Arthur Burton, ed., *Case Studies in Counseling and Psychotherapy*. New York: Prentice Hall, 1959.

Rogers, Carl R. 'Significant Trends in the Client-Centered Orientation'. In Daniel Brower and Leonard E. Abt, eds, *Progress in Clinical Psychology*, Vol. 4. New York: Grune and Stratton, 1960.

Rogers, Carl R., Alan W. Walker, and Richard A. Rablen. 'Development of a Scale to Measure Process Changes in Psychotherapy'. *Journal of Clinical Psychology* 16, no. 1 (1960): 79–85.

Rogers, Carl R. 'The Developing Values of the Growing Person'. *Psychiatric Institute Bulletin, University of Wisconsin* 1, no. 13 (1961).

Rogers, Carl R. 'Ellen West and Loneliness'. *Review of Existential Psychology and Psychiatry* 1, no. 2 (1961): 94–101. Also published in Howard Kirschenbaum and Valerie Land Henderson, eds, *The Carl Rogers Reader*. Boston: Houghton Mifflin, 1989.

Rogers, Carl R. 'Introduction to the Symposium'. *Psychiatric Institute Bulletin, University of Wisconsin* 1, no. 10(a) (1961).

Rogers, Carl R. 'The Loneliness of Contemporary Man, as Seen in the Case of Ellen West'. *Review of Existential Psychology and Psychiatry* 1, no. 2 (1961): 94–101.

Rogers, Carl R. 'The Meaning of the Good Life'. In A. E. Kuenzli, ed., *Reconstruction in Religion: A Symposium*. Boston: Beacon, 1961.

Rogers, Carl R. 'Panel Presentation: The Client-Centered Approach to Certain Questions Regarding Psychotherapy'. *Annals of Psychotherapy* 2 (1961): 51–53.

Rogers, Carl R. 'The Place of the Person in the New World of Behavioral Sciences'. *Personnel and Guidance Journal* 39, no. 6 (1961): 442–51. Also published as 'The Behavioral Sciences and the Person'. In Carl R. Rogers, *On Becoming a Person*. Boston: Houghton Mifflin, 1961.

Rogers, Carl R. 'The Potential of the Human Individual. The Capacity for Becoming Fully Functioning'. In Arthur Burton, ed., *The Conception of Man*. 1961. Also published in *Journal of Education* 22 (1964/1965): 1–14.

Rogers, Carl R. 'The Process Equation of Psychotherapy'. *American Journal of Psychotherapy* 15, no. 1 (1961): 27–45. Also published in Joseph T. Hart and T. M. Tomlinson, *New Directions in Client-Centered Therapy*. Boston: Houghton Mifflin, 1970.

Rogers, Carl R. 'A Theory of Personality with Schizophrenics and a Proposal for Its Empirical Investigation'. In J. G. Dawson, H. K. Stone, and N. P. Dellis, eds, *Psychotherapy with Schizophrenics*. Baton Rouge: Louisiana State University Press, 1961.

Rogers, Carl R. 'Two Divergent Trends'. In *Existential Psychology*. New York: Random House, 1961.

Rogers, Carl R. 'What We Know about Psychotherapy'. *Pastoral Psychology* 12 (1961): 31–38.

Rogers, Carl R. 'Comment on Article by F. L. Vance'. *Journal of Counseling Psychology* 9, (1962): 16–17.

Rogers, Carl R. 'The Interpersonal Relationship: The Core of Guidance'. *Harvard Educational Review* 32, no. 4 (1962): 416–29.

Rogers, Carl R. 'Niehbuhr on the Nature of Man'. In S. Doniger, ed., *The Nature of Man*. New York: Harper and Brothers, 1962.

Rogers, Carl R. 'Some Learnings from a Study of Psychotherapy with Schizophrenics'. *Pennsylvania Psychiatric Quarterly* (1962): 3–15.

Rogers, Carl R. 'A Study of Psychotherapeutic Change in Schizophrenics and Normals: The Design and Instrumentation'. *Psychiatric Research Reports* 15 (1962): 51–60.

Rogers, Carl R. 'Toward Becoming a Fully Functioning Person'. In A. W. Combs, ed., *Perceiving, Behaving, Becoming, 1962 Yearbook*. Washington, DC: Association for Supervision and Curriculum Development, 1962.

Rogers, Carl R. 'The Actualizing Tendency in Relation to "Motives" and to Consciousness'. In Marshall R. Jones, ed., *Nebraska Symposium on Motivation*. Lincoln: University of Nebraska, 1963.

Rogers, Carl R. 'The Concept of the Fully Functioning Person'. *Psychotherapy: Theory, Research, and Practice* 1, no. 1 (1963): 17–26. Also published in a revised version, 'The Goal: The Fully Functioning Person', in Carl R. Rogers, *Freedom to Learn: A View of What Education Might Become*. Columbus, OH: Charles E. Merrill, 1969; and in Carl R. Rogers, *Freedom to Learn for the '80s*. Columbus, OH: Charles E. Merrill, 1983.

Rogers, Carl R. 'Learning to Be Free'. In Seymour M. Farber and Robert H. Wilson, eds, *Conflict and Creativity: Control of the Mind*. New York: McGraw-Hill, 1963. Also published in Carl R. Rogers and Barry Stevens, *Person to Person: The Problem of Being Human*. Walnut Creek, CA: Real People Press, 1967.

Rogers, Carl R. 'Psychotherapy Today: Or, Where Do We Go from Here?' *American Journal of Psychotherapy* 17, no. 1 (1963): 5–16.

Rogers, Carl R. 'Toward a Science of the Person'. *Journal of Humanistic Psychology* 3 (Fall 1963). Also published in T. W. Wann, ed., *Behaviorism and Phenomenology: Contrasting Bases for Modern Psychology*. Chicago: University of Chicago Press, 1964.

Rogers, Carl R. 'Freedom and Commitment'. *Humanist* 24, no. 2 (1964): 37–40. Also published as Chapter 13 in Carl R. Rogers, *Freedom to Learn: A View of What Education Might Become*. Columbus, OH: Charles E. Merrill, 1969; and in Carl R. Rogers, *Freedom to Learn for the '80s*. Columbus, OH: Charles E. Merrill, 1983.

Rogers, Carl R. 'Toward a Modern Approach to Values: The Valuing Process in the Mature Person'. *Journal of Abnormal and Social Psychology* 68, no. 2 (1964): 160–67.

Rogers, Carl R. 'An Afternoon with Carl Rogers'. *Explorations* 3 (1965): 104.

Rogers, Carl R. 'Can We Meet the Need for Counseling? A Suggested Plan'. *Marriage and Family* 2, no. 3 (September 1965): 4–6.

Rogers, Carl R. 'Dealing with Psychological Tensions'. *Journal of Applied Behavioral Science* 1, no. 1 (1965): 6–24.

Rogers, Carl R. Foreword to H. Anderson, *Creativity in Childhood Adolescence*. Palo Alto, CA: Science and Behavior Books, 1965.

Rogers, Carl R. 'A Humanistic Conception of Man'. In Richard Farson, ed., *Science and Human Affairs*. Palo Alto, CA: Science and Behavior Books, 1965. Also published in G. B. Carr, ed., *Marriage and Family in a Decade of Change*. Reading, MA: Addison-Wesley, 1972.

Rogers, Carl R. 'Psychology and Teacher Training'. In D. B. Gowan and C. Richardson, eds, *Five Fields and Teacher Education*. Ithaca, NY: One Publications/Cornell University Press, 1965.

Rogers, Carl R. 'Some Questions and Challenges Facing a Humanistic Psychology'. *Journal of Humanistic Psychology* 5 (Spring 1965): 105–107.

Rogers, Carl R. 'Some Thoughts Regarding the Current Philosophy of the Behavioral Sciences'. *Journal of Humanistic Psychology* 5 (Fall 1965): 182–93.

Rogers, Carl R. 'The Therapeutic Relationship: Recent Theory and Research'. *Australian Journal of Psychology* 17, no. 2 (1965).

Rogers, Carl R. 'To Facilitate Learning'. In M. Provus, ed., *Innovations for Time to Teach*. Washington, DC: National Education Association, 1966.

Rogers, Carl R. 'Autobiography'. In E. W. Boring and G. Lindzey, eds, *A History of Psychology in Autobiography,* Vol. 5. New York: Appleton/Century/Crofts, 1967.

Rogers, Carl R. 'Carl Rogers Speaks out on Groups and the Lack of a Human Science: An interview'. *Psychology Today* 1 (December 1967): 19–21, 62–66.

Rogers, Carl R. 'Client-Centered Therapy'. In A. M. Freedman and H. I. Kaplan, eds, *Comprehensive Textbook of Psychiatry.* Baltimore, MD: Williams and Wilkins, 1967.

Rogers, Carl R. 'The Facilitation of Significant Learning'. In L. Siegel, ed., *Contemporary Theories of Instruction.* San Francisco: Chandler, 1967.

Rogers, Carl R. 'The Interpersonal Relationship in the Facilitation of Learning'. In T. Leeper, ed., *Humanizing Education.* National Education Association, Association for Supervision and Curriculum Development, 1967: 1–18. Also published in J. T. Hart and T. M. Tomlinson, eds, *New Directions in Client-Centered Therapy.* Boston: Houghton Mifflin, 1970; and in Howard Kirschenbaum and Valerie Land Henderson, eds, *The Carl Rogers Reader.* Boston: Houghton Mifflin, 1989.

Rogers, Carl R. 'A Plan for Self-Directed Change in an Educational System'. *Educational Leadership* 24, no. 8 (1967): 717–31.

Rogers, Carl R. 'The Process of the Basic Encounter Group'. In James F. Bugental, *The Challenges of Humanistic Psychology.* New York: McGraw-Hill, 1967. Also published in J. T. Hart and T. M. Tomlinson, eds, *New Directions in Client-Centered Therapy.* Boston: Houghton Mifflin, 1970.

Rogers, Carl R. 'What Psychology Has to Offer to Teacher Education'. In *Teacher Education and Mental Health – Association for Student Teaching.* Cedar Falls: State College of Iowa, 1967: 37–57.

Rogers, Carl R. 'Graduate Education in Psychology: A Passionate Statement'. *OPA Quarterly* 21, no. 4 (1968).

Rogers, Carl R. 'The Interpersonal Relationship in the Facilitation of Learning'. In *The Virgil E. Herrick Memorial Lecture Series.* Columbus, OH: Charles E. Merrill, 1968.

Rogers, Carl R. 'Interpersonal Relationships. USA 2000'. *Journal of Applied Behavioral Science* 4, no. 3 (1968): 265–80.

Rogers, Carl R. 'A Practical Plan for Educational Revolution'. In R. R. Goulet, ed., *Educational Change: The Reality and the Promise.* New York: Citation Press, 1968.

Rogers, Carl R. 'Review of J. Kavanaugh's Book, *A Modern Priest Looks at His Outdated Church'. Psychology Today* 13 (1968).

Rogers, Carl R., and Michael Polanyi. 'Dialogue Between Michael Polanyi and Carl Rogers'. *ETC: A Review of General Semantics XXV* 1, no. 3 (1968). Also published in Carl R. Rogers and William R. Coulson, *Man and the Science of Man.* Columbus, OH: Charles E. Merrill, 1968; and in Howard Kirschenbaum and Valerie Land Henderson, eds, *Carl Rogers: Dialogues*. Boston: Houghton Mifflin, 1989.

Rogers, Carl R. 'Community: The Group'. *Psychology Today* 3 (December 1969): 27–61.

Rogers, Carl R. 'The Increasing Involvement of the Psychologist in Social Problems. Some Comments, Positive and Negative'. *Journal of Applied Behavioral Sciences* 5, no. 1 (1969): 3–7.

Rogers, Carl R. 'The Intensive Group Experience'. In *Psychology Today: An Introduction*. Del Mar, CA: CRM Books, 1969.

Rogers, Carl R. 'Self-Directed Change for Educators. Experiments and Implications'. In E. Morphet and D. E. Jesser, eds, *Preparing Educators to Meet Emerging Needs*. New York: Citation Press/*Scholastic* magazine, 1969.

Rogers, Carl R. 'Some Personal Learnings about Interpersonal Relationships'. *Word* 7, no. 2 (1969): 6–10.

Rogers, Carl R. 'Carl Rogers Resigns from USIU'. *AHP Newsletter* 7, no. 1 (1970).

Rogers, Carl R. 'Carl Rogers Says, "It Is My Observation …"'. *AHP Newsletter* 7, no. 1 (October 1970): 7.

Rogers, Carl R. Foreword and Chapters 9, 16, 22, 25, 26, 27 in J. T. Hart and T. M.Tomlinson, eds, *New Directions in Client-Centered Therapy*. Boston: Houghton Mifflin, 1970. All have been published elsewhere, except the Foreword and Chapter 27, 'Looking Back and Ahead: A Conversation with Carl Rogers conducted by J. T. Hart'.

Rogers, Carl R. 'The Person of Tomorrow'. Commencement Address, Sonoma State College Pamphlet, June 1969. Also published in *USIU Doctoral Society Journal* 3, no. 1 (1970): 11–16; and in G. B. Carr, ed., *Marriage and Family in a Decade of Change*. Reading, MA: Addison–Wesley, 1972; and *Colorado Journal of Educational Research* 12, no. 1 (1972).

Rogers, Carl R. 'Rogers on Change'. *Educate* 3, no. 3 (1970).

Rogers, Carl R. 'Views of USIU'. *AHP Newsletter* 7, no. 1 (1970).

Rogers, Carl R. 'Can Schools Grow Persons?' *Educational Leadership* (December 1971).

Rogers, Carl R. 'Facilitating Encounter Groups'. *American Journal of Nursing* 71, no. 2 (1971).

Rogers, Carl R. 'Forget You Are a Teacher: Carl Rogers Tells Why'. *Instructor* (August/September 1971): 65f.

Rogers, Carl R. 'Psychological Maladjustments vs Continuing Growth'. In *Developmental Psychology*. Del Mar, CA: CRM Books, 1971.

Rogers, Carl R. 'Some Elements of Effective Interpersonal Communication'. *Washington State Journal of Nursing* (May/June 1971): 3–11.

Rogers, Carl R., Willard B. Frick, Abraham H. Maslow, and Gardner Murphy. 'Interview with Dr Carl Rogers'. In *Humanistic Psychology: Interviews with Maslow, Murphy, and Rogers*. Columbus, OH: Charles E. Merrill, 1971.

Rogers, Carl R. 'Bringing Together Ideas and Feelings in Learning'. *Learning Today* 5 (Spring 1972): 32–43.

Rogers, Carl R. 'Comment on Brown and Tedeschi's Article'. *Journal of Humanistic Psychology* 12 (Spring 1972): 16–21.

Rogers, Carl R. 'Carl Rogers, Gardener'. *Human Behavior* 1 (November/December 1972): 16.

Rogers, Carl R. Foreword to L. N. Solomon and B. Berzon, eds, *New Perspectives on Encounter Groups*. San Francisco: Jossey-Bass, 1972.

Rogers, Carl R. Introduction to Haruko Tsuge, 'My Experience in Encounter Group'. *Voices* no. 2, Issue 28 (1972).

Rogers, Carl R. 'Some Social Issues Which Concern Me'. *Journal of Humanistic Psychology* 12, no. 2 (Fall 1972): 45–60.

Rogers, Carl R. 'Comment on Pitts' Article'. *Journal of Humanistic Psychology* 13, no. 1 (Winter 1973): 83–84.

Rogers, Carl R. 'An Encounter with Carl Rogers'. In C. W. Kemper, ed., *Res Publica, Claremont Men's College* 1, no. 1 (1973): 41–51.

Rogers, Carl R. 'The Good Life as an Ever-Changing Process'. Ninth in newspaper series, *America and the Future of Man*, published by Regents of the University of California, and distributed by Copley News Service, 1973.

Rogers, Carl R. 'My Philosophy of Interpersonal Relationships and How It Grew'. *Journal of Humanistic Psychology* 13, no. 2 (Spring 1973): 3–19.

Rogers, Carl R. 'Some New Challenges'. *American Psychologist* 28, no. 5 (1973): 379–87. Also published in Carl R. Rogers, *A Way of Being*. Boston: Houghton Mifflin, 1980; and in Howard Kirschenbaum and Valerie Land Henderson, eds, *The Carl Rogers Reader*. Boston: Houghton Mifflin, 1989.

Rogers, Carl R. 'To Be Fully Alive'. *Penney's Forum* 3 (Spring/Summer 1973).

Rogers, Carl R. 'After Three Years: My View and That of Outside Evaluators'. *Education* 95, no. 2 (1974): 183–89.

Rogers, Carl R. 'Can Learning Encompass Both Ideas and Feelings?' *Education* 95, no. 2 (1974): 103–14; also published, slightly revised, in 1980 in *A Way of Being*. Boston: Houghton Mifflin, 1980: 263–91; and in *Educational Digest* (April 1975): 40, 56–59.

Rogers, Carl R. 'Dear Bonnie'. *Education* 95, no. 2 (1974): 190–96.

Rogers, Carl R. Foreword to Harold Lyon, *It's Me and I'm Here*. New York: Delacorte Press, 1974.

Rogers, Carl R. 'In Retrospect: Forty-Six Years'. *American Psychologist* 29, no. 2 (1974): 115–23.

Rogers, Carl R. 'Interview on "Growth"'. In W. Oltmans, ed., *On Growth: The Crisis of Exploding Population and Resource Depletion*. New York: G. P. Putnam's Sons, 1974.

Rogers, Carl R. 'Introduction'. *Education* 95, no. 2 (Winter 1974): 172.

Rogers, Carl R. 'The Project at Immaculate Heart: An Experiment in Self-Directed Change'. *Education* 95, no. 2 (Winter 1974): 172–89.

Rogers, Carl R. 'Questions I Would Ask Myself If I Were a Teacher'. *Education* 95, no. 2 (1974): 134–39. Also published in *Educational Forum* 51, no. 2 (1987): 115–22.

Rogers, Carl R., and John K. Wood. 'The Changing Theory of Client-Centered Therapy'. In Arthur Burton, ed., *Operational Theories of Personality*. New York: Brunner/Mazel, 1974.

Rogers, Carl R. 'Client-Centered Theory: Carl R. Rogers'. In Arthur Burton, ed., *Operational Theories of Personality*. New York: Brunner/Mazel, 1974.

Rogers, Carl R. 'Client-Centered Psychotherapy'. In H. I. Kaplan, B. J. Sadock, and A. M. Freeman, eds, *Comprehensive Textbook of Psychiatry II*. Baltimore, MD: Williams and Wilkins, 1975.

Rogers, Carl R. 'Empathic – An Unappreciated Way of Being'. *Counseling Psychologist* 5, no. 2 (1975): 2–10. Also published in Carl R. Rogers, ed., *A Way of Being*. Boston: Houghton Mifflin, 1980.

Rogers, Carl R. 'An Interview with Carl Rogers'. *Practical Psychology for Physicians* 2, no. 8 (1975): 43–49.

Rogers, Carl R. Preface to To Thi Anh, *Eastern and Western Cultural Values: Conflict or Harmony?* Manila, Philippines: East Asian Pastoral Institute, 1975.

Rogers, Carl R. 'Beyond the Watershed in Education'. *Teaching–Learning Journal* (Winter/Spring 1976): 43–49.

Rogers, Carl R. 'Beyond the Watershed: And Where Now?' *Educational Leadership* 34, no. 8 (1977): 623–31.

Rogers, Carl R. 'Nancy Mourns'. In Dorothy Nevill, ed., *Humanistic Psychology: New Frontiers*. New York: Gardner, 1977.

Rogers, Carl R. 'Personal Power at Work'. *Psychology Today* 10, no. 11 (1977): 60–62, 93–94.

Rogers, Carl R. 'The Politics of Education'. *Journal of Humanistic Education* 1, no. 1 (1977): 6–22. Also published in Carl R. Rogers, *Freedom to Learn for the '80s*. Columbus, OH: Charles E. Merrill, 1983; and in Howard Kirschenbaum and Valerie Land Henderson, eds, *The Carl Rogers Reader*. Boston: Houghton Mifflin, 1989.

Rogers, Carl R. Preface to R. Fairfield, *Person-Centered Graduate Education*. Elmhurst, IL: Hagle and Co., 1977.

Rogers, Carl R., and T. L. Holdstock. 'Person-Centered Personality Theory'. In R. Corsini, ed., *Current Personality Theories*. Itasca, IL: F. E. Peacock, 1977.

Rogers, Carl R. 'Carl R. Rogers Papers'. *Quarterly Journal of the Library of Congress* 35 (October 1978): 258–59.

Rogers, Carl R. 'Do We Need a Reality?' *Dawnpoint* 1, no. 2 (1978): 6–9.

Rogers, Carl R. 'The Formative Tendency'. *Journal of Humanistic Psychology* 18, no. 1 (Winter 1978): 23–26.

Rogers, Carl R. 'From Heart to Heart: Some Elements of Effective Interpersonal Communication'. *Marriage Encounter* 7, no. 2 (1978): 8–15.

Rogers, Carl R., et al. 'Evolving Aspects of Person-Centered Workshops'. *Self and Society* 6, no. 2 (1978): 43–49. Also published in *AHP Newsletter* (January 1979): 11–14.

Rogers, Carl R. 'The Foundations of the Person-Centered Approach'. *Education* 100, no. 2 (1979): 98–107. Also published in Carl R. Rogers, *A Way of Being*. Boston: Houghton Mifflin, 1980.

Rogers, Carl R. 'Groups in Two Cultures'. *Personal and Guidance Journal* 38, no. 1 (September 1979): 11–15.

Rogers, Carl R., et al. 'Learning in Large Groups: Their Implications for the Future'. *Education* 100, no. 2 (1979): 108–16.

Rogers, Carl R. 'Some New Directions: A Personal View'. In T. Hanna, ed., *Explorers of Humankind*. San Francisco: Harper and Row, 1979.

Rogers, Carl R. 'Growing Old – Or Older and Growing'. *Journal of Humanistic Psychology* 20, no. 4 (Fall 1980): 5–16.

Rogers, Carl R. 'Building Person-Centered Communities. The Implications for the Future'. In Alberto Villoldo and Ken Dytchwald, eds, *Revisioning Human Potential. Glimpses into the 21st Century*. Los Angeles: Tarcher, 1981.

Rogers, Carl R. 'Education: A Personal Activity'. *Educational Change and Development* 3, no. 3 (1981): 1–12.

Rogers, Carl R., and J. Elliott-Kemp. *The Effective Teacher: A Person-Centered Development Guide*. Sheffield, England: PAVIC, 1981.

Rogers, Carl R. 'Notes on Rollo May'. *Perspectives. Humanistic Psychology Institute* 2, no. 1 (1981): 1. Also published in *Journal of Humanistic Psychology* 22 (Summer 1982); and in Howard Kirschenbaum and Valerie Land Henderson, eds, *Carl Rogers: Dialogues*. Boston: Houghton Mifflin, 1989.

Rogers, Carl R. 'Some Unanswered Questions'. *Journey* 1, no. 1 (1981): 1–4.

Rogers, Carl R. 'My Politics'. *Journey* 1, no. 6 (1982): 8.

Rogers, Carl R. 'A Psychologist Looks at Nuclear War: Its Threat, Its Possible Prevention'. *Journal of Humanistic Psychology* 22, no. 4 (Fall 1982): 9–20. Also published in Howard Kirschenbaum and Valerie Land Henderson, eds, *The Carl Rogers Reader*. Boston: Houghton Mifflin, 1989.

Rogers, Carl R. 'Reply to Rollo May's Letter to Carl Rogers'. *Journal of Humanistic Psychology* 22, no. 4 (1982): 85–89.

Rogers, Carl R. 'Carl Rogers Speaks to Montessorians'. *NAMTA Quarterly* 8, no. 4 (1983): 11–15.

Rogers, Carl R. 'I Can't Read!' *Visualtek News* (Summer 1983).

Rogers, Carl R. 'I Walk Softly through Life'. *Voices* 18, no. 4 (1983): 6–14.

Rogers, Carl R. 'A Visit to Credo Mutwa'. *Journey* 2, no. 4 (1983): 4–5.

Rogers, Carl R. 'Gloria – A Historical Note'. In Ronald F. Levant and John M. Shlien, eds, *Client-Centered Therapy and the Person-Centered Approach: New Directions in Theory, Research, and Practice*. New York: Praeger, 1984.

Rogers, Carl R. 'The New World Person'. *Odyssey South Africa* 8, no. 2 (1984): 16–19.

Rogers, Carl R. 'Person-Centered Approach Foundations'. In R. Corsini, ed., *Encyclopedia of Psychology*. New York: John Wiley, 1984.

Rogers, Carl R. 'A Way of Meeting Life: An Interview with Carl Rogers'. *The Laughing Man* 5, no. 2 (1984) 22–23. Also published in part in J. I. Harmann, 'Unconditional Confidence as a Facilitative Precondition', in

G. Lietaer et al., *Client-Centered and Experiential Psychotherapy in the Nineties.* Leuven, Belgium: Leuven University Press, 1990.

Rogers, Carl R., and David Ryback. 'One Alternative to Nuclear Planetary Suicide'. *Counseling Psychologist* 12, no. 2 (1984): 3–12. Also published in Ronald F. Levant and John Shlien, eds, *Client-Centered Therapy and the Person-Centered Approach: New Directions in Theory, Research, and Practice.* New York: Praeger, 1984.

Rogers, Carl R. 'Comment on Slack's Article'. *Journal of Humanistic Psychology* 25, no. 2 (Spring 1985): 43–44.

Rogers, Carl R. 'Reaction to Gunnison's Article on the Similarities Between Erickson and Rogers'. *Journal of Counseling and Development* 63, no. 9 (1985).

Rogers, Carl R. 'Toward a More Human Science of the Person'. *Journal of Humanistic Psychology* 25, no. 4 (Spring 1985): 7–24.

Rogers, Carl R. 'Carl Rogers on the Development of the Person-Centered Approach'. *Person-Centered Review* 1, no. 3 (August 1986): 257–59.

Rogers, Carl R. 'Carl Rogers Says: An Introductory Comment for *The Person-Centered Review*'. *The Person-Centered Review* 1 (February 1986): 3–14.

Rogers, Carl R. 'A Client-Centered/Person-Centered Approach to Therapy'. In I. L. Kutash and A. Wolf, eds, *Psychotherapist's Casebook. Theory and Technique in the Practice of Modern Times.* San Francisco: Jossey-Bass, 1986.

Rogers, Carl R. 'Client-Centered Therapy'. In I. L. Kutash and A. Wolf, *Psychotherapist's Casebook: Theory and Technique in Practice.* San Francisco: Jossey-Bass, 1986.

Rogers, Carl R. 'Commencement Held May 14'. *Teachers College/Columbia University, New York* 14, no. 2 (Summer 1986).

Rogers, Carl R. 'The Dilemmas of a South-African White'. *Person-Centered Review* 1, no. 1 (1986): 15–35.

Rogers, Carl R. 'The Interpersonal Relationship'. *Human Relations* 3 (1986): 151–55.

Rogers, Carl R. 'Reflection of Feelings'. *Person-Centered Review* 1, no. 4 (1986): 375–77.

Rogers, Carl R. 'Rogers, Kohut and Erickson: A Personal Perspective on Some Similarities and Differences'. *Person-Centered Review* 1, no. 2 (1986): 125–40.

Rogers, Carl R. 'The Rust Workshop: A Personal Overview'. *Journal of Humanistic Psychology* 26, no. 3 (Summer 1986): 23–45. Also published in Howard Kirschenbaum and Valerie Land Henderson, eds, *The Carl Rogers Reader.* Boston: Houghton Mifflin, 1989.

Rogers, Carl R. 'This is Me. The Development of My Professional Thinking and My Personal Philosophy'. In Painter et al., eds, *Human Relations.* Needham Heights, MA: Ginn Press, 1986, 126–31. Also published in Howard Kirschenbaum and Valerie Land Henderson, eds, *The Carl Rogers Reader.* Boston: Houghton Mifflin, 1989.

Rogers, Carl R., Rollo May, and Abraham H. Maslow. 'American Politics and Humanistic Psychology'. Dallas, TX: Saybrook Publishing, 1986.

Rogers, Carl R. 'Politics and Innocence: A Humanistic Debate'. San Francisco: Saybrook Publishing, 1986.

Rogers, Carl R. 'Client-Centered? Person-Centered?' *Person-Centered Review* 2, no. 1 (1987): 11–13.

Rogers, Carl R. 'Carl Rogers Column on Reaching 85'. *Person-Centered Review* 2, no. 2 (May 1987): 150–152.

Rogers, Carl R. 'Comment on Shlien's Article, "A Countertheory of Transference"'. *Person-Centered Review* 2, no. 2 (1987): 182–88.

Rogers, Carl R. 'Comments on the Issue of Equality in Psychotherapy'. *Journal of Humanistic Psychology* 27, no. 1 (Winter 1987): 38–40.

Rogers, Carl R. 'Journal of South-African Trip. January 14–March 1'. *Counseling and Values* 32, no. 1 (1987): 21–37. Special issue on Carl Rogers and the person-centered approach to peace.

Rogers, Carl R., and Richard E. Farson. 'Active Listening'. In R. G. Newman, M. A. Danziger, and M. Cohen, eds, *Communication in Business Today*. Washington, DC: Heath and Company, 1987.

Rogers, Carl R., and Ruth Sanford. 'Inside the World of the Soviet Professional'. *Journal of Humanistic Psychology* 27, no. 3 (Summer 1987): 277–304. Also published in Howard Kirschenbaum and Valerie Land Henderson, eds, *The Carl Rogers Reader*. Boston: Houghton Mifflin, 1989.

Rogers, Carl R. 'Reflections on Our South African Experience'. *Counseling and Values* 32, no. 1 (1987): 17–20. Special issue on Carl Rogers and the person-centered approach to peace. Also published in Edward McIlduff and David Coghlan, eds, *The Person-Centered Approach and Cross-Cultural Communication*, Vol. 1. (1991): 87–90.

Rogers, Carl R. and R. C. Sanford, 'Client-Centered Psychotherapy'. In H. I. Kaplan and B. J. Sadock, eds, *Comprehensive Textbook of Psychiatry*, Vol. 5. Baltimore, MD: Williams and Wilkins, 1989.

Rogers, Carl R. 'What Understanding and Acceptance Mean to Me'. *Journal of Humanistic Psychology* 35, no. 4 (Fall 1995).

Books about Carl R. Rogers and the person-centered approach

Amodeo, J., and K. Amodeo. *Being Intimate: A Guide to Successful Relationships*. New York: Arkana, 1986.

Anderson, Rob. *Students as Real People: Interpersonal Communication and Education*. Rochelle Park, NJ: Hayden, 1979.

Anderson, Rob, and Kenneth N. Cissna. *The Martin Buber–Carl Rogers Dialogue: A New Transcript with Commentary*. Ithaca: State University of New York Press, 1997.

Anderson, Rob, and Kenneth N. Cissna. *Moments of Meeting: Buber, Rogers, and the Potential for Human Dialogue*. Albany: State University of New York Press, March 2002.

Aspy, David N. *Toward a Technology for Humanizing Education*. Champaign, IL: Research Press, 1972.

Aspy, David N., and F. N. Roebuck. *Kids Don't Learn from People They Don't Like.* Amherst, MA: Human Resources Development Press, 1977.

Aspy, David N., and J. B. Buhler (1974), *Physical Health for Educators.* Denton, TX: North Texas State University Press.

Auw, A. *Gentle Roads to Survival.* Lower Lake, CA: Aslan Publishing, 1991.

Axline, Virginia. *Dibs, in Search of Self: Personality Development in Play Therapy.* Boston: Houghton Mifflin, 1965.

Axline, Virginia. *Play Therapy.* Boston: Houghton Mifflin, 1947.

Barrett-Lennard, Godfrey T. *Carl Rogers' Helping System: Journey and Substance.* London/Thousand Oaks, CA: Sage Publications, 1998.

Barton, Anthony. *Three Worlds of Therapy: An Existential-Phenomenological Study of the Therapies of Freud, Jung, and Rogers.* Palo Alto, CA: National Press Books, 1974.

Bohart, A. C., and K. Tallman. *How Clients Make Therapy Work.* Washington, DC: American Psychological Association, 1999.

Bohart, A. C., and L. S. Greenberg, eds. *Empathy Reconsidered: New Directions in Psychotherapy.* Washington, DC: American Psychological Association, 1997.

Boukydis, C. C. F. Z. *Support for Parents and Infants: A Manual for Parent Organizations and Professionals.* Boston: Routledge and Kegan Paul, 1985.

Boy, A. V., and G. P. Pine. *A Person-Centered Foundation for Counseling and Psychotherapy,* 2nd ed. Springfield, IL: Charles C. Thomas, 1999.

Boy, A. V., and G. P. Pine. *Child-Centered Counseling and Psychotherapy.* Springfield, IL: Charles C. Thomas, 1995.

Boy, A. V., and G. P. Pine. *The Counselor in the Schools: A Reconceptualization.* Boston: Houghton Mifflin, 1968.

Bozarth, Jerold D. *Person-Centred Therapy: A Revolutionary Paradigm.* Llangarron, Ross-on-Wye: PCCS Books, 1998.

Brazier, David, ed. *Beyond Carl Rogers: Towards a Psychotherapy for the Twenty-First Century.* London: Constable, 1993.

Breggin, P. R. *The Heart of Being Helpful: Empathy and the Creation of a Healing Presence.* New York: Springer, 1997.

Buchanan, L., and R. Hughes. *Experiences of Person-Centred Counselling Training.* Llangarron, Ross-on-Wye: PCCS Books, 2000.

Butler, J. M., L. N. Rice, and A. K. Wagstaff. *Quantitative Naturalistic Research.* Englewood Cliffs, NJ: Prentice Hall, 1963.

Cain, David, and Julius Seeman. *Humanistic Psychotherapies: Handbook of Research and Practice.* Washington, DC: American Psychological Association, 2001.

Campbell, P., and E. McMahon. *The Focusing Steps.* Kansas City, MO: Sheed and Ward, 1991.

Carkhuff, R. R. *Beyond Counseling and Therapy.* New York: Holt, Rinehart and Winston, 1967.

Carkhuff, R. R. *The Development of Human Resources: Education, Psychology and Social Change.* New York: Holt, Rinehart and Winston, 1971.

Carkhuff, R. R. *Helping and Human Relations: A Primer for Lay and Professional Helpers. Vol. 1. Selection and Training.* New York: Holt, Rinehart and Winston, 1969.

Carkhuff, R. R. (1984). *The productive teacher*. Human Resource Development Press, Inc. Amherst, MA.

Carkhuff, R. R., and W. A. Anthony. *The Skills of Helping: An Introduction to Counseling*. Amherst, MA: Human Resource Development Press, 1979.

Carkhuff, R. R., and Berenson, B.G. (1976). *Teaching as Treatment: An Introduction to Counseling and Psychotherapy*. Human Resource Development Press, Amherst: Massachusetts.

Carkhuff, R. R. (1977). *The Skills of Teaching: Interpersonal Skills*. Amherst, MA: Human Resources Development Press.

Carkhuff, R. R. *Art of Helping*. Amherst, MA: Human Resources Development Press, 1983.

Ciaramicoli, A. P., and K. Ketcham. *The Power of Empathy: A Practical Guide to Creating Intimacy, Self-Understanding, and Lasting Love in Your Life*. New York: Dutton/Penguin Books, 2000.

Cohen, David. *Carl Rogers: A Critical Biography*. London: Constable, 1997.

Combs, A. W. *Being and Becoming*. New York: Springer, 1999.

Combs, A. W., and D. L. Avila. *Helping Relationships: Basic Concepts for the Helping Professions*. Boston: Allyn and Bacon, 1985.

Cornelius-White, J. H. D., and A. P. Harbaugh. *Learner-Centered Instruction*. Thousand Oaks, CA, London, New Delhi, Singapore: SAGE Publications, 2010.

Cornelius-White, J. H. D., ed. *Carl Rogers – The China Diary*. Ross-on-Wye, UK: PCCS Books, 2012.

Coulson, W. R. *Groups, Gimmicks and Instant Gurus*. New York: Harper and Row, 1972.

Coulson, W. R. *A Sense of Community*. Columbus, OH: Charles E. Merrill, 1973.

Coulson, W. R., D. Land, and Betty Meador. *The La Jolla Experiment: Eight Personal Views*. La Jolla, CA: Center for Studies of the Person, 1977.

Curran, C. A. *Counseling in Catholic Life and Education*. New York: Macmillan, 1952.

Danish, S. J., and A. E. Hauer. *Helping Skills: A Basic Training Program*. New York: Behavioral Publications, 1973.

DeCarvalho, Roy Jose. *The Founders of Humanistic Psychology*. New York: Praeger, 1991.

DeCarvalho, Roy Jose. *The Growth Hypothesis in Psychology: The Humanistic Psychologies of Abraham Maslow and Carl Rogers*. Lampeter, England: Mellen, 1991. Also published by San Francisco: EM Text, 1991.

Derlega, V. J. *The Therapy Relationship as a Personal Relationship*. New York: Guilford Press, 1991.

Devonshire, C. M., and J. W. Kremer. *Toward a Person-Centered Resolution of Intercultural Conflicts*. Dortmund, Germany: Pädagogische Arbeitsstelle, 1980.

Dillon, J. T. *Personal Teaching*. Columbus, OH: Charles E. Merrill, 1971.

Du Toit, D., H. Grobler, and R. Schenck, eds. *Person-Centred Communication: Theory and Practice*. Halfway House, South Africa: International Thomson Publishing, 1997.

Duncan, B. L., A. D. Solovey, and G. S. Rusk. *Changing the Rules: A Client-Directed Approach to Therapy*. New York: Guilford Press, 1992.

Egan, G. *Face to Face*. Monterey, CA: Brooks/Cole, 1973.

Egan, G. *The Skilled Helper: A Model for Systematic Helping and Interpersonal Relating*. Belmont, CA: Wadsworth, 1975.

Egendorf, A. *Healing from the War: Trauma and Transformation after Vietnam*. Boston: Shambala/Random House, 1986.

Eisenberg, N., and J. Strayer, eds. *Empathy and Its Development*. New York: Cambridge University Press, 1990.

Erskine, R. G., J. P. Moursund, and R. L. Trautmann. *Beyond Empathy: A Therapy of Contact-in-Relationship*. Philadelphia, PA: Brunner/Mazel, 1999.

Esser, U., H. Pabst, and G.-W. Speierer, eds. *The Power of the Person Centered Approach: New Challenges, Perspectives, Answers*. Köln, Germany: GwG, 1996.

Evans, Richard I., ed. *Carl Rogers: The Man and His Ideas*. New York: E. P. Dutton, 1975.

Evans, Richard I., ed. *Dialogue with Carl Rogers*. New York: Praeger, 1981.

Fairfield, Roy. Preface to *Person-Centered Graduate Education*. Elmhurst, IL: Hagle and Co., 1977.

Fairhurst, J., ed. *Women Writing in the Person-Centered Approach*. Llangarron, Ross-on-Wye, UK: PCCS Books, 1999.

Farber, Barry A., Debora C. Brink, and Patricia M. Raskin, eds. *The Psychotherapy of Carl Rogers: Cases and Commentary*. New York: Guilford Press, 1996.

Farson, Richard. *Birthrights*. New York: Macmillan, 1974.

Fierman, L. B. *The Therapist Is the Therapy*. Northvale, NJ: Jason Aronson, 1997.

Flanagan, K. *Focusing on Your Emotional Intelligence*. Dublin: Marino, 1998.

Friedman, M. *The Healing Dialogue in Psychotherapy*. New York: Jason Aronson, 1985.

Friedman, N. *Experiential Therapy and Focusing*. New York: Half Court Press, 1982.

Fusek, L., ed. *New Directions in Client-Centered Therapy: Practice with Difficult Client Populations*. Monograph Series 1. Chicago: Chicago Counseling and Psychotherapy Center, 1991.

Gendlin, Eugene T. *Experiencing and the Creation of Meaning*. New York: Free Press of Glencoe, 1962.

Gendlin, Eugene T. *Focusing*, revised ed. New York: Bantam Books, 1981.

Gendlin, Eugene T. *Focusing-Oriented Psychotherapy. A Manual of the Experiential Method*. New York: Guilford Press, 1996.

Gendlin, Eugene T. *Let Your Body Interpret Your Dreams*. Wilmette, IL: Chiron, 1986.

Ginott, H. *Group Psychotherapy with Children*. New York: McGraw-Hill, 1961.

Goodman, G. *Companionship Therapy: Studies in Structured Intimacy*. San Francisco: Jossey-Bass, 1972.

Goodman, G., and E. Esterly. *The Talk Book. The Intimate Science of Communicating in Close Relationships.* New York: Ballantine Books, 1988.

Gordon, Thomas. *Group-Centered Leadership.* Boston: Houghton Mifflin, 1955.

Gordon, Thomas. *Leader Effectiveness Training: LET.* New York: P. H. Wyden Books, 1977. Republished by Bantam Books, 1980.

Gordon, Thomas. *Parent Effectiveness Training: The No-Lose Program for Raising Responsible Children.* New York: P. H. Wyden Books, 1970.

Gordon, Thomas. *Teaching Children Self-Discipline.* New York: Times Books, 1989.

Gordon, Thomas, and N. Burch. *TET: Teacher Effectiveness Training.* New York: P. H. Wyden Books, 1974.

Gordon, Thomas, and W. S. Edwards. *Making the Patient Your Partner: Communication Skills for Doctors and Other Caregivers.* London: Auborn House, 1995.

Gorlow, L., E. L. Hoch, and E. F. Telschow. *The Nature of Non-Directive Group Psychotherapy.* New York: Columbia University, 1952.

Graham, K. M., S. J. Saunders, M. C. Flower, C. B. Timney, M.White–Campbell, and A. Z. Pietropaolo. *Addictions Treatment for Older Adults: Evaluation of an Innovative Client Centered Approach.* New York: Haworth, 1995.

Greenberg, L. S., J. C. Watson, and Germain Lietaer, eds. *Handbook of Experiential Psychotherapy.* New York: Guilford Press, 1998.

Greenberg, L. S., and J. D. Safran. *Emotion in Psychotherapy.* New York: Guilford Press, 1987.

Greenberg, L. S., L. N. Rice, and R. Elliott. *Facilitating Emotional Change: The Moment-by-Moment Process.* New York: Guilford Press, 1993.

Greenberg, L. S., and S. C. Paivio. *Working with Emotions in Psychotherapy.* New York: Guilford Press, 1997.

Greenberg, L. S., and S. Johnson. *Emotionally-Focused Therapy for Couples.* New York: Guilford Press, 1988.

Guerney, B. G. *Psychotherapeutic Agents: New Roles for Non-Professionals, Parents and Teachers.* New York: Holt, Rinehart and Winston, 1969.

Guerney, B. G. *Relationship Enhancement Manual.* State College, PA: Ideals, 1988.

Guerney, B. G. *Relationship Enhancement: Marital/Family Therapists' Manual.* State College, PA: Ideals, 1987.

Guerney, B. G. *Relationship Enhancement: Skill-Training Programs for Therapy, Problem Prevention, and Enrichment.* San Francisco: Jossey–Bass, 1977.

Guerney, L. *Parenting: A Skills Training Manual.* State College, PA: Ideals, 1978.

Guidano, V. F. *The Self in Process.* New York: Guilford Press, 1993.

Harré, R. *The Singular Self: An Introduction to the Psychology of Personhood.* London: Sage Publications, 1997.

Hart, J. T., and T. M. Tomlinson, eds. *New Directions in Client-Centered Therapy.* Boston: Houghton Mifflin, 1970.

Harwood, I. N. H., and M. Pines, eds. *Self Experiences in Group: Intersubjective and Self-Psychological Pathways to Human Understanding.* London: Jessica Kingsley, 1998.

Haugh, S., and Tony Merry, eds. *Empathy*. Llangarron, Ross-on-Wye, UK: PCCS Books, 2001.

Hedges, L. *Listening Perspectives in Psychotherapy*. New York: Jason Aronson, 1991.

Hermans, H. J. M., and E. Hermans-Jansen. *Self-Narratives: The Construction of Meaning in Psychotherapy*. New York: Guilford Press, 1995.

Heron, J. *Sacred Science: Person-Centred Inquiry into the Spiritual and the Subtle*. Llangarron, Ross-on-Wye, UK: PCCS Books, 1998.

Hill, J. *Person-Centred Approaches in Schools*. Llangarron, Ross-on-Wye, UK: PCCS Books, 1994.

Hinterkopf, E. *Integrating Spirituality in Counseling: A Manual for Using the Experiential Focusing Method*. Alexandria, VA: American Counseling Association, 1998.

Hirayama, E. *The Process of Personal Growth in Encounter Groups*. Japan, 1998.

House, R., and N. Totton, eds. *Implausible Professions: Arguments for Pluralism and Autonomy in Psychotherapy and Counselling*. Llangarron, Ross-on-Wye, UK: PCCS Books, 1997.

Hughes, R., and L. Buchanan. *Experiences of Person-Centred Counselling Training*. Llangarron, Ross-on-Wye, UK: PCCS Books, 2000.

Hutterer, R., G. Pawlowsky, P. F. Schmid, and R. Stipsits, eds. *Client-Centered and Experiential Psychotherapy: A Paradigm in Motion*. Frankfurt am Main, Germany: Peter Lang, 1996.

Ickes, W., ed. *Empathic Accuracy*. New York: Guilford Press, 1997.

Johnson, E. R. *Existential Man: The Challenge of Psychotherapy*. New York: Pergamon Press, 1971.

Johnson, S. M. *The Practice of Emotionally Focused Marital Therapy: Creating Connection*. New York: Brunner/Mazel, 1996.

Jones, A., and R. Crandall. *Handbook of Self-Actualization: A Special Issue of the Journal of Social Behavior and Personality,* Vol. 6. Corte Madera, CA: Select Press, 1991.

Kelly, E. W., Jr. *Relationship-Centered Counseling: An Integration of Art and Science*. New York: Springer, 1994.

Kiesler, D. J. *Therapeutic Metacommunication*. Palo Alto, CA: Consulting Psychologists Press, 1988.

Kinget, G. M. *On Becoming Human: A Systematic View*. New York: Harcourt and Brace, 1975.

Kirschenbaum, Howard. *On Becoming Carl Rogers*. New York: Delacorte Press, 1979.

Kirschenbaum, H. (2007). *The Life and Work of Carl Rogers*. Ross-on-Wye, UK: PCCS Books.

Kohut, H. *Self-Psychology and the Humanities: Reflections on a New Psychoanalytic Approach*. New York: W. W. Norton, 1985.

Krau, E. *The Realization of Life Aspirations through Vocational Careers.* Westport, CT: Praeger, 1997.

Lago, C., and M. MacMillan, eds. *Experiences in Relatedness: Group Work and the Person-Centred Approach*. Llangarron, Ross-on-Wye, UK: PCCS Books, 1999.

Landreth, G. *Play Therapy: The Art of the Relationship.* Muncie, IN: Accelerated Development, 1991.

Landreth, G., L. Homeyer, G. Glover, and D. Sweeney. *Play Therapy Interventions with Children's Problems.* Northvale, NJ: Jason Aronson, 1996.

Langer, I., F. Schulz v. Thun, and R. Tausch. *How to Speak Clearly*, 7th ed. Munich: Reinhard, 2001.

Lawrence, J. *Balancing Empathy and Interpretation: Relational Character Analysis.* Northvale, NJ: Jason Aronson, 1995.

Levant, R. F., and J. M. Shlien, eds. *Client-Centered Therapy and the Person-Centered Approach: New Directions in Theory, Research and Practice.* New York: Praeger, 1984.

Levin, D. M. *Language Beyond Postmodernism: Saying and Thinking in Gendlin's Philosophy.* Evanston, IL: Northwestern University Press, 1997.

Levine, P. *Waking the Tiger: Healing Trauma.* Berkeley, CA: North Atlantic Books, 1997.

Lietaer, Germain. *Client-Centered/Experiential Psychotherapy and Counseling: Bibliographical Survey 1988–1990/1991; 1993/1994; 1996/1997; 1999.* Leuven, Belgium: Counseling Centrum, 1991; 1994; 1997; 2000. Four brochures of approximately 100 pages each.

Lietaer, Germain, J. Rombauts, and R. Van Balen, eds. *Client-Centered and Experiential Psychotherapy in the Nineties.* Leuven, Belgium: Leuven University Press, 1990.

Lyon, H. C. *Learning to Feel – Feeling to Learn.* Columbus, OH: Charles E. Merrill, 1971.

Lyon, H. C. *It's Me and I'm Here!* New York: Delacorte, 1974.

Lyon, H. C. *Tenderness Is Strength.* New York: Harper Row, 1977.

MacMillan, M., and D. Clark. *Learning and Writing in Counselling.* London: Sage Publications, 1998.

Mahrer, A. R. *Therapeutic Experiencing: The Process of Change.* New York: W. W. Norton, 1986.

Marques-Teixeira, J., and S. Antunes, eds. *Client-Centered and Experiential Psychotherapy.* Linda a Velha, Portugal: Vale and Vale, 2000.

Martin, D. G. *Counseling and Therapy Skills.* Monterey, CA: Brooks/Cole, 1983.

Martin, D. G. *Learning-Based Client-Centered Therapy.* Monterey, CA: Brooks/Cole, 1972.

McCombs, B. L. (2008) *The School Leader's Guide to Learner Centered Education: From Complexity to Simplicity.* Thousand Oaks, CA: Corwin Press.

McConville, M. *Adolescence: Psychotherapy and the Emergent Self.* San Francisco: Jossey-Bass, 1995.

McGuire, K. N. *Building Supportive Community: Mutual Self-Help through Peer Counseling.* Eugene, OR: Focusing Northwest, 1981.

McGregor, Douglas. *The Human Side of Enterprise.* New York: McGraw-Hill Book Company, 1960.

McIlduff, E., and D. Coghlan. *The Person-Centered Approach and Cross-Cultural Communication: An International Review.* Vols 1 and 2. Linz, Austria: Sandkorn, 1991, 1993.

McLeod, J. *Narrative and Psychotherapy.* London: Sage Publications, 1997.

McLeod, J. *Qualitative Research in Counselling and Psychotherapy.* London: Sage Publications, 2001.

Mearns, Dave. *Developing Person-Centred Counselling.* London: Sage Publications, 1994.

Mearns, Dave. *Person-Centered Counselling Training.* London: Sage Publications, 1997.

Mearns, Dave, and Brian Thorne. *Person-Centered Counselling in Action.* London: Sage Publications, 1998, 1999.

Mearns, Dave, and Brian Thorne. *Person-Centered Therapy Today: New Frontiers in Theory and Practice.* London: Sage Publications, 2000.

Mearns, Dave, and W. Dryden, eds. *Experiences of Counseling in Action.* London: Sage Publications, 1990.

Merry, Tony. *Invitation to Person-Centred Psychology.* London: Whurr Publishers, 1995.

Merry, Tony. *Learning and Being in Person-Centered Counselling.* Llangarron, Ross-on-Wye, UK: PCCS Books, 1999.

Merry, Tony, ed. *Person-Centred Practice: The BAPCA Reader.* Llangarron, Ross-on-Wye, UK: PCCS Books, 1999.

Merry, Tony, and B. Lusty. *What Is Person-Centred Therapy?* Loughton, England: Gale Centre Publications, 1993.

Milhollan, Frank, and Bill E. Forisha. *From Skinner to Rogers: Contrasting Approaches to Education.* Lincoln, NE: Professional Educators Publications, 1972.

Morton, J. ed. *Person-Centred Approaches to Dementia Care.* Bicester, England: Winslow Press, 1999.

Moustakas, C. E. *Children in Play Therapy.* New York: McGraw–Hill, 1953.

Moustakas, C. E. *The Child's Discovery of Himself.* New York: Ballantine Books, 1966.

Moustakas, C. E., ed. *Existential Child Therapy.* New York: Basic Books, 1966.

Moustakas, C. E. *Individuality and Encounter: A Brief Journey into Loneliness and Sensitivity Groups.* Cambridge, MA: Doyle, 1968.

Moustakas, C. E. *Phenomenological Research Methods.* Thousand Oaks, CA: Sage Publications, 1994.

Moustakas, C. E. *Psychotherapy with Children.* New York: Harper and Row, 1959.

Nichols, M. P. *The Lost Art of Listening.* New York: Guilford Press, 1996.

Nye, Robert D. *Three Psychologies: Perspectives from Freud, Skinner, and Rogers.* Monterey, CA: Brooks/Cole, 1981.

O'Leary, Charles J. *Couple and Family Counselling: A Person-Centred Approach.* London: Sage Publications, 1999.

Page, R. C., and D. N. Berkow. *Creating Contact, Choosing Relationship: The Dynamics of Unstructured Group Therapy.* San Francisco: Jossey-Bass, 1995.

Patterson, C. H. *The Therapeutic Relationship: Foundations for an Eclectic Psychotherapy.* Monterey, CA: Brooks/Cole, 1985.

Patterson, C. H. *Understanding Psychotherapy. Fifty Years of Client-Centered Theory and Practice.* Llangarron, Ross-on-Wye, UK: PCCS Books 2000.

Patterson, C. H., and S. C. Hidore. *Successful Psychotherapy: A Caring, Loving Relationship.* Northvale, NJ: Jason Aronson, 1997.

Pentony, P. *Models of Influence in Psychotherapy.* New York: Free Press/Macmillan, 1981.

Porter, E. H. *An Introduction to Therapeutic Counselling.* Boston: Houghton Mifflin, 1950.

Pörtner, M. *Trust and Understanding: The Person-Centred Approach in Everyday Care for People with Special Needs* Translation Llangarron, Ross-on-Wye, UK: PCCS Books, 2000.

Prouty, Garry F. *Theoretical Evolutions in Person-Centered/Experiential Therapy: Application to Schizophrenic and Retarded Psychoses.* Westport, CT: Praeger, 1994.

Rennie, D. L. *Person-Centered Counselling: An Experiential Approach.* London: Sage Publications, 1998.

Reynolds, W. J. *The Measurement and Development of Empathy in Nursing.* Abingdon, England: Ashgate, 2000.

Rice, L. N., and L. S. Greenberg, eds. *Patterns of Change: Intensive Analysis of Psychotherapy Process.* New York: Guilford Press, 1984.

Rogers, Carl R. *A Personal Approach to Teaching: Beliefs That Make a Difference.* Boston: Allyn and Bacon, 1982.

Rogers, Carl R. *Perspectives on Helping Relationships and the Helping Profession: Past, Present and Future.* Boston: Allyn and Bacon, 1985.

Rogers, Carl R. *A Theory of Therapy: Guidelines for Counseling Practice.* London: Sage Publications, 1989.

Rogers, Natalie. *The Creative Connection: Expressive Arts as Healing.* Palo Alto, CA: Science and Behavior Books, 1993. Also published by Llangarron, Ross-on-Wye, UK: PCCS Books, 1993.

Rogers, Natalie. *Emerging Woman: A Decade of Mid-Life Transitions.* Point Reyes, CA: Personal Press, 1980.

Rose, A., and A. Auw. *Growing Up Human.* New York: Harper and Row, 1974.

Rubenstein, Ben O. *Freud and Rogers – A Comparative Study of Two Psychological Systems.* New York: Michigan Academy of Science, Arts, and Letters, 1960.

Ryan, V., and K. Wilson. *Case Studies in Non-Directive Play Therapy.* London: Bailliere Tindall, 1996.

Ryback, David. *Putting Emotional Intelligence to Work.* Woburn, MA: Butterworth-Heinemann, 1998.

Sanders, P. *An Incomplete Guide to Using Counselling Skills on the Telephone.* Llangarron, Ross-on-Wye, UK: PCCS Books, 1996.

Seeman, Julius. *Personality Integration: Studies and Reflections.* New York: Human Sciences Press, 1983.

Segrera, A. S., ed. *Proceedings of the First International Forum on the Person-Centered Approach.* Oaxtepec, Mexico, 1982 and Mexico City: Universidad Iberoamericana, 1984.

Seruya, B. B. *Empathic Brief Psychotherapy*. Northvale, NJ: Jason Aronson, 1997.

Schmid, P. F. *Carl Rogers Bibliography, 1922–1987*. 9th ed. Vienna, Austria: IPS of APG, 1999–2000. Available at www.pfs-online.at.

Schmid, P. F. *The Person-Centered Approach Bibliography, 1940–1999*. 8th ed. Vienna, Austria: IPS of APG, 1999–2000. Available at www.pfs-online.at.

Schmid, P. F., and W. Wascher, eds. *Towards Creativity: A Person Centered Reading and Picture Book*. Linz, Austria: Sandkorn, 1994.

Sherman, E. *Working with Older Persons*. Boston: Kluwer-Nijhoff, 1984.

Silverstone, Liesl. *Art Therapy: The Person-Centred Way*. 2nd ed. London: Jessica Kingsley, 1997.

Snyder, W. U. *Casebook of Non-Directive Counseling*. Boston: Houghton Mifflin, 1947.

Snygg, D., and A. W. Combs. *Individual Psychology: A New Frame of Reference for Psychology*. New York: Harper, 1949. Also published in revised edition by Harper, 1959.

Solomon, Lawrence N., and B. Berzon, eds. *New Perspectives on Encounter Groups*. San Francisco: Jossey-Bass, 1972.

Steffenhagen, R. A. *Self-Esteem Therapy*. New York: Praeger, 1990.

Stillwell, William. *Questing Voices*. La Jolla, CA: Center for Studies of the Person, 1998.

Stillwell, William. *Three Voices: Interviews into Person-Centered Approaches with Ernie Meadows, Maria Bowen, Bob Lee*. La Jolla, CA: Center for Studies of the Person, 2000.

Suhd, Melvin M., ed. *Positive Regard: Carl Rogers and Other Notables He Inspired*. Palo Alto, CA: Science and Behavior Books, 1995.

Tausch, A.-M. *Speaking Against Fear*. Reinbek: Rowohlt, 2001.

Tausch, R., and A.-M. Tausch. *Speaking Therapy*. Göttingen: Hogrefe, 1990.

Tausch, R., and A.-M. Tausch. *Experiential Psychology*. Göttingen: Hogrefe, 1998.

Tausch, R., and A.-M. Tausch. *Ways to Us and Others*. Reinbek: Rowohlt, 1999.

Tausch, R., and A.-M. Tausch. *Soft Dying*. Reinbek: Rowohlt, 2000.

Tausch, R. *Help with Stress and Burden,* 9th ed. Reinbek: Rowohlt, 2000.

Taylor, C. *The Ethics of Authenticity*. Cambridge, MA: Harvard University Press, 1992.

Teich, Nathaniel, ed. *Rogerian Perspectives: Collaborative Rhetoric for Oral and Written Communication*. Norwood, NJ: Ablex Publishers, 1992.

Thorne, Brian J. *Behold the Man*. London: Darton, Longman and Todd, 1991.

Thorne, Brian J. *Carl Rogers*. London: Sage Publications, 1992.

Thorne, Brian J. *Counselling and the Spiritual Journey*. Birkenhead, England: Time+Space, 1997.

Thorne, Brian J. *Person-Centred Counselling: Christian Spiritual Dimensions*. London: Whurr Publishers, 1998.

Thorne, Brian J. *Person-Centered Counselling and Christian Spirituality: The Secular and the Holy*. London: Whurr Publishers, 1998.

Thorne, Brian J. *Person-Centered Counselling: Therapeutic and Spiritual Dimensions*. London: Whurr Publishers, 1991.

Thorne, Brian J, A. Newsome, and K. Wyld. *Student Counselling in Practice*. 3rd ed. London: University of London Press, 1981.

Thorne, Brian J., and E. Lambers, eds. *Person-Centered Therapy: A European Perspective*. London: Sage Publications, 1998.

Toukmanian, S. G., and D. L. Rennie, eds. *Psychotherapy Process Research: Paradigmatic and Narrative Approaches*. Newbury Park, CA: Sage Publications, 1992.

Truax, C. B., and R. R. Carkhuff. *Toward Effective Counseling and Psychotherapy: Training and Practice*. Chicago: Aldine, 1967.

Van Belle, Harry Albert. *Basic Intent and Therapeutic Approach of Carl R. Rogers: A Study of His View of Man in Relation to His View of Therapy, Personality, and Interpersonal Relations*. Toronto, ON: Wedge Publishing Foundation, 1980. Also published by Burnaby, BC: Academy Press, 1980.

von Broembsen, F. *The Sovereign Self: Toward a Phenomenology of Self-Experience*. Northvale, NJ/London: Jason Aronson, 1999.

Weiser, A. *The Power of Focusing: A Practical Guide to Emotional Self-Healing*. Oakland, CA: New Harbinger Publications, 1996.

West, J. *Child-Centered Play Therapy*. London: Edward Arnold, 1996.

Wexler, D. A., and L. N. Rice, eds. *Innovations in Client-Centered Therapy*. New York: John Wiley, 1974.

Whitlock, G. E. *Person-Centered Learning: Confluent Learning Processes*. London: University Press of America, 1984.

Wilkins, P. *Personal and Professional Development for Counsellors*. London: Sage Publications, 1996.

Wilson, K., P. Kendrick, and V. Ryan. *Play Therapy: A Non-Directive Approach for Children and Adolescents*. London: Bailliere Tindall, 1992.

Wood, J. T. *How Do You Feel? A Guide to Your Emotions*. Englewood Cliffs, NJ: Prentice Hall, 1974.

Worsley, R. *Process-Work in Person-Centred Therapy: Phenomenological and Existential Perspectives*. Houndmills, Basingstoke, England: Palgrave, 2001.

Wosket, V. *The Therapeutic Use of Self: Counseling Practice, Research and Supervision*. London: Routledge, 1999.

Wright, L., F. Everett, and L. Roisman. *Experiential Psychotherapy with Children*. Baltimore, MD: Johns Hopkins University Press, 1986.

Wyatt, G., ed. *Congruence*. Llangarron, Ross-on-Wye: PCCS Books, 2001.

Yalom, Irvin D. *Existential Psychotherapy*. New York: Basic Books, 1980.

Yalom, Irvin D. *Love's Executioner and Other Tales of Psychotherapy*. New York: Basic Books, 1989.

Zeig, Jeffrey K., ed. Introduction to *The Evolution of Psychotherapy Fundamental Issues*. New York: Brunner/Mazel, 1987.

Articles about Carl R. Rogers and the person-centered approach

American Psychological Association. 'Distinguished Scientific Contribution Awards for 1956—Carl R. Rogers'. *American Psychologist* 12, no. 3 (March 1957): 125–33.

American Psychological Association Symposium. 'Carl Rogers: Giving People Permission to Be Themselves'. *Science* 198 (October 7, 1977).

Anderson, Rob. 'Frisbee and the Art of Self-Maintenance'. *Dawnpoint: A Magazine from the Association for Humanist Psychology* (Winter 1978): 32–33.

Anderson, Rob. 'Phenomenological Dialogue, Humanistic Psychology, and Pseudo Walls: A Response and Extension'. *Western Journal of Speech Communication* 46, no. 4 (Fall 1982): 344–57.

Anderson, Rob, and Kenneth Cissna. 'The Contributions of Carl R. Rogers to a Philosophical Praxis of Dialogue'. *Western Journal of Speech Communication* 54 (Spring 1990): 125–47.

Arnett, Ronald C. 'Rogers and Buber: Similarities, Yet Fundamental Differences'. *Western Journal of Speech Communication* 46, no. 4 (Fall 1982): 358–72.

Aspy, D. N. *Towards a Technology for Humanizing Education*. Champaign, IL: Research Press Co, 1971.

Aspy, David N., and Flora N. Roebuck. 'From Humane Ideas to Humane Technology and Back Again Many Times'. *Education* (1974).

Aspy, D. N. and F. N. Roebuck. *Research Summary: Effects of Training in Interpersonal Skills. Interim Report*. NIMH Grant Number 5P01 MH 19871, 1974. ERIC Document ED 106733.

Aspy, D. N. and F. N. Roebuck. 'The Relationship of Teacher-Offered Conditions of Meaning to Behaviors Described by Flanders Interaction Analysis'. *Education* 95, no. 3 (1975): 216–18, 234.

Aspy, D. N. and F. N. Roebuck. *Kids Don't Learn from People They Don't Like*. Amherst, MA: Human Resources Development Press, 1977.

Assagioli, Roberto, MD. 'Self-Realization and Psychological Disturbances'. Greenville, DE: Psychosynthesis Research Foundation, 1961.

Association for Humanistic Psychology. 'Carl Rogers: A Celebration'. *AHP Perspective* (May 1987): 4–11. A Special Issue in Memoriam to Carl Rogers.

Bakan, David. 'On Evil as a Collective Phenomenon'. *Journal of Humanistic Psychology* 22, no. 4 (Fall 1982): 91–92.

Barrett-Lennard, Godfrey T. 'The Client-Centered System: A Developmental Perspective'. University of Waterloo (April 1973).

Barrett-Lennard, Godfrey T. 'The Empathy Cycle: Refinement of a Nuclear Concept'. *Journal of Counseling Psychology* 28, no. 2 (1981).

Barrett-Lennard, Godfrey T. 'Experiential Learning Groups'. *Psychotherapy: Theory, Research, and Practice* 11, no. 1 (Spring 1974).

Barrett-Lennard, Godfrey T. 'A New Model of Communicational-Relational Systems in Intensive Groups'. *Human Relations* 32 (November 1979): 841–49.

Barrett-Lennard, Godfrey T. 'Outcomes of Residential Encounter Group Workshops'. *Interpersonal Development* 5 (1974/1975): 86–93.

Barrett-Lennard, Godfrey T. 'Process, Effects, and Structure in Intensive Groups: A Theoretical- Descriptive Analysis'. In C. L. Cooper, ed., *Theories of Group Processes*. London/New York: John Wiley, 1975.

Barrett-Lennard, Godfrey T. 'Some Effects of Participation in Encounter Group Workshops: An Analysis of Written Follow-Up Reports. *Interpersonal Development* 5 (1973/1974): 35–41.

Barrett-Lennard, Godfrey T. 'The Relationship Inventory: Issues and Advances in Theory, Method, and Use'. In L. Greenberg and W. M. Pinsoff, eds, *The Psychotherapeutic Process: A Research Handbook*. New York: Guilford Press, 1986.

Barrett-Lennard, Godfrey T. 'South Pacific Adventure: Carl and Helen Rogers in Australia'. *Person-Centered Review* 2, no. 3 (August 1987): 299–306.

Barrett-Lennard, Godfrey T. 'Toward a Person-Centered Theory of Community'. *Journal of Humanistic Psychology* 34 (Summer 1994).

'Behavior Theories and a Counseling Case: A Symposium'. *Journal of Counseling Psychology* 3, no. 2 (1956).

Barrineau, P. 'Person-Centered Dream Work'. *Journal of Humanistic Psychology* 32, no. 1 (Winter 1992).

Bengis, Ingrid. 'What We Do Not Say Is That We Are All, Every Last One of Us, Scared of Love's Power to Create and Destroy'. *Ms. Magazine* (1973).

Bergin, Allen. 'Carl Rogers' Contribution to a Fully Functioning Psychology'. In Alvin R. Mahrer and Leonard Pearson, eds, *Creative Developments in Psychotherapy*. Cleveland, OH: Case Western Reserve University, 1971.

Bern, Sandra, and Daryl Bern. 'Training the Woman to Know Her Place'. *Journal of Humanistic Psychology*. Newsletter.

Berzon, Betty, and Lawrence N. Solomon. 'Research Frontiers—the Self-Directed Therapeutic Group: Three Studies'. *Journal of Counseling Psychology* 13, no. 4 (1966).

Bixler, Ray, and Julius Seeman. 'Suggestions for a Code of Ethics for Consulting Psychologists'. *Journal of Abnormal and Social Psychology* 41, no. 4 (1946).

Bohart, A. 'Empathy in Client-Centered Therapy: A Contrast with Psycho-analysis and Self-Psychology'. *Journal of Humanistic Psychology* 31 (Winter 1991).

Bohart, A., O'Hara, M. and Lietner, L. (2010) 'Empirically Violated Treatments: Disenfranchisement of Humanistic and Other Psychotherapies.' *Psychotherapy Research* 8, no. 2: 141–57.

Bold, Kathryn. 'Carl Rogers in Retrospect'. *La Jolla Light* (1982).

Bondarenko, A. F. 'My Encounter with Carl Rogers: A Retrospective View from the Ukraine'. *Journal of Humanistic Psychology* (Winter 1999).

Bowen, M.V. (1979) 'Learning in Large Groups: Their Implication for the Future'. *Education* 100, no. 2: 108–116.

Bowen, M. V., Justyn, J., Kass J., Miller, M., Rogers, C. R., Rogers, N., and Wood, J. K., (1978) 'Evolving Aspects of Person-Centered Workshops.' *Self and Society*, 6, no. 2: 43–49.

Bozarth, Jerold D. 'Beyond Reflection: Emergent Modes of Empathy'. Athens, GA: University of Georgia, 1987.

Bozarth, Jerold D. 'Not Necessarily Necessary But Always Sufficient'. Athens, GA: University of Georgia, 1987.

Bozarth, Jerold D. 'Person-Centered Assessment'. *Journal of Counseling and Development* 69 (May/June 1991).

Bozarth, Jerold D. 'Person-Centered Facilitation, the Group and the Development of the Person-Centered Association'. *Renaissance*, 15–16.

Bozarth, Jerold D. 'Rejoinder: Perplexing Perceptual Ploys'. *Journal of Counseling and Development* 69 (May/June 1991).

Bozarth, Jerold D. 'Some Commonalties and Divergencies in the Client Centered Approach'. Athens, GA: University of Georgia, 1987.

Braaten, Leif J. 'The Effects of Person-Centered Group Therapy'. *Person-Centered Review* 4, no. 2 (May 1989): 183–209.

Braaten, Leif J. 'How Do Clients Discriminate Between the Person-Centered Facilitating Conditions in Group Psychotherapy? A Factorial Model'. Oslo, Norway: University of Oslo.

Braaten, Leif J. 'The Self Development Project List: A New Instrument to Measure Positive Goal Attainment'. Reprint from *Small Behavior* 20, no. 1 (February 1989): 3–23.

Braaten, Leif J. 'Thirty Years with Rogers. Necessary and Sufficient Conditions of Therapeutic Personality Change'. *Person-Centered Review* 1, no. 1 (February 1986): 37–49.

Brenman, Margaret. 'Research in Psychotherapy Round Table: 1947'. *American Journal of Orthopsychiatry* 18, no. 1 (January 1948).

Brink, Debora C. 'The Issues of Equality and Control in the Client or Person-Centered Approach'. *Journal of Humanistic Psychology* 24, no. 1 (Winter 1987): 27–37.

Brown, Robert C. 'Rejoinder to Rogers by Robert C. Brown and James T. Tedeschi'. *Journal of Humanistic Psychology* 12, no. 2 (Fall 1972).

Brown, Robert C., and J. Tedeschi. 'Graduate Education in Psychology: A Comment on Rogers' Passionate Statement'. *Journal of Humanistic Psychology* (Spring 1972).

Burstow, Bonnie. 'Humanistic Psychotherapy and the Issue of Equality'. *Journal of Humanistic Psychology* 27, no. 1 (Winter 1987): 9–25.

Cartwright, Rosalind Dymond. 'Patterns of Perceived Interpersonal Relations'. *Sociometry* 19, no. 3 (1956).

Caspary, W. 'Carl Rogers – Values, Persons, and Politics: The Dialectic of Individual and Community'. *Journal of Humanistic Psychology* (Fall 1991).

Ceshur Connection. 'Carl Rogers Memorial Issue'. *Ceshur Connection* 2, nos 1 and 2 (December 1987).

Ceshur Connection. *The International Newsletter of the Centre for Studies in Human Relations* 1, no. 1 (April 1985); A, nos. 2 and 3 (November 1985/June 1986); 1, no. 4 (December 1986).

Cissna, Kenneth N., and Rob Anderson. 'The 1957 Martin Buber–Carl Rogers Dialogue, as Dialogue'. *Journal of Humanistic Psychology* (Winter 1994).

Cissna, Kenneth N., and Rob Anderson. 'The Person-Centered Approach to Interpersonal Communication'. *Florida Communication Journal* 20, no. 2 (1992).

Cooper, Shirley. 'A Look at the Effect of Racism on Clinical Work'. *Social Case-Work* (February 1973): 76–84.

De Rasa, Alison. "Getting to Know You": Modern Day Theme Song for Mothers and Daughters'. *San Diego Tribune, The Tribune Scene* (May 10, 1979).

De Rosenber, Annette, and Sara Jenton. 'Remaining Human in the Nuclear/Computer Age'. *University Without Walls.* San Diego: University of California, San Diego, 1983.

'The Development of Client-Centered Therapy – Looking Back and Ahead: A Conversation with Carl Rogers'. In J. T. Hart and T.M. Tomlinson, eds. *New Directions in Client-Centered Therapy.* Boston: Houghton Mifflin, 1970.

Dolliver, Robert H. 'Carl Rogers' Emphasis on His Own Direct Experience'. *Journal of Humanistic Psychology, Carl Rogers Issue* 35, no. 4 (Fall 1995).

Dolliver, Robert H. 'Carl Rogers' Personality Theory and Psychotherapy as a Reflection of His Life Experience and Personality'. *Journal of Humanistic Psychology, Carl Rogers Issue* 35, no. 4 (Fall 1995).

Fenly, Leigh. 'Carl Rogers: Bestowing the Freedom to Be: An Interview by Leigh Fenly'. *San Diego Union* (July 1, 1978).

Fenly, Leigh. 'Meditation Plan Sounds Familiar to Authors'. *San Diego Union* (October 12, 1982).

Ford, G. 'Rogerian Self-Actualization: A Clarification of Meaning'. *Journal of Humanistic Psychology* (Spring 1991).

Friedman, Maurice. 'Comment on the Rogers–May Discussion of Evil'. *Journal of Humanistic Psychology* 2, no. 4 (Fall 1982): 93–96.

Friedman, Maurice. 'Reflections on the Buber–Rogers Dialogue'. *Journal of Humanistic Psychology* (Winter 1994).

Fuller, Robert. 'Carl Rogers, Religion, and the Role of Psychology in American Culture'. *Journal of Humanistic Psychology* 22, no. 4 (Fall 1982): 21–32.

Geller, Leonard. 'The Failure of Self-Actualization Theory, a Critique of Carl Rogers and Abraham Maslow'. Reprint of article in *Journal of Humanistic Psychology.*

Gendlin, Eugene T. 'Carl Rogers (1902–1987)'. *American Psychologist* (February 1988).

Gillette, Tom, Betty Meador, and Bruce Meador. 'On Carl Rogers'. *Voices* (Spring 1971).

Ginther, Claire. 'A Legacy Enhanced: Natalie Rogers' Person-Centered Expressive Therapy Institute Expands on the Work of Her Famous Father'. *Psychiatric Times* (December 1996).

Gordon, Thomas, C. Rogers, and D. L. Grummon. 'Developing a Program of Research in Psychotherapy'. Chicago: Psychological Service Center Press, 1952.

Graf, C. 'On Genuineness and the Person-Centered Approach: A Reply to Quinn'. *Journal of Humanistic Psychology* (Spring 1994).

Greening, Thomas. 'Carl Rogers: 1902–1987'. *Journal of Humanistic Psychology* 27, no. 2 (Spring 1987): 134–40.

Greening, Thomas. 'Commentary by the Editor'. *Journal of Humanistic Psychology: Carl Rogers Issue* 35, no. 4 (Fall 1995).

Gunnison, Hugh. 'The Uniqueness of Similarities: Parallels of Milton H. Erickson and Carl Rogers'. *Journal of Counseling Development* 63, no. 9 [no year listed]: 561–654.

Haigh, Gerard. 'I Walk Softly Through Life: An Interview with Carl Rogers'. *Voices* 18, no. 4 (Winter 1983): 6–14.

Hall, Mary Harrington. 'Carl Rogers Speaks out on Groups and the Lack of a Human Science: An Interview'. *Psychology Today* (December [no year listed]): 19–21, 62–66.

Hatase, Minoru. 'A Comparative Study of Encounter Group Experiences in Japan and the USA through a Follow-Up Survey of Japanese Participants in La Jolla Program'. *Japanese Journal of Humanistic Psychology* no. 2 (1984): 79–97.

Hearn, Curry B. 'Personality Integration and Perception of Interpersonal Relationship'. *Journal of Personality and Social Psychology* 18, no. 2 (1971).

Henderson, Val. 'Choreography in Long-Term Relationships'. *Journey* 1, no. 3 (March 1982).

Heppner, P. Paul, Mark E. Rogers, and Lucienne A. Lee. 'Carl Rogers: Reflections on His Life'. *Journal of Counseling and Development* 63 (September 1984).

Hill-Hain, Alicia. 'A Dialogue with Carl Rogers: Cross-Cultural Challenges of Facilitating Person-Centered Groups in South Africa'. *Journal for Specialists in Group Work* 13 (May 1988).

Hobbs, Tony. 'The Rogers Interview: Discussion of Carl's Ideas on Therapy and Education'. *Changes* 4, no. 4 (October 1986).

Jacobs, David. 'Successful "Empathy" Training: A Demonstration with Implications for the General Theoretical Problem of Evaluating Capacity from Performance'. Reprint of article in *Journal of Humanistic Psychology* (1980).

Kahn, E. 'A Critique of Non-Directivity in the Person-Centered Approach'. *Journal of Humanistic Psychology* (Fall 1999).

Kemper, Cynthia Warwick. 'An Encounter with Carl Rogers'. Interview. *Respublica, Claremont Men's College* 1, no. 1 (1973): 41–51.

Kirschenbaum, Howard. 'Denigrating Carl Rogers: William Coulson's Lost Crusade'. *Journal of Counseling and Development* 69 (May/June 1991): 411–13.

Kramer, Robert. 'The Birth of Client-Centered Therapy: Carl Rogers, Otto Rank and "The Beyond"'. *Journal of Humanistic Psychology* 35, no. 4 (Fall 1995).

Krause, Merton S. 'Alternative Psychologies – An Analytical Reconstruction of Rogers' Theory of Personality'. Chicago: University of Chicago Counseling Center discussion papers 4, Institute for Juvenile Research no. 6 (1958).

Kubler-Ross, Elizabeth. 'A Letter to a Child with Cancer'. *Shanti Nilaya* (1979).

Kutash, Irwin L., ed. Foreword, Preface, Contents, Editor's Information, and Contributors. In *Psychotherapists' Casebook*. San Francisco: Jossey-Bass Publishers, 1986.

Larson, Dale. 'Therapeutic Schools, Styles, and Schoolism: A National Survey'. *Journal of Humanistic Psychology* 20, no. 3 (1980).

Lazarus, Arnold A., and Clifford N. Lazarus. 'Let Us Not Forsake the Individual Nor Ignore the Data: A Response to Bozarth'. *Journal of Counseling and Development* 69 (May/June 1991).

Lepkowski, Wil. 'The Social Thermodynamics of Ilya Prigogine'. *Chemical and Engineering News* (April 1979).

Lukas, Betty. 'Backyard Pioneering'. *Los Angeles Times* (July 31, 1980).

Lukas, Betty. 'The World According to Ilya Prigogine'. *Quest* (December 1980).

Macy, Francis U. 'Mission to Moscow Succeeds'. *AHP Perspective* (February 1986).

Macy, Francis U. 'The Legacy of Carl Rogers in the U.S.S.R.'. *Journal of Humanistic Psychology* 27, no. 3 (Summer 1987).

May, Rollo. 'The Problem of Evil: An Open Letter to Carl Rogers'. *Journal of Humanistic Psychology* 22, no. 3 (Summer 1982): 10–21.

McWhinney, Bonnie. 'Seven Years Later—"Dear Carl"'. With a Response: "Dear Bonnie" by Carl Rogers'. *Education* 95, no. 2 (1974): 190–96.

Merry, Tony. 'Counselling and Creativity: An Interview with Natalie Rogers'. *British Journal of Guidance and Counselling* 25, no. 2 (1997): 263–73.

Metzler, Karen M. 'Growing Up Hospitalized and Handicapped'. *ACCH Newsletter* (1973): 15–19.

Nelson, Marie Coleman. 'What's Inside the Pants? With Comment By Nathaniel J. Raskin: A Positive Alternative to the Paradigmatic Encounter'. *Voices* 13, no. 2 (1977).

Noel, Joseph R. 'I-We-Thou Multi-Centered Counseling and Psychotherapy'. *Psychotherapy: Theory, Research and Practice* 18, no. 4 (1977).

Odom, Linda. 'A Study of Family Communication Patterns and Personality Integration in Children'. *Child Psychiatry and Human Development* 1, no. 4 (Summer 1971): 275–85.

O'Hara, Maureen. 'Alert! Alert! Alert!' *Inside AHP* (1989): 16.

O'Hara, Maureen. 'Carl Rogers: Scientist and Mystic'. *Journal of Humanistic Psychology* 35, no. 4 (Fall 1995).

O'Hara, Maureen. 'Comment on Carl Rogers' "Towards a More Human Science of the Person"'. *Journal of Humanistic Psychology* 25, no. 4 (Fall 1985): 25–30.

O'Hara, Maureen. 'Constructing Emancipatory Realities'. In Walter T. Anderson, ed., *The Truth About Truth: De-constructing and Reconstructing the Postmodern World*. Palo Alto, CA: Jeremy Tarcher, 1995.

O'Hara, Maureen. 'Emancipatory Therapeutic Practice in a Turbulent Transmodern Era: A Work of Retrieval'. *Journal of Humanistic Psychology,* 37, no. 3 (1997): 7–33.

O'Hara, Maureen. 'Evolving Aspects of the Person-Centered Approach'. *Newsletter of the Association of Humanistic Psychology* (1979): 11–14.

O'Hara, Maureen. 'Feminist Analysis of a Session of Psychotherapy between Carl Rogers and a Female Client "Silvia"'. In Barry A. Farber, Patricia Raskin, and Debora Brink, eds, *Carl Rogers: Casebook and Critical Perspectives*. New York: Guilford Publications, 1996.

O'Hara, Maureen. 'Foreword'. In J. Wood, *Carl Rogers' Person-Centered Approach: Toward an Understanding of Its Implications*. Ross-on-Wye, UK: PCCS Books, 2008: iii–viii.

O'Hara, Maureen. 'Heuristic Inquiry as Psychotherapy: The Client-Centered Approach'. *Person Centered Review*, 1, no. 2 (1986): 172–83.

O'Hara, Maureen. 'Humanistic Psychology, Co-constructionism and the Global Search for Deep Democracy'. *AHP Perspective* (November 1990).

O'Hara, Maureen. 'The Hundredth Humanistic Psychologist'. *Perspective: Association for Humanistic Psychology* (July 1983).

O'Hara, Maureen. 'The "Hundredth Monkey Phenomenon"': A Look at the Darker Side of "New Age" Ideology'. *Omni* (October 1985).

O'Hara, Maureen. 'Is it Time to Deconstruct Constructivism?' *Journal of Constructivist Psychology* 8, no. 4 (1995): 293–303.

O'Hara, Maureen. 'Jealousy in Non-Monogamous Marriages'. In *Carl Rogers on Personal Power*. New York: Delacorte, 1977: 224–29.

O'Hara, Maureen. 'Moments of Eternity: What Carl Rogers Has to Offer Brief Therapists'. In Jeffrey K. Zeig, ed., *Brief Therapy: Lasting Impressions*. Phoenix, AZ: The Milton H. Erickson Foundation Press, 2002.

O'Hara, Maureen. 'Of Myths and Monkeys'. *Whole Earth Review*. 55 (Fall 1986): 30–34.

O'Hara, Maureen. 'Of Myths and Monkeys: A Critical Look at a Theory of Critical Mass'. *Journal of Humanistic Psychology* 25, no. 1 (1985): 61–78.

O'Hara, Maureen. 'Our Foremothers as Gurus'. *Perspective: Association for Humanistic Psychology* (November 1983).

O'Hara, Maureen. 'Person-Centered Approach as Conscientização: The Works of Carl Rogers and Paulo Freire'. *Journal of Humanistic Psychology* 29, 1 (Winter 1989).

O'Hara, Maureen. 'Reflections of Sheldrake, Wilber and New Science'. *Journal of Humanistic Psychology* 24, no. 2 (1984): 116–20.

O'Hara, Maureen. 'Relational Empathy: From Egocentricism to Postmodern Contextualism'. In A. Bohardt and L. Greenberg, eds, *Empathy and Psychotherapy: New Directions in Theory, Research and Practice*. Washington, DC: American Psychological Association, 1997.

O'Hara, Maureen. 'Relational Humanism: A Psychology for a Pluralistic World'. In F. Wertz, ed., *The Humanistic Movement: Recovering the Person in Psychology*. Lake Worth, FL: Gardner Press, 1994.

O'Hara, Maureen. 'When I Use the Term Humanistic Psychology'. *Journal of Humanistic Psychology* 29, no. 2 (Spring 1989).

O'Hara, Maureen, and John K. Wood. 'Patterns of Awareness: Consciousness and the Group Mind'. *Gestalt Journal* 6, no. 2: 103–16.

'Peacemakers: An Interview with Carl Rogers'. *Holistic Living News* 7, no. 3 (December 1984/January 1985).

Peters, H. 'Prouty's Pre-Therapy Applied to Mentally Handicapped People'. *Journal of Humanistic Psychology* (Fall 1999).

Pitts, Carl E. 'Twelve Years Later: A Reply to Carl Rogers'. *Journal of Humanistic Psychology* 13, no. 1 (Winter 1973): 75–81.

Prigogine, Ilya. 'Prigogine's Science of Becoming'. *Brain Mind Bulletin* 4, no. 13 (May 21, 1979).

Prouty, Garry F. 'Pre-Therapy: A Method of Treating Pre-Psychotic and Retarded Patients'. *Psychotherapy: Theory, Research and Practice* 13, no. 3 (Fall 1976): 290–94.

Prouty, Garry F. 'Protosymbolic Method: A Phenomenological Treatment of Schizophrenic Hallucinations'. *Journal of Mental Imagery* 2 (1977): 339–42.

Quinn, R. 'Confronting Carl Rogers: A Developmental-Interactional Approach to Person-Centered Therapy'. *Journal of Humanistic Psychology* (Winter 1993).

Raskin, Nathaniel. 'Becoming – A Therapist, a Person, a Partner, a Parent, a ...' *Psychotherapy Theory, Research and Practice* 15, no. 4 (1978): 362–70.

Raskin, Nathaniel. 'Carl Rogers: A Biographical Supplement from the International Encyclopedia'. *Social Science*: 671–75.

Raskin, Nathaniel. 'Client-Centered Counseling and Psychotherapy'. *Clinical Psychological* 1, sec. 1 (1952): 236–48.

Raskin, Nathaniel. 'The Development of Non-Directive Therapy'. *Journal of Consulting Psychology* 12 (1948): 92–110.

Raskin, Nathaniel. 'Learning Through Human Encounters'. *Improving College and University Teaching* 23, no. 2 (Spring 1975): 71–74.

Raskin, Nathaniel. 'An Objective Study on the Locus of Evaluation Factor in Psychotherapy'. In W. Wolff and J. A. Poecker, eds, *Success in Psychotherapy*. New York: Gunn and Stratton, 1952.

Raskin, Nathaniel. 'Play Therapy with Blind Children'. *Nart News* 4, no. 2 (1954).

Raskin, Nathaniel. 'The Scope of Carl Rogers'. *VOICES Editorial Amalgam* (Fall 1978): 12–13.

Raskin, Nathaniel J., and Ferdinand Van Der Veen. 'Client-Centered Family Therapy: Some Clinical and Research Perspectives'. In J. T. Hart and T. M. Tomlinson, eds. *New Directions in Client-Centered Therapy*. New York: Houghton Mifflin, 1970.

'Renaissance'. *Quarterly Newsletter of the Person-Centered Therapy Network* 1, no. 4 (Fall 1984) 2, no. 3 (Summer 1985).

Rhodes, William C., Julius Seeman, Charles D. Spielberger, and Robert F. Stepbach. 'The Multi-Problem Neighborhood Project'. *Community Mental Health* 4, no. 1 (February 1966): 3–12.

Roache, Joel. 'Confessions of a Househusband'. *Ms Magazine*.

Robinson, Edward H. 'Education for the 1980s and Beyond: An Interview With Carl Rogers'. *Humanistic Education and Development* (March 1985).

Roethlisberger, F. J. 'Readings in Human Relations'. Harvard Business School, Division of Research (1954).

Rogers, David E., MD. 'AIDS: An Expanding Tragedy'. National Commission on AIDS. Washington, 1993.

Rogers, David E., MD. 'The Doctor Himself Must Become the Treatment'. *Alpha Omega Honor Medical Society* 3, no. 4 (1974): 124–29.

Rogers, Helen. 'A Wife's Eye View of Carl Rogers'. *Voices*. American Academy of Psychotherapists 1, no. 1 (Fall 1965).

Rogers, Natalie. 'Changes in Self-Concept in the Case of Mrs. Ett'. *Personal Counselor*. Chicago: University of Chicago, 1947: 278–91.

Rogers, Natalie. 'The Creative Connection: The Concept, and the Healing Aspects of Movement and Writing'. Part 1. *Somatics* 9, no. 2 (Spring/Summer 1993): 10–12.

Rogers, Natalie. 'The Creative Connection: The Concept, and the Healing Aspects of Movement and Writing'. Part 2. *Somatics* 9, no. (Fall/Winter 1993–94): 10–17.

Rogers, Natalie. 'Discovering Spirituality Through the Arts'. *Create* 3 (1992): 93–101.

Rogers, Natalie. 'Express Yourself'. *AHP Perspective* (April 1985): 14–15.

Rogers, Natalie. 'Fostering Creative Expression in the Soviet Union'. *New Realities* (March/April 1990): 28–34.

Rogers, Natalie. 'On Carl Rogers' 87th Birthday: A Daughter's Evocation'. *Noetic Sciences Review* (Spring 1989): 24–25.

Rogers, Natalie. 'Pain Transformed: Expressive Therapy in the Soviet Union'. *AHP Perspective* (August/September 1991): 10–11.

Rogers, Natalie. 'Person-Centered Expressive Arts Therapy'. *Creation Spirituality* (March/April 1993): 28–30.

Rogers, Natalie. 'Sacred Space: Using Expressive Arts to Build Community'. *Earth Circles* 4, no. 3 (Fall 1993): 1–6.

Rogers, Natalie. 'Using Expressive Arts to Communicate Across Boundaries'. *AHP Perspective* (July 1992): 16.

Rogers, Natalie. 'Women, Power, and the Future'. *Journal of Humanistic Education* 5 (Spring 1981): 1–7.

Rogers, Natalie, Francis Macy, and Claire Fitzgerald. 'Fostering Creative Expression in the Soviet Union: A US Team Reports on Facilitating Workshops in the USSR'. *New Realities* (1989): 28–34.

Ryback, David. 'Towards Power and Joy in Humanistic Teaching'. *Journal of Humanistic Education* (Spring 1980).

Sackett, Samuel J. 'The Application of Rogerian Theory to Literary Study'. *Journal of Humanistic Psychology* 35, no. 4 (Fall 1995).

Sanford, Ruth. 'Unconditional Positive Regard: A Misunderstood Way of Being'. Long Island, NY: Center for Interpersonal Growth, 1984.

Seeman, Julius. 'Client-Centered Therapy'. In D. Brower and L. E. Abt, eds, *Progress in Clinical Psychology*, Vol. 2. New York: Grune, 1956: 98–113.

Seeman, Julius. 'Counselor Judgments of Therapeutic Process and Outcome'. In C. R. Rogers and R. F. Dymond, eds, *Psychotherapy and Personality Change*. Chicago: University of Chicago Press, 1954.

Seeman, Julius. 'Deception in Psychological Research'. *American Psychologist* 24, no. 11 (1969): 1025–28.

Seeman, Julius. 'An Investigation of Client Reactions to Vocational Counseling'. *Journal of Consulting Psychology* 12, no. 2 (1949): 794–97.

Seeman, Julius. 'On Continuity and Change in the Person-Centered Approach'. *Renaissance* 8, no. 2 (1987): 99–108.

Seeman, Julius. 'On Supervising Student Research'. *American Psychologist* 28, no. 10 (1973): 900–906.

Seeman, Julius. 'Personality Integration as a Criterion of Therapy Outcome'. *Psychotherapy: Theory, Research and Practice* 1, no. 1 (August 1963).

Seeman, Julius. 'Personality Integration in College Women'. *Journal of Personality and Social Psychology* 4, no. 1 (1966): 91–93.

Seeman, Julius. 'Perspectives in Client-Centered Therapy in Women'. In B.B. *Handbook of Clinical Psychologists*. New York: McGraw-Hill, 1965: 1215–29.

Seeman, Julius. 'The Psychological Center: A Historical Note'. *American Psychologist* 23, no. 7 (1968): 522–23.

Seeman, Julius. 'Psychotherapy'. *Annual Review of Psychology* 12 (1961): 157–61.

Seeman, Julius. 'Psychotherapy and Perceptual Behavior'. *Journal of Clinical Psychology* 17, no. 1: 34–37.

Seeman, Julius. 'Reaction to Bozarth'. *Journal of Counseling and Development* 69 (May/ June 1991).

Seeman, Julius. 'A Study of Client Self-Selection of Tests in Vocational Counseling'. *Educational and Psychological Measurement* 8, no. 3 (Autumn 1948): 327–46.

Seeman, Julius. 'A Study of Preliminary Interview Methods in Vocational Counseling'. *Journal of Consulting Psychology* 12, no. 5 (1948): 321–30.

Seeman, Julius. 'A Study of the Process of Non-Directive Therapy'. *Journal of Consulting Psychology* 12, no. 3 (1949): 157–67.

Seeman, Julius. 'Teacher Judgments of High and Low Adjustments'. *Journal of Educational Research* 57, no. 4 (December 1963): 213–16.

Seeman, Julius. 'A Therapeutic Approach to Reading Difficulties'. *Journal of Consulting Psychology* 18, no. 6 (1954): 451–53.

Seeman, Julius, Edyth Barry, and Charlotte Ellinwood. 'Interpersonal Assessment of Play Therapy Outcome'. *Psychotherapy: Theory, Research and Practice* 1, no. 2 (January 1964): 63–66.

Seeman, Julius, and N. J. Raskin. 'Research Perspectives in Client-Centered Therapy'. In O. H. Mowrer, ed., *Psychotherapy, Theory and Research*. New York: Ronald Press, 1953: 205–34.

Seeman, Julius, and Larry Seeman. 'Emergent Trends in the Practice of Clinical Psychology'. *Professional Psychology* (May 1973): 151–57.

Seeman, Julius, and Paul Williams. 'Applied Research and Public Policy: A Study in Urban Relocation'. *Community Mental Health Journal* 7, no. 2 (1971): 99–106.

Shapiro, Deane, and Steven Zifferblatt. 'Zen Meditation and Behavioral Self-Control: Similarities, Differences, and Clinical Application'. *American Psychologist* 31, no. 7 (July 1976): 519–32.

Shaw, Suzanne M. 'Teachers in Transition: The Need for Freedom Within'. *Education* 95, no. 2 (1974): 140–44.

Shedlin, Arthur J. 'A Student-Centered Class'. *Personal Counselor: A Newsletter* 2, no. 2 (1947): 116–31.

Shedlin, Arthur J. 'Case of Mr. San: Second Interview'. *Personal Counselor: A Newsletter* 2, no. 1 (1947): 44–56.

Shedlin, Arthur J. 'Case of Mr. San: Third Interview'. *Personal Counselor: A Newsletter* 2, no. 2 (1947): 77–94.

Shedlin, Arthur J. 'Case of Mr. San: Fourth Interview'. *Personal Counselor: A Newsletter* 2, no. 3 (1947): 180–93.

Shedlin, Arthur J. 'Case of Mr. San: Sixth Interview'. *Personal Counselor: A Newsletter* 2, no. 6 (1947): 341–48.

Sheehy, Gail. 'Why Mid-Life Crisis Time for Couples'. *New York Magazine*, 31–35.

Shlien, John M. 'Theory as Autobiography: The Man and the Movement'. *Contemporary Psychology* 37, no. 10 (1992): 1082–84.

Slack, Sylvia. 'Reflections on a Workshop with Carl Rogers'. *Journal of Humanistic Psychology* 25, no. 2 (Spring 1985): 35–42.

Slater, Philip E. 'Sexual Adequacy in America'. *Intellectual Digest* (November 1973): 17–20.

Sollod, Robert. 'Carl Rogers and the Origins of Client-Centered Therapy'. *Professional Psychology* (February 1978): 93–104.

Solomon, Lawrence N. 'Building the Image of Peace'. *Journal of Humanistic Psychology* 26, no. 4 (Fall 1986): 108–16.

Solomon, Lawrence N. 'Humanism and the Training of Applied Behavioral Scientists'. *Journal of Applied Behavioral Science* 7, no. 5 (1971): 531–47.

Solomon, Lawrence N. 'A Personal Growth Program for Self-Directed Groups'. *Journal of Applied Behavioral Science* 6, no. 5 (1970): 427–51.

Solomon, Lawrence N. 'A Note on the Ethical Implications of Values Research'. *Journal of Humanistic Psychology* 10, no. 1 (Spring 1970): 30–32.

Solomon, Lawrence N. 'Declaration: The Person-Centered Approach and International Relations International Tension-Reduction Through the Person-Centered Approach'. Special Issue: Carl Rogers'-Centered Approach to Peace and Citizen Diplomacy. *Journal of Humanistic Psychology* 27, no. 3 (Summer 1987).

Stephenson, William. 'Scientific Creed – 1961: Philosophical Credo, Scientific Creed – 1961: Abductive Principles, Scientific Creed. 1961: The Centrality of Self'. *Psychological Record* 11, no.1 (January 1961).

Stillwell, William. 'The Process of Mysticism: Carlos Castaneda'. *Journal of Humanistic Psychology* 19, no. 4 (Fall 1979): 6–29.

Super, Donald E. 'Comment on Carl Rogers' Obituary'. *American Psychologist* (August 1989): 1161.

Swenson, Gay Leah. 'Grammar and Growth: A "French Connection."' *Education* 95, no. 2 (1974): 115–27.

Swenson, Gay Leah. 'When Personal and Political Processes Meet: The Rust Workshop'. *Journal of Humanistic Psychology* 27, no. 3 (Summer 1987): 309–32.

Tausch, Reinhard. 'Facilitative Dimensions in Interpersonal Relations: Verifying the Theoretical Assumptions of CRR'. *College Student Journal* 12, no. 1 (1978): 2–11.

Tausch, Reinhard. 'The Supplementation of Client-Centered Communication Therapy with Other Validated Therapeutic Methods: A Client-Centered Necessity'. In G. Lietaer, J. Rombauts, and R. Van Balen, eds, *Client-Centered and Experiential Psychotherapy in the Nineties*. Leuven, Belgium: Leuven University Press, 1990: 447–55.

Thayer, Louis. 'An Interview with Carl R. Rogers: Toward Peaceful Solutions to Human Conflict. Parts 1 and 2'. *Michigan Journal of Counseling and Development* 17, no. 1 (Summer 1987).

Thayer, Louis. 'A Person-Centered Approach to Family Therapy'. In A. M. Horne and M. M. Ohlsen, eds, *Family Counseling and Therapy*. Itasca, IL: F. E. Peacock Publishers, 1982: 175–212.

Thomas, Murphy, and Julius Seeman. 'Criterion Measures for Therapy Outcome: A Study on Personality Integration'. *Psychotherapy: Theory, Research and Practice* 8, no. 1 (Spring 1971): 26–30.

Thomas, Murphy, and Julius Seeman. 'Personality Integration and Cognitive Processes'. *Journal of Personality and Social Psychology* 24, no. 2 (1972): 154–61.

Tobin, S. 'A Comparison of Psychoanalytic Self-Psychology and Carl Rogers's Person-Centered Therapy'. *Journal of Humanistic Psychology* (Winter 1991).

Toms, Michael. 'Expressive Therapy: Creativity as a Path to Peace: A Conversation with Natalie Rogers', ed. Mary McClary. *New Realities* (January/February 1988): 13–17.

Tritt, Donald. 'Cognitions of Self as Learner: A Necessary Objective in Experiential Education'. *Psychological Reports* 69 (1991): 591–98.

Ueland, Brenda. 'Recent Trends in the Client-Centered Framework'. In J. T. Hart and T. M. Tomlinson, eds, *New Directions in Client-Centered Therapy*. New York: Houghton Mifflin, 1970: 23–32.

Ueland, Brenda. 'Tell Me More: On the Fine Art of Listening'. *Utne Reader* (1992): 104–109.

Van Der Veen, Ferdinand. 'Client Perception of Therapist Conditions as a Factor in Psychotherapy'. In J. T. Hart and T. M. Tomlinson, eds, *New Directions in Client-Centered Therapy*. New York: Houghton Mifflin, 1970: 214–22.

Van Der Veen, Ferdinand. 'You Can't Feel Your Thoughts: A Clinical Note on the Experience of Schizophrenia'. *Voices* (Spring 1974): 26–31.

Van Der Veen, Ferdinand, and N. Raskin. 'Client-Centered Family Therapy: Some Clinical and Research Perspectives'. In J. T. Hart and T. M. Tomlinson, eds, *New Directions in Client-Centered Therapy*. New York: Houghton Mifflin, 1970: 387–406.

Van Kalmthout, Martin A. 'The Religious Dimension of Rogers's Work'. *Journal of Humanistic Psychology* 35, no. 4 (Fall 1995).

Villas-Boas Bowen, Maria. 'Personality Differences and Person-Centered Supervision'. *Person-Centered Review* 1, no. 3 (August 1986): 291–309.

Villas-Boas Bowen, Maria. 'Special Characteristics of the Rust Workshop and Their Influence on My Facilitation Process'. *Journal of Humanistic Psychology* 27, no. 3 (Summer 1987).

Wager, Jon. 'Field Study as a State of Mind'. In L. Borzak, ed., *Field Study: A Sourcebook for Experiential Learning*. Beverly Hills, CA: Sage Publications, 1981: 18–49.

White, Alvin M. 'Effective Approaches to Faculty Development'. In *Effective Approaches to Faculty Development*. Washington, DC: Association of American Colleges.

White, Alvin M. 'Humanistic Mathematics: An Experiment'. *Education* 95, no. 2 (1974): 128–33.

White, Alvin M. 'Process and Environmental in Teaching and Learning'. Prepublication of chapter in *Interdisciplinary: Examples and Explorations*. San Francisco: Jossey-Bass, 1979.

Wood, John K. 'Carl Rogers, Gardener'. *Human Behavior* (December 1972): 17–22.

Wood, John K. 'Person-Centered Group Therapy'. In G. Gazda, E. J. Ginter, and A. M. Horne, *Group Counseling and Group Psychotherapy: Theory and Application*. Boston: Allyn & Bacon, 2001.

APPENDIX 1

MODIFIED FLANDERS INTERACTION ANALYSIS OBSERVATION FORM[1] (Copyright: 2013. Harold C. Lyon Jr, with thanks to Matthias Siebeck, MD. for reformatting this Modified Flanders Interaction Analysis Observation Form as a word processing document.)

Name of Observer:
Name of Teacher:　　Subject of teaching:
Date:
Setting:

[1] To make the form, join pages 236 and 237 at columns 21 and 22.

TABLE 1 Flanders' Interaction Analysis Categories (FIAC)

			0 (60)	1 (61)	2	3	4	5	6	7	8	9	10 (70)	11	12	13	14	15	16	17	18	19	20 (80)	21
Teacher – talk	Response	**1. Accepts Feeling.** Accepts and clarifies an attitude or the feeling tone of a pupil in a non threatening manner																						
		2. Praises or encourages. Praises or encourages pupil action or behaviour. Jokes that release tension, but not at the expense of another individual; nodding head, saying um, hmm or go on are included																						
		3. Accepts or uses ideas of pupils. Clarifying, building or developing ideas suggested by a pupil. Teachers' extensions of pupil ideas are included but as teacher brings more of his own ideas into play, shift to category five.																						
	Initiation	**4. Asks questions.** Asking a question about content or procedures; based on teacher ideas, with the intent that the pupil will answer																						
		5. Lecturing. Giving facts or opinions about content or procedures; expressing his own ideas, giving his own explanation or citing an authority other than a pupil																						
		6. Giving directions. Directions, commands or orders to which a student is expected to comply																						
Pupil Talk		**7. Criticizing or justifying authority.** Statements intended to change pupil behaviour from non acceptable to acceptable pattern; bawling someone out; stating why the teacher is doing what he is doing; extreme self-reference																						
	Response	**8. Pupil-talk – response.** Talk by pupils in response to teacher. Teacher initiates the contact or solicits pupil statement or structures the situation. Freedom to express own ideas is limited																						
	Initiation	**9. Pupil-talk – initiation.** Talk by pupils that they initiate. Expressing own ideas; initiating a new topic; freedom to develop opinions and a line of thought, like asking thoughtful questions; going beyond the existing structure.																						
Silence		**10. Silence or confusion.** Pauses, short periods of silence and periods of confusion in which communication cannot be understood by the observer.																						
			0 (60)	1 (61)	2	3	4	5	6	7	8	9	10 (70)	11	12	13	14	15	16	17	18	19	20 (80)	21

Time	0 – 60	61 – 120
Symbol	x	o

Additional Criteria	
Empathy	
Prizing	
Genuineness	
Humour	

Problem-Based (1 to 5):	

NOTES:

22	23	24	25	26	27	28	29	30 (90)	31	32	33	34	35	36	37	38	39	40 (100)	41	42	43	44	45	46	47	48	49	50 (110)	51	52	53	54	55	56	57	58	59	60 (120)	N/%
22	23	24	25	26	27	28	29	30 (90)	31	32	33	34	35	36	37	38	39	40 (100)	41	42	43	44	45	46	47	48	49	50 (110)	51	52	53	54	55	56	57	58	59	60 (120)	N

ROPES	Tell	Show	Do
Review			
Overview			
Present			
Exercise			
Summary			

Teacher Talk (%)	
Student Talk (%)	
Silence (%)	
Indirect / Direct	
Direct (#s 5-7)	
Indirect (#s 1-4)	

APPENDIX 2

MODEL DIAGNOSIS OF TEACHING REPORT FOR TEACHER

Name of University: Name of faculty member
Class: Date:
Observer:

EXPLANATION OF TEACHING DIAGNOSTIC TOOLS USED

Flanders Interactive Analysis: Flanders Interactive Analysis is a tool to diagnose classroom interaction. The Flanders Interaction Analysis (FIA) is descriptive or diagnostic rather than evaluative. The system has been used extensively in classroom observation studies (Wragg, 1999, Aspy, 1980). It was one of the primary vehicles for the largest study of effective teaching (200,000 hours of classroom analysis) conducted in 42 US states and 7 countries including Germany where Prof. Reinhard Tausch and his wife Anna Marie Tausch corroborated the findings of the larger US study with what Carl Rogers labeled as "Teutonic thoroughness." From the 10 diagnostic categories listed below, the ratio (I/D) of Indirect (items 1-4) to Direct (items 5-6) responses, if higher than .7 (more Indirect) tends to correlate with more effective teacher outcomes (see list in paragraph below) while, when less than .4 (more Direct) correlates with less effective outcomes. Hattie and Cornelius-White have since corroborated the high effect sizes of person-centered teaching in their extensive meta-analyses.

Empathy, Prizing, Genuiness: The above studies found that teachers with three traits – empathy, prizing (caring about students), and genuineness (or congruence) in the teacher had significantly higher desirable outcomes among their students including the following: increased standard achievement scores; less absenteeism; fewer discipline problems; increased IQ scores; increased self-concept scores;

improved attitudes toward school; increased levels of cognitive functioning (more thinking); increased creative responses; much greater percentage of "student talk" than in the average classroom, and increases in teacher energy and satisfaction levels. These teachers also tended to integrate humor into the classroom and be in better physical condition than average teachers.

ROPES: The effective teachers also responded to student feelings, asked thinking questions, facilitated skill development, transfer, and application by organizing their presentations in a way which: 1) Reviewed the content to access learner's abilities; 2) Overviewed the content with the students, motivating them and showing why it will be important to them; 3) Presented the content in small simple steps, asking questions while doing this; 4) Exercised the content to provide learners time to practice the skills, and 5) Summarized to obtain a follow-up after learning. ("What have you learned this hour?") These teachers integrated these steps in multi-sensory Tell-Show-Do steps. (Review, Overview, Present, Exercise, Summary = ROPES). eLearning also offers an effective mode for facilitating the ROPES steps. The average teacher uses only 2–3 of these steps. More effective teachers tend to use more steps.

Each 1-minute block of your presentation was observed for the following Flanders Interaction Analysis Categories

Teacher Talk	Indirect-	1.	Accepts Feelings
	Influence	2.	Praises or Encourages
	Indirect-	3.	Accepts or Uses Ideas of Student
	Influence	4.	Asks Questions
	Direct-	5.	Lecturing
	Influence	6.	Giving Directions
	Direct Influence	7.	Criticizing of Justifying Authority
Student Talk		8.	Student Talk: Response
		9.	Student Talk: Initiation
		10.	Silence or Confusion

YOUR DIAGNOSIS PROFILE COMPARED TO THE AVERAGE AND MOST EFFECTIVE TEACHER PROFILES

	You	*Average teachers*	*Most effective teachers*
% Teacher Talk	%	80%	30%
% Student Talk	%	10%	50%
% Silence or confusion	%	10%	20%

Continued

TABLE Continued

	You	Average teachers	Most effective teachers
Praising & encouraging	%	5%	24%
Response to feelings	%	0%	26%
Indirect (items 1-4) to Direct Ratio (items 5-6) (I/D):	%	<.4	>.7
# of ROPES Cells used★	%	2	11-15
Empathy	Yes or no	Not usually	Yes
Prizing (caring)	Yes or no	Sometimes	Yes
Genuineness (congruence)	Yes or no	Not usually	Yes
Humor	Yes or no	Not usually	Yes

★You used the following ROPES cells:

SAMPLE NARRATIVE REPORT

RECOMMENDATIONS OF OBSERVER: A good lecture! You stimulated the students to begin thinking by starting with repeated questions – especially the first 18 minutes of your lecture. You presented the symptoms of two patients (swollen hands and pathological foot), which is always the best problem-based method to teach clinical reasoning and diagnosis. Some students who came into this lecture to relax and not think, or to communicate with their classmates, found that impossible during the first 18 minutes of the lecture in the way you held the students attention with repeated questions, which always stimulates student thinking.

You taught in an informal friendly style, smiling frequently and standing before the students instead behind the podium. Your informal teaching manner showed that you care for students (prizing or caring) and that you are a genuine person (congruent). So you showed evidence of two of the three most important traits found in the research to be present in the most effective teachers (empathy, prizing, genuineness), as difficult as it is to see this in a lecture. Extensive research on teaching shows that students who have teachers with these three traits also have the following positive outcomes: increased achievement scores, less absenteeism, fewer disciplinary problems, increased IQ scores (if students are children), increased self-concept scores, increased levels of cognitive functioning or more thinking, increased creative or divergent responses, and more "student talk" than with average teachers.

You had some good Power Point slides, which helped you make your teaching points graphically, though some had small text and were difficult to read. You have a relaxed engaging manner, which shows the students your competence and confidence in the subject you teach.

During the first four minutes of the lecture, you talked in such a quiet voice while giving directions and perhaps reviewing the material that I could not hear you from the back and I suspect many students in the rear of the lecture hall were not able to hear you.

You had 80% Teacher Talk, which compares to the average in the large studies who also had 80% and the most effective teachers who have only 30% (however those data include small seminars where there is normally much less teacher talk). You had 13% Student Talk compared to the average of 10%. This student-talk resulted from your frequent question asking – especially during the first 18 minutes. You asked questions 18% of the time compared to the average teacher who asks questions only 8% of the time and the most effective who question 30% of the time. There was a slack period after the first 18 minutes when you lectured without questions for about 17 minutes while talking about your slides. You might wish to liven up this segment of your class with more interesting graphic case-based material and by asking more questions about the content, which always stimulates students to think.

Your ratio of Indirect to Direct teaching was .51. The most effective teachers have a ratio >.7 (very Indirect). Research shows less effective teachers being more Direct with a ratio of <.4. Indirect teaching is the amount of the first 4 categories on the Flanders: accepts feelings, praises or encourages, accepts or uses ideas of students, and asks questions. Direct teaching is the next 3 categories: lecturing, giving directions, and criticizing. The most effective teachers in the research are more indirect than direct. Asking more questions will increase your I/D ratio.

Compared to many faculty, you are a relaxed question-asker and face the "fears" which keep many teachers from having more interactive lectures. Among these fears is a fear of losing control and chaos. Another fear is that students will not answer their questions. The students learn to out-wait the teacher rather than risking answering questions, as they know if they wait long enough the teacher will become uncomfortable and give them the answers. Another common fear is that students will ask questions the teacher cannot answer. Some also fear that they will not be able to cover all the material if they allow interaction. But you have the courage to risk these fears and ask questions, which facilitates student thinking, so often difficult to do in long lectures. You mostly have the patience after asking a question to wait for the students to answer, even during that uncomfortable time when no one is answering. I would recommend not only asking more questions the last half of your lecture but also using more inflection in your voice while asking questions as well as when lecturing as your voice became very flat the last two thirds of your lecture during which student background "noise" increased gradually. You praised or acknowledged students 6% of the time compared to the best teachers who do this 24% of the time. I recommend you acknowledge students who risk answering your questions more often ("Good question! Good answer!"), which reinforces student interactive participation in your lecture.

You used 5 of the ROPES steps effective teachers use to organize teaching. Though no one uses all 15, I highly recommend you use the Overview step, which motivates students to be attentive to your lecture. A brief Overview step tells students what they will get out of your lecture and motivates them to pay attantion: "If you pay attention for the next 45-minutes, you will know how to recognize, diagnose and treat the most common CRPS symptoms." Also more opportunity to Exercise the content you presented would lead to more indelible learning. And a Summary at the end will help put the teaching into context. A good interactive way to summarize is to ask students what they learned today.

I recommend you use more complete patient cases along with your direct questioning of students to create productive problem-solving teaching. With the two visual image cases presented in your lecture, I recommend you add pictures of faces for each patient (could be a picture of any appropriate face). Research shows that students create what is called an "illness script" in their minds, associating the face of a patient with a particular diagnosis in the process of "pattern recognition" which, along with the hypothetical deductive reasoning process, is essential in learning clinical reasoning and diagnosis. At Dartmouth Medical School we learned to put up human faces with all cases we taught as learning is more indelible when the students sees a human face – any real face.

Silence and confusion (you had 7% compared to the average of 10%) is a good thing as the students are thinking about your questions.

Given how much material you need to cover in this 45-minute lecture, you might wish to consider creating an on-line interactive case, which could be introduced in the class by projecting it, instead of your slide cases. There may be some cases already authored for CRPS in the hundreds of interactive multi-media cases already created, many of which are available for faculty to use or modify for use. The students could work on a case either before class and discuss it in class or you could present it in class for them to interact with. And another could be assigned to them for after class to work on on-line at home. Use of multi-media cases, which have been thoroughly evaluated, could perhaps save you some of the time you need to cover all your teaching points and certainly engage the students more interactively. And research shows they are efficient in cutting the time it takes for students to master the content.

You gave a good lecture and you are potentially a great teacher! Thank you for inviting me to your lecture! I consider it your "teaching art" and am honored be invited into it. If you wish me to come again to diagnose a subsequent lecture to see how much you have improved, I will be happy to come.

Prof. Harold C. Lyon
Guest Professor of Medical Education
halclyon@yahoo.com

INDEX